FAMILIES IN POVERTY

Karen Seccombe
Portland State University

Volume 1 in the Series
Families in the Twenty-First Century

General Editor

Susan J. Ferguson
Grinnell College

PEARSON

New York   San Francisco   Boston
London   Toronto   Sydney   Tokyo   Singapore   Madrid
Mexico City   Munich   Paris   Cape Town   Hong Kong   Montreal

Senior Series Editor: Jeff Lasser
Series Editorial Assistant: Erikka Adams
Senior Marketing Manager: Kelly M. May
Production Editor: Won McIntosh
Editorial Production Service: WestWords, Inc.
Composition Buyer: Linda Cox
Manufacturing Buyer: JoAnne Sweeney
Electronic Composition: WestWords, Inc.
Cover Designer: Joel Gendron

For related titles and support materials, visit our online catalog at www.ablongman.com.

Between the time website information is gathered and then published, it is not unusual for some sites to have closed. Also, the transcription of URLs can result in typographical errors. The publisher would appreciate notification where these errors occur so that they may be corrected in subsequent editions.

Seccombe, Karen.
    Families in poverty / Karen Seccombe
        p. cm. -- (Familes in the 21st century series; v. 1)
    Includes bibliographical references and index.
    ISBN 0-205-50254-7
        1. Family--Economic aspects--United States. 2. Family policy--United States. 3.
    Poverty--United States. I. Title

HQ536.S3983 2007
306.85086'9420973--dc22

                                        2006050068

Printed in the United States of America

10 9 8 7 6 5 4 3 2 1   11 10 09 08 07 06

CONTENTS

FAMILIES IN THE TWENTY-FIRST CENTURY

The family is one of the most private and pervasive social institutions in U.S. society. At the same time, public discussions and debates about the institution of the family persist. Some scholars and public figures claim that the family is declining or dying, or that the contemporary family is morally deficient. Other scholars argue that the family is caught in the larger culture wars currently taking place in the United States. Regardless of one's perspective that the family is declining or caught in broader political struggles, family scholars are working to address important questions about the family, such as, what is the future of marriage? Is divorce harmful to individuals, to the institution of the family, or to society? Why are rates of family violence so high? Are we living in a post-dating culture? How does poverty and welfare policy affect families? How is child rearing changing now that so many parents work outside the home, and children spend time with other caretakers? How are families socially constructed in different societies, cultures, and time periods?

Most sociologists and family scholars agree that the family is a dynamic social institution that is continually changing as individuals and other social structures in society change. The family also is a social construction with complex and shifting age, gender, race, and social class meanings. As we begin the twenty-first century, many excellent studies are currently investigating the changing structures of the institution of the family and the lived experiences and meanings of families. *Families in the Twenty-First Century* is a series of short texts and research monographs that provides a forum for the best of this burgeoning scholarship. One goal of this series is to recognize the diversity of families that exist in the United States and globally. A second goal is for the series to better inform pedagogy and future family scholarship about this diversity of families. The series also seeks to connect family scholarship to a broader audience beyond the classroom, by informing the public and ensuring that family studies are central to contemporary policy debates and to social action. Each short text contains the most outstanding current scholarship on the family from a variety of disciplines, including sociology, demography, policy studies, social work, human development, and psychology. Moreover, each short text is authored by a leading family scholar or scholars who bring their unique disciplinary perspective to an understanding of contemporary families.

Families in the Twenty-First Century provides the most contemporary scholarship and up-to-date findings on the family. Each volume provides a brief overview of significant scholarship on that family topic, including critical current debates or areas of scholarly disagreement. In addition to providing an assessment of the latest findings related to their family topic, authors also examine the family utilizing an intersectional framework of race-ethnicity, social class, gender, and sexuality. Much of the research is interdisciplinary with a number of theoretical frameworks and methodological approaches presented. A particular strength of the series is that the short texts appeal to undergraduate students as well as to family scholars, but they also are written in a way that makes them accessible to a larger public of well-informed individuals.

About This Volume

Poverty is a social problem, with profound consequences for family members of all ages. *Families in Poverty* brings together the best scholarship and data available to describe the extent of poverty among U.S. families, the problems poor families face, and the prospects for alleviating family poverty. The author, Karen Seccombe (Portland State University), draws upon the most recent qualitative and quantitative data to help readers understand the extent, causes, and consequences of poverty. Seccombe examines how poverty is measured and defined in the United States and how labor market issues, such as unemployment and the minimum wage, affect poverty trends on a national level and families on an individual level. She also discusses and evaluates U.S. policies and programs designed to eliminate or reduce family poverty. Seccombe shows that the consequences of poverty on both children and adults are complex and varied. Moreover, she encourages readers to think and take action about how to reduce or eliminate poverty.

Topics covered include poverty trends and data, the definition and measurement of poverty, the explanations of poverty, anti-poverty policies, Temporary Assistance to Needy Families (TANF), the Earned Income Credit, and the effects of poverty on children and adults.

Families in Poverty is appropriate for use in any class concerned with family structure, social inequality, gender, social welfare, and government policy. This book is a valuable resource to teachers and students in beginning and advanced courses in sociology, psychology, family studies, women's studies, human development, social work, public policy, and other disciplines. It also finds an audience among those who work in various human service fields, including human development, social work, education, counseling, health services, and the government.

Future Volumes in the Series

Global Families—Meg Wilkes Karraker, University of St. Thomas

Families and Social Class—Shirley A. Hill, University of Kansas

Family Policy—Janet Z. Giele, Brandeis University

Remarriages and Stepfamilies—Lawrence H. Ganong and Marilyn Coleman, University of Missouri

Susan J. Ferguson
General Editor
Grinnell College

PREFACE

Families in Poverty is one of several books in the new series *Families in the Twenty-First Century* that focus on critical issues facing families today. In this book, I draw upon recent quantitative and qualitative data to help the reader understand the extent, causes, and consequences of poverty for families in the United States. Toward this goal, I describe the trends in poverty in the United States; define how poverty is measured and provide a critique of various measures; and describe the consequences of poverty on children and adults. The book offers and critiques several explanations for poverty, from the structural to individualistic perspectives; discusses labor market issues such as unemployment, minimum wage, and employer-sponsored fringe benefits; and describes and critiques several key programs in the United States designed to eliminate or reduce the incidence or the effects of poverty on families (e.g., food stamps, Medicaid, Head Start). I discuss the evolution of the 1996 welfare reform legislation and the Temporary Assistance to Needy Families (TANF) program, describe and evaluate the effects of welfare reforms, and compare and contrast U.S. family anti-poverty policies with those of other industrialized nations.

My goal is to make accessible to readers the most recent data available from important sources such as the U.S. Census Bureau, U.S. Department of Labor, Centers for Disease Control and Prevention (CDC), U.S. Department of Health and Human Services, U.S. Department of Agriculture (USDA), and the Center on Budget and Policy Priorities. Infused with these quantitative data, I provide elaborate qualitative stories that give meaning and richness to the empirical studies. Qualitative data can personalize the issues for the reader in profound ways, and it also can bring problems and solutions alive. I hope the result is a relatively easy-to-read book that brings together the best and most recent quantitative and qualitative data to better understand the extent of poverty among U.S. families, the problems poor families face, and ultimately, to argue that poverty is not insurmountable and that real solutions do exist. Although this book primarily focuses on poverty in the United States, some comparative data from developed and developing nations are presented to illustrate key concepts, and differences in our family and anti-poverty policies and subsequent outcomes.

I strive for optimism within an innately disheartening topic. I emphasize throughout the book that poverty is far more than a personal problem. Its causes and consequences are rooted in our social structure. Poverty is a social problem, and its solutions require that we look deeply at our social institutions and evaluate how they may encourage or perpetuate poverty. The good news is that we have the resources to do this. Now, do we have the will?

ACKNOWLEDGMENTS

No one, including sole authors, ever really writes a book by oneself. I am no different. I am grateful to the School of Community Health at Portland State University for providing me with the time, resources, and intellectual climate in which to tackle this project. My graduate students at the University of Florida and Portland State University conducted many of the interviews presented here, and I am forever grateful for their dedication to our projects. However, many of those people who helped me the most really have nothing to do with academia. In particular, I want to thank the good friends and support network I have cultivated, because without them, I could not have written this book. As always, my family provided the inspiration, assistance, and distractions that make writing a book possible. To my sweet daughters Natalie and Olivia, and to my husband Rich: Thank you.

This book has been inspired by the many women and men that I have met in Florida and Oregon as I pursued my research on poverty, welfare, and access to healthcare. You have confirmed for me that the personal is indeed political.

ABOUT THE AUTHOR

Dr. Karen Seccombe is professor of Community Health at Portland State University. She received her MSW from the University of Washington, specializing in health and welfare policy, and her Ph.D. in sociology from Washington State University, focusing on family sociology and social stratification. She taught at the University of Alaska and the University of Florida prior to coming to Portland State University. She is the author of several books, including *"So You Think I Drive a Cadillac?" Welfare Recipients' Perspective on the System and Its Reform,* 2nd ed. (Allyn and Bacon, 2007), *Just Don't Get Sick: Access to Health Care in the Aftermath of Welfare Reform* (Rutgers University Press, 2007), and *Marriages and Families: Relationships in Social Context* (with Rebecca Warner, Wadsworth, 2004). Dr. Seccombe's research interests focus on the health and well-being of poor families. She has published her research in leading journals, including the *Journal of Marriage and Family, Journal of Health and Social Behavior, Journal of Family Issues, Gender and Society,* and *Inquiry.* Her current work focuses on the access to healthcare among families who have recently left welfare for work, funded by the Agency for Healthcare Research and Quality. Dr. Seccombe is the recipient of two excellence in teaching awards, and she was awarded the Distinguished Alumni Award for 2006 representing the Behavioral and Social Sciences at California State University, Chico, her alma mater.

Dr. Seccombe lives in Portland, Oregon with her husband Richard, and daughters Natalie Rose, age 5, and Olivia Lin, age 3. As a family they enjoy spending time at their cabin in the mountains, exploring the beauty and many hidden gems of the Pacific Northwest, and sampling all the child-friendly restaurants and other fun places in Portland.

1

Putting A Face
on Poverty

Dee

Dee is a 31-year-old woman with short-cropped hair, a warm smile, and a hearty laugh that is highly contagious. Quite simply, she is happy to be alive. After years of submitting to physical and sexual abuse by her domineering husband, she is finally free. She has a newfound skip in her walk. The weight of the abuse, lies, secrets, and fears has finally been lifted from her shoulders.

It took Dee a long time to get from there to here. She makes few apologies for herself. "I just didn't know that I was worth more than that," she says. She grew up in a home that was impoverished economically, socially, and spiritually. She saves her apologies for her 11-year-old daughter, Clare. "Can she ever forgive me for making her live like that—for seeing her momma bleeding on the floor? For seeing her daddy leaning over me with a bat, laughing? For listening to us as we cursed each other?"

It took both police intervention and the kindly help from her church members to leave her abuser. When the police took him to jail after a particularly brutal encounter, her pastor and several church members insisted that she and Clare move to safety. They found Dee and Clare temporary shelter in a neighboring community at the home of a church member's sibling. For the first time in a long while, maybe forever, Dee felt safe.

The road ahead was not an easy one for either Dee or Clare. However, Dee is a loving and devoted mother, and she was convinced that she owed Clare a better life. She was willing to make the transition and climb the ladder out of despair for her daughter's sake. But how would she begin?

She was thankful for the free food and lodging that she and Clare received; she did not know that people could be so kind. Because of their help, she was able to maintain her pride and forgo applying for welfare benefits. "Welfare—now that's just not my thing," she said. Dee knew that soon she would be on her own and would need to support herself and Clare. Her immediate family would be of no help to her. Her parents were lifelong alcohol and drug abusers, wallowing in self-pity. Her brother was in jail, and she had not seen him in years. Her grandparents were dead, and she had no close aunts and uncles to whom she could turn for aid. Dee knew that, other than the generous care from her church family that was bound to expire soon, she was on her own and needed to find a job quickly.

Dee had not worked since shortly after her daughter was born. Her husband had simply not permitted it. He was angry when one of her co-workers expressed concern about the bruising on her arm, and he told her that she must quit and never go back. He would not even allow her to pick up her final paycheck. When she protested, he beat her harder. Besides, he reasoned, he was man enough to support the family. Why wasn't she woman enough to take care of the new baby? Dee remembers that quitting her job was one of the saddest days of her life. Although she made only minimum wage and the work stocking shelves of the store could be difficult, she made several new friends. Her boss also liked her and promised her a significant raise if she would reduce her absenteeism. Dee knew she missed too many days of work, but what could she do, with the bruises and all?

Dee remembered fondly her days of working, so she was eager to find a job to propel her into her new life. She combed the want ads, but her eagerness soon turned to anxiety. She did not see very many jobs that she felt qualified for. She acknowledged that her math skills were somewhat limited. "I get nervous with fractions and all, but I can read real good," she told me. However, Dee knew nothing about computers. She had never used one, her family had never owned one, and her high school did not have them back when she was in school. Many of the jobs she saw wanted specific computer skills, yet she did not even know how to type on a keyboard or use a word processor, let alone understand the nuances of an Excel spreadsheet.

Dee made many telephone calls, and even had a few job interviews, but she was not offered any jobs. She did not know why, but one potential employer hinted that her appearance was not appropriate for the job. She left the interview with her head held high, but she did cry all the way back to the bus. On the bus ride home, she looked at her reflection in a window and was forced to agree that her broken tooth was very noticeable and unattractive.

I've had that broken tooth for years now, so I guess I've forgotten about it. But yeah, it's ugly. I broke it in a fall I took when he hit me. He knocked me down and I hit my mouth on some steps in the yard. Wow, did it bleed! I'd like to fix the darn thing, but, well, do you know how much that costs? Lots more than I have.

After searching the want ads and repeatedly coming up empty, she began to feel a sense of desperation. Her usual optimism was beginning to fade. She knew that the kindness of strangers sharing their home was running out, and that she must do what she feared: apply for a job in the fast-food industry. She had no experience with this type of job, and honestly dreaded the thought of working there. She had heard intimate details about these jobs years ago from her friend in high school who bemoaned the dismal working conditions. Yet, she knew that the fast-food industry was always eager for new employees, and therefore she could find work quickly. She was right—by noon she was offered a job: 30–39 hours per week with a variable schedule, $6.00 an hour, and no benefits. She quickly took it, pleased because it was 85 cents an hour over minimum wage.

Although making french fries, flipping burgers, pouring sodas, and waiting on customers was not what she had hoped for, Dee went to work and did not complain much. She had little in common with her co-workers, because most were teenagers much younger than her. She felt that several of them were quite rude, mocking her as a "lifer," while they were just working there before leaving for college, and presumably, a better life.

Yeah, they yak about going off to college, and a few of them snicker at me, "Having fun with your career Dee?" they'll say. I try to just ignore them. A woman's got to do what a woman's got to do. Besides, I'll be getting a raise soon, and I'll be earning more than them anyway.

The hours at her job did vary dramatically each week. One week she worked 39 hours, and the next week it was 30, resulting in a reduction in her weekly pay of about $55. This is a sizable sum to a family trying to piece its life together. When she asked her manager for more hours on a regular basis, he just sighed and told her that this is the nature of the industry. She should not expect anything different. Nonetheless, she always volunteered to fill the shifts of her high school co-workers who wanted the time off to attend a big party or school function. However, the manager made sure that Dee's hours remained below a certain threshold; otherwise, he would have to pay her fringe benefits, such as health insurance. This situation frustrated Dee: "How am I supposed to better myself if he won't let me work?" she asks.

On average, Dee earned about $900 per month at her job, although a small portion of that was taken out in taxes. Working year-round, she could be expected to gross about $10,800 a year. By federal calculations, she and Clare live in poverty. For these wages, she sometimes worked days, evenings, and weekends, and her schedule was never the same from one week to another.

Within a month of employment, Dee and Clare moved out of their friends' home and rented a one-bedroom trailer for $425 in a neighborhood generally regarded as "the other side of the tracks." The location did not matter much to Dee, because she felt safe living so far away from her husband, and secure knowing that she alone was in charge of her destiny. The trailer was bare the first month, but subsequent paychecks allowed Dee and Clare to peruse the local Goodwill and Salvation Army stores and purchase well-worn but inexpensive furniture, pictures, dishes, and knickknacks. They purchased a double bed for the bedroom and slept in it together. Food, clothing, utilities, and bus passes used most of the remaining money from her paycheck. There was little left over for entertainment. Fortunately, neither of them had been sick or had an injury that required medical attention, because they would have had no way to pay for it. The trailer proved to be very cold and drafty in the winter months. Lacking additional money to keep it adequately heated, Dee and Clare wore coats in the house, and sometimes wore hats as well to stay warm.

> We're trying to make it homey, you know, buying this and that. It's hard because we don't have much money, but I've found some really great deals at the stores. I found a set of pretty nice dishes for under $15. I wish we had more space—Clare would like to have her own room of course, but that just can't happen right now. We've both been healthy, knock on wood. This trailer does get mighty cold. Maybe it's better to only have one bed after all so we can help each other stay warm [laughter].

Clare was often left on her own after school hours when Dee had to work nights or weekends. Clare would sometimes stay with a neighbor, but the sitter cost Dee $3.50 an hour, a large chunk of her hourly wage. Therefore, Clare often stayed home alone with the door locked until Dee returned from work. Dee asked Clare to try to be extra quiet and to have only one light on to avoid alerting the neighbors that she was home alone.

Too proud to complain, Dee hoped to avoid programs like welfare, food stamps, or Medicaid. Her goal was to be on her own and self-sufficient. In some respects, she has met her goals. Why then is life so hard, she wonders? She works diligently at a job she truly dislikes, but with so few options available to her, she guesses that she will work there forever.

What Are Dee's Options?

This brief story gives us a glimpse into Dee's life. What are her options for the future? The manager has promised a pay raise to $6.50 an hour after a few more months of work. The pay increase would give Dee another $75 per month, which she desperately needs. However, despite this pay raise, and likely the next, she and Clare will remain impoverished, with little chance of significantly improving their lives.

We all clamor for more "good jobs at good pay" for workers. Dee is one of many women who are looking for one of these jobs. She would like to raise her daughter Clare without welfare, and she recognizes the need for a permanent full-time job. Instead, however, she has been stymied by the tremendous growth in low-paying, part-time, temporary positions.

Dee's case is important for several reasons. First, it shows us that people without significant job skills often wind up in the low-paying service sector working at jobs that are part-time, sub-contracted, temporary in nature, or that occur at night (Mishel, Bernstein, and Allegretto 2005; Douglas-Hall and Koball 2004). Low-wage jobs have been described as those that would offer below-poverty wages for a family of three or four, paying less than roughly $8.50 to $9.00 an hour, in 2005 (Schochet and Rangarajan 2004). Using this definition, between one-quarter and one-third of all workers could be classified as low-wage workers (Carnevale and Rose 2001; Mitnik, Zeidenberg, and Dresser 2002).

Millions of workers earn only the minimum wage, which was $5.15 an hour in 2006, although some states have increased their minimum wage above this federally mandated minimum. The federal wage of $5.15 an hour has not been increased since 1997, and inflation has deteriorated its purchasing power by at least 17 percent since then. The real value of the minimum wage peaked in 1968 when it was equivalent to a wage of $7.54 an hour in 2005 dollars. Once an adjustment for inflation is taken into account, the purchasing power of the minimum wage now has declined to its lowest level since 1955, with a brief exception in 1989 (Bernstein and Shapiro 1 September 2005). An individual working full-time at the current minimum wage makes $10,712 per year—about $2,000 below the 2005 poverty threshold for a family of two, and $4,500 below the threshold for a family of three (U.S. Census Bureau 1 February 2006). Working full-time every week of the year, the current minimum wage covers only 40 percent of the estimated cost of raising two children in 2005, down from 48 percent in 1997 when the minimum wage was last raised. The purchasing power of the minimum wage has been eroded, leaving low-income families struggling to stay economically afloat (Children's Defense Fund 2005c).

There is strong public support for helping low-income workers to meet their families' needs and advance economically. A survey conducted by Jobs for the

Future revealed that 94 percent of Americans agree that "as a country, we should make sure that people who work full-time should be able to earn enough to keep their families out of poverty," and a W. K. Kellogg Foundation poll found that 77 percent agreed that the government should help families that leave welfare for work but remain poor (Children's Defense Fund 2005c).

Low-wage workers are disproportionately female, minority, young, and without a college education. Low-wage workers also are much more likely to live in households with children that are headed by single females, that contain fewer adults, and that have fewer secondary workers (Schochet and Rangarajan 2004). Many low-income workers live in families with other earners and therefore have total family incomes above the poverty level. However, with the rise in single-parent families, an increasing number of low-wage earners are the sole support of their families. Dee is one of these types of workers.

Low-wage work also is characterized by offering irregular work hours. Employees working in jobs with these types of schedules, referred to as **nonstandard work schedules,** represent the fastest-growing category of workers in the United States (Presser 2003). Dee's situation is not unique. Women with only high school diplomas or less are disproportionately found working irregular schedules that include night and weekend shifts, and varying hours. Forty-three percent of women with a high school education or less work at least some weekend days or have varying shifts, compared with 36 percent of women who have more than a high school education.

According to sociologist Harriet Presser, most women with children do not want this arrangement and prefer the assurance of a steady job with an established pay scale and fringe benefits. More than half (53 percent) of women Presser surveyed whose youngest child was between the ages of 5 and 13, reported that the main reason they worked non-standard schedules was because it was a requirement of the job, such as cashiers, maids, nursing aids, cooks, waitresses, and fast-food retail, and that they could not get any other job. Only 30 percent of women listed beneficial reasons for working these shifts, such as it allowed for better childcare arrangements (18 percent), it allowed better arrangements for care of other family members (7 percent), it offered time for school (2 percent), or it provided better pay (3 percent).

Many jobs are now temporary in nature and offer little or no job security. Manpower is one of the largest private employers in the United States, ranking 140th in the *Fortune* 500, employing more than 2.5 million workers a year (Manpower 2005). Every morning, its workers scatter into factories and offices around the country, looking for a day's work. As other industrial giants lay off workers, Manpower and many other temporary agencies are booming.

Turnover rates in many low-tier jobs are high, even in those low-tier jobs considered to be "permanent." Sometimes people quit work in hopes of finding something better or to turn to welfare. However, persons in these jobs are also considerably more likely to be laid off than are other workers. They are the expendable workforce. They work in the service industry, in clerical work, and on assembly lines performing routine tasks. To the management, people in these largely unskilled or semi-skilled jobs are interchangeable. A high turnover rate is not a problem for management, and in fact, may even be considered desirable so that health insurance premiums and payments of other benefits can be avoided. These disposable workers generally earn less than those on the regular payroll, and they also must live with the uncertainty that their jobs could permanently end on any given day when they clock out at 5:00 p.m. Their anxiety is high, and for many, unemployment insurance is not an option.

Dee's case is also significant because it shows us that these jobs have important implications for the availability and costs of childcare. Childcare is often in short supply, it is expensive, and it consumes a considerable portion of family income (Johnson 2005). One national study found that among the working poor families headed by single mothers who paid for childcare, 40 percent spent more than half of their cash income on childcare, and another 25 percent spent 40 to 50 percent. Likewise, among the working poor families headed by married couples who paid for childcare, 23 percent spent more than half their cash income on childcare, and another 21 percent spent between 40 and 50 percent (Wertheimer 2003).

Nonstandard schedules affect the degree to which centers, family, friends, and neighbors are able to provide childcare, thereby decreasing availability and increasing costs. Dee's work requires late nights and weekend hours when childcare centers are not open, and informal childcare might not be available. Clare, arguably, is too young to remain at home alone at night while her mother works. Yet, large numbers of young children are left alone to care for themselves. According to Census Bureau data, 10 percent of 5–11-year-olds, and 34 percent of 12–14-year-olds are in "self-care" (Johnson 2005). Low-income children are less than half as likely as their upper-income peers to be in after-school sports and clubs (Fields et al. 2001). Programs for low-income children are either unavailable in their neighborhoods, are not affordable, or the children face other obstacles, such as transportation. Therefore, millions of young children spend significant amounts of time after school, on weekends, or at night, alone caring for themselves.

Kate

Kate and Tony were married for more than five years before they decided that the time was right to have children. Their marriage was happy in the early years, and Kate sighed when she said that they looked like the all-American couple. However, as happens with many other couples, the stress of children, budgets, and jobs took its toll, and over time their marriage fell apart.

They met years before at a softball game. Tony was playing on a city-sponsored league, and Kate went to watch the game with one of her friends from work. Her friend introduced them after the game, and as Kate likes to tell it, "Nature then took its course." They dated for a year and then married. Kate, who was 23 years old when she married Tony, wanted children right away. But Tony suggested that they work and try to save beforehand.

Both worked, and they worked hard. Tony was employed by a trucking company and was responsible for much of the scheduling of the freight. Kate worked as a cashier at a discount store, and the management was so impressed by her eye for detail that they quickly promoted her to an assistant manager position. This promotion pleased them both—Tony liked spending the extra money she earned on things for the house, such as a large-screen television, and Kate hoped to save some of the money for the baby. "Those were the good old days. We liked being together. We had dreams," Kate told me. Their lives were comfortable: a two-bedroom condo, a late-model car for her, and a new truck for Tony. They seemed to have most gadgets that any family would want, although she acknowledged that they were saving very little toward their goal of having a baby. Each paycheck seemed destined for one of their mounting bills. Conversations about money and spending habits were often tense, but both just assumed that these differences were natural and a part of every relationship.

When the first baby came, a son they named Elliott, both were thrilled, but they noticed that the budget seemed to be getting tighter and less comfortable. Several months after Elliott was born, Kate became pregnant again, this time unplanned. After the initial shock wore off, both she and Tony were happy to welcome another child into the family. Emma was born only 13 months after Elliott.

> Yeah, Elliott, I had been waiting for Elliott for years. You think you know how much a baby costs, but I don't think there's any way that you can really know. Diapers, formula, clothes, a crib, a car seat, the swing, and daycare, wow, daycare! The costs were just incredible. I managed to get some toys and clothing items from a friend whose baby had outgrown them. But the costs were still incredible. And then when Emma came, which was a complete surprise, you can't reuse everything. I mean, we can't put them in the same crib, or use the same car seat, now can we?

Kate and Tony tried to continue in their jobs after the babies were born; however, they found that the costs of childcare were eating up most of Kate's check. She earned $12.25 an hour as an assistant manager of the store, amounting to about $1,700 a month after taxes. Her daycare bill for two children was nearly

$1,200 a month. She searched for less expensive daycare, but shuddered at the quality of what she found: "It made me cry, thinking of having my babies there all day. No way." She also found daycare that was far more expensive than what she paid, and she came to the realization that her bills were squarely in the middle, unlikely to decrease substantially. So Kate and Tony faced a decision experienced by many parents today—is the job satisfaction she felt worth the extra hassles she experienced every morning trying to get everyone ready for their day, worth the gnawing guilt she felt when she dropped her children off, and worth the relatively low take-home pay she had after paying for childcare? After a few months of soul searching, she decided the answer was no, and so she quit.

> I thought it over long and hard. I took my time. Basically, Tony agreed with the decision—he had to face it too, I just wasn't making much money after the daycare bills. I didn't completely want to quit because I liked my job. And they liked me too, you know. But, it was all so stressful, and for what, like a couple of hundred a month? No, I had to quit. It doesn't seem fair that raising babies has to put you in the poorhouse.

Tony made $15.50 an hour at his job, or about $2,000 a month after taxes, and had full health benefits for his family. Yet, they found that they could not make ends meet on his salary alone. He began to work overtime to augment his pay, but it was still not enough. Even with his overtime earnings, Tony was forced to sell his truck, which was his pride and joy. Creditors hounded them because they could not pay their bills, and their lives were racked with stress.

Meanwhile, Kate felt increasingly lonely and isolated at home with the children all day. Emma was a particularly fussy baby, and often cried for hours on end. Elliott was learning how to walk and seemed to be bent on tearing the house apart. Kate had a few friends to call in times of stress, but for the most part, without money to pay a babysitter, she had to endure her days alone.

Kate and Tony began to argue about nearly every detail in their lives. Why didn't he earn more money? Why did he have to sell his truck when she got to keep her car? Why didn't he help more with the kids? Why was the house always such a mess? Their communication, and eventually their love, deteriorated. After several years of the bitter fights, Tony had an affair, and when Kate confronted him with the evidence she found, he confessed, she said, "With an air of 'I don't care anymore.'" He acknowledged that the woman meant little to him, but he told Kate that the sex was great, and he was in no hurry to give it up. Not long afterwards, Kate filed for divorce.

Kate moved in briefly with a friend, along with Elliott, who was then 5, and 4-year-old Emma. She went back to work, and her childcare bills were reduced because Elliott was in kindergarten. However, she was very disappointed when her boss told her that she would have to start again as a cashier, earning only $8.00 an hour, rather than coming back as an assistant manager, because there were other "very qualified girls," as he put it, in line for management jobs. Her boss told her that with her "eye for detail" she could likely be promoted within two to three years.

Kate found a shabby two-bedroom apartment for herself and the children, at a cost of $500 a month. This rental price took almost half of her take-home pay. She quickly recognized that with only $550 remaining in her check she could not afford to purchase necessities such as food, clothing, utilities, Emma's childcare, or gas to get to work. She desperately needed the court-ordered child support of $600 from Tony to make ends meet. This child support was crucial to her family's well-being, but it arrived only sporadically. The children needed new shoes, winter coats, and school supplies. They were living without a telephone because they could not afford the cost. She sold her car to pay off some of her bills, but the bills continued to accumulate. Winter was coming, and how would she pay for the heat? Food usually ran low at the end of the month, and sometimes it ran out completely.

> I'd get pretty creative at the end of the month. We'd eat a little dab of this and a little dab of that. I would try to have at least a couple of types of jelly in the house so they wouldn't have to eat the same kind with their peanut butter sandwich day in and day out. After a while when it got really bad and I'd completely run out, a friend told me about the food places where I could get a bag of groceries. I hated going there and feeling like a beggar, but they were always real nice. They knew that I can't let my kids go hungry.

Although Kate had high hopes for her job, she found that getting to work on time was a logistical nightmare. She lived near a bus stop, but there were no direct routes to her job. Instead, she had to take two buses to get to work, which took her more than an hour to go the 5-mile distance. Many days the buses failed to coordinate their schedules. Perhaps a bus was late, which kept her waiting. Or perhaps a bus was early, meaning that she would miss her connection and wait even longer for the next one. Difficulties associated with transportation resulted in frequently being late for work, and her boss had already reprimanded her twice. Kate hoped to buy a car soon, but realistically, with no ability to save money, that was impossible.

In the months following the divorce, Tony would visit the children at his court-arranged time, which was every other weekend. However, as time marched on, Tony's visits became more and more sporadic, as did his child support checks. Within 18 months, he rarely saw the children at all, nor did he send a monthly check to support them. The situation made Kate very angry; she felt that it was his responsibility to continue to be a father to their children.

He'd probably blame it on me. You know, all the fighting and all. We would argue a lot. I would try not to, on account of the kids. They need to know their dad. And we need his money. But, things being what they are, we would just fight. So he would come around less and less after that. And the money would rarely come at all. So when I did see him, we'd argue even more than before. "Where the hell have you been?" I'd say. Now, I don't even plan on him or the money. Why set ourselves up to be disappointed?

Instead of relying on child support payments to make ends meet, Kate turned to the welfare office for help. She applied for food stamps, and received about $300 a month in assistance. She also applied for Medicaid because she could not get health insurance from her job until she had completed one year with the company; however, she was turned down because she earned too much money. Therefore, she and the children were uninsured for the first year after the divorce, and they faced several bills for needed medical care. "Nothing serious, but it still cost a lot," she said. She also applied for subsidized housing, but was told that the wait would likely be more than two years. She withdrew her application when she recognized that she would probably have to live in a large, unkempt housing project on the other side of town, which also would require Elliott to change schools. She looked into the possibility of subsidized childcare, but was told that her earnings were too far above the threshold for assistance. Therefore she had to pay the full cost, but given her financial circumstances she could no longer be as fussy about childcare as she had been in the past. Kate was forced to choose from the selection of providers that years ago had made her cringe. She crossed her fingers, hoped for the best, and tried to justify her low-cost choice, "I just crossed my fingers and prayed that she didn't have to stay there too much longer. But, to be honest, it was safe and all. It was okay, I guess. Not so bad."

Kate and her children trudged along, day after day, with few of the bright spots that money can provide. There was little in the budget for entertainment that would lift the spirits. No pizza on Friday night, no money for a trip to the zoo, and no trips to the beach. Nothing could be purchased unless it was truly needed for survival. She tried not to think about her former late-model car, the large-screen television, or her two-bedroom condo—they had all become distant memories and reminders of a previous life. Kate's task, as she described it, was to "hold on until I can become eligible for a promotion to assistant manager." She longs for the day that she can again earn more than $12 an hour.

Why Is Kate's Family Poor?

Kate and her children are poor for many reasons, one of which is that they fail to receive the court-ordered child support payments that are owed to them. They join the ranks of millions of people who also slip in or near poverty because, alone and without child support, they cannot earn enough for a decent standard of living.

According to the law, noncustodial parents have a legal responsibility to support their children. For much of this country's history, this financial support was provided through a private arrangement between the former spouses; the noncustodial parent (usually the father) negotiated with the mother a child support order, a legal document delineating the amount and circumstances surrounding the financial support of noncustodial children (Garfinkel, Meyer, and McLanahan 1998). Not surprisingly, the amount of awards varied widely, even among similar types of families. In the recent past, the administrative authority for child support was left to the local courts, and an individual judge had the power to decide whether the residential father should be required to pay, and what the payment should be. Enforcement was minimal; usually the burden of pursuing overdue payments was left to the mother.

Prior to 1979, data on child support are sketchy. By 1979, the Census Bureau added questions pertaining to child support to its Current Population Survey (CPS). These data began to provide a clearer picture, and the news was not good. Only 60 percent of mothers with children who were eligible for child support had a legal arrangement requiring the father to pay. Furthermore, of the 60 percent of fathers with child support orders, only one-half of them paid the full amount due on a regular basis, one-quarter paid only a portion of what was due, and one-quarter paid nothing at all (U.S. Bureau of the Census 1983).

Since then, the federal government has stepped up efforts to improve the collection of child support payments. A series of laws were passed aimed at increasing and standardizing child support orders, and increasing collection rates (Garfinkel, Meyer, and McLanahan 1998). These include the Child Support Enforcement (CSE) amendment to Title IV of the Social Security Act, and establishing the federal Office of Child Support Enforcement (OCSE), which requires all states to establish comparable state offices and which provides federal funding to augment state funding for enforcement.

How successful are these stepped-up efforts? Unfortunately, overall trends in child support have not improved dramatically. For 40 percent of single parents, there is no child support agreement—of the 13.4 million custodial parents in 2002, only 7.9 million (59 percent) had some type of legal or nonlegal support agreement for their children. Forty-one percent did not have any type of set agreement. Why would a custodial parent fail to have a child support agreement? Reasons include sentiments such as "did not feel the need to make it legal" (33 percent), "other parent pays what they can" (26 percent), "other parent could not afford to pay" (23 percent), and "did not want other parent to pay" (19 percent) (Grall 2003).

Moreover, of the 7.9 million who did have some sort of agreement, only three-quarters of custodial mothers received any payment at all, and less than half

(45 percent) received their full payment on a regular basis. The average child support bill due was $5,138 annually in 2002, but the average amount received was only $3,198, or nearly $2,000 short per year, enough to lift a family out of poverty (Grall 2003). Yet, the vast majority of these fathers are employed for pay, and less than 10 percent live below the poverty line themselves (Grall 2005).

Kate also faces a number of structural barriers that impede her success. One of those barriers is a lack of reliable transportation. Research has found that the lack of affordable and reliable transportation presents a barrier to securing employment even more serious than the lack of childcare (Kaplan 1998). The poor cannot afford to buy or maintain reliable automobiles (Seccombe et al. 2005). Welfare programs limit the automobile assets that a person could have, even if he or she managed to purchase a car. The personal asset value of an automobile (value minus debt) varies by state, but in several states it cannot be worth more than $4,650 before it is counted against eligibility for assistance (U.S. Department of Health and Human Services 2004). This situation poses a dilemma for a rational person—How can I find and maintain a respectable job, if I am not allowed to have reliable (i.e., more expensive) transportation?

Public transportation and walking are the primary alternatives to the private automobile. Although public transportation is available in larger communities, it can be expensive, unreliable, time-consuming, and inconvenient. Bus service is usually reduced or eliminated on weekends and at night. Moreover, public transportation is completely unavailable in many smaller communities.

Bicycling or walking are options; however, communities built since the 1950s are often spread out. They are not geared toward pedestrians or cyclists, but geared instead toward private automobile ownership. Few communities have a strong, central, vibrant downtown core for work. Instead, people work in strip malls spread throughout the city limits and fringe areas. Sidewalks may not exist, traffic whizzes by, and without a central core, walking, bicycling, or relying on public transportation becomes difficult or dangerous. Walking through high-crime neighborhoods or crossing highways, especially at night, poses special problems. Walking can also add an hour or two to childcare bills, and it may necessitate being away from one's children for 9, 10, or 11 hours a day. For better or worse, life without a car is difficult in most cities and towns in the United States. Even with the best intentions, it is not surprising that women without cars find it difficult to maintain steady work.

Robert and Maria

Robert and Maria virtually grew up together in the same working-class neighborhood within a medium-size city. Both lived in neatly kept, but modest homes. They went to school together and played kickball with the neighborhood children. Both remember their childhoods with a sparkle in their eye: "Those were the days," Robert claimed. "Things were safe back then. The neighborhood kids played until well after dark. We didn't have to worry about gangs, crime, or drugs back then."

Robert and Maria began dating in their senior year of high school and married a few years later. Both went to a nearby community college to further their education, although Robert dropped out after a year to get a full-time job in construction. Maria finished a degree in cosmetology, and soon after began working at a hair salon, work that she continues today. Together they earned *"good money"* and bought a house in their old neighborhood not far from the street that they grew up on. Robert came from a large family, with two brothers and four sisters. Maria only had one brother, who was 13 years her senior, and so in many ways she felt like a single child. She was often lonely, except for her neighborhood friends, and therefore, not surprisingly, Robert and Maria agreed that when the time was right, they too would have a large family.

They worked and saved diligently for several years after marrying. Purchasing a home meant security to them. They did not really care whether they had fancy cars or took expensive vacations. For Maria and Robert, home and family were the priorities in life, and they devoted their time to one another, fixing up their modest home and spending time with their extended family. They sometimes went to a movie together, or went bowling. However, for the most part, they were quiet homebodies and perfectly content.

After four years of marriage, at the age of 25, Maria had their first child, whom they named Adrian, after Maria's father. Two years later, Maria had a daughter, Sarah. Three years later, she bore twin sons, Jake and Levi. With four children, they decided that their family felt complete. Maria was pleased; because her children were so close in age, no one would ever feel lonely.

Maria and Robert had a clear and shared idea of roles within their family. Robert's primary job was the family breadwinner, a role in which he took great pride. Although his earnings fluctuated somewhat month-to-month, he generally earned around $3,000 a month, which was enough to support the family on their frugal budget. He also received a generous health insurance and retirement plan, adding to the security of the family. Maria's role was to stay at home and take care of the children, a role which she also cherished. This was the model they had known as children, and they wanted to duplicate it for their own children. Therefore, Maria quit working after the children were born, assuming that she would never work again, or at least not until all the children were grown.

Their life continued in this pattern for several years. It was able to continue because of the economic boom of the 1990s in which construction jobs were in demand. Unfortunately, the next decade ushered in an economic recession that drastically altered their lives.

The change was subtle at first. In an effort to scale back the rising costs of labor, a few newly hired workers at Robert's worksite were laid off. Then Robert's employer-sponsored health insurance coverage was reduced, requiring him to pay a higher monthly fee for insurance, along with increased deductibles and copayments. These costs took a large bite out of the monthly budget. Two years later, health insurance benefits were eliminated altogether. The owner apologized profusely, but said that the rapidly increasing costs of providing insurance to his workers could cause the company to fold. It would be better to eliminate health coverage, he reasoned, than it would be to eliminate more jobs.

When Robert told Maria that insurance benefits had been eliminated, she felt a stab of terror in her heart. With four active children still under the age of 9, she knew the importance of health insurance coverage. In the past year alone, Adrian had broken his arm on his skateboard, Sarah had needed stitches, and Levi had been in and out of the doctor's office several times for recurrent ear infections. Jake had been healthy, but like the others he still needed routine medical and dental care. Moreover, looking ahead, Levi and Jake, like their two older siblings, were going to need extensive orthodontic work. How would they pay these bills, she asked?

> You just can't imagine the fear unless you've been in this situation. I would almost rather have had him take a 50 percent pay cut. We can get food from relatives, and they can help us with school clothes and this and that. But how are we supposed to pay for all those high-price fancy doctor bills?

It did not take long for her fears to be realized. Maria developed a bladder infection and was racked with pain. She tried every home remedy she could think of, to no avail, but waited nearly a week until Robert's payday before seeking professional treatment. The doctor scolded her for waiting so long, and then wrote her a prescription for some little white pills that would clear up her infection. Within two days she was feeling fine, but at a cost of $140.

The next month, Levi had another severe ear infection. The doctor suggested more extensive tests to try to establish the root cause of the repeated infections. How much would these tests cost, she asked? Were they really necessary? Could the doctor do a few of the tests or did he need to do them all? After negotiating the best avenue of treatment at the least cost, Maria and Robert were billed almost $650, and they chose a payment plan to spread the costs over six months, with interest.

The next two years continued this way, with routine care foregone, urgent care delayed or reduced, and medicines rationed. Dental care for the children, which had seemed so important years before, was put on hold. Nonetheless, healthcare bills mounted, and by the end of the second year, they were more than $4,000 in debt. Robert occasionally looked for another job that would provide health insurance benefits for his family, but few of these were available, and all would mandate a drastic pay cut as well as loss of seniority. He and Maria felt that the best course of action would be for him to stay at his current job. Once they got out of debt, they would see about purchasing a health insurance policy on their own.

Robert and Maria, despite their best intentions, never got out of medical debt. Suddenly and without warning, Robert's appendix burst. Although he tried to forgo care at first, thinking it was just a stomachache, it quickly became clear that this was like no other ache or pain he had experienced. He fretted over how much this problem would cost, and therefore, tried a number of home remedies to relieve the pain, without success. Finally, Maria drove him to the emergency room, where he was immediately prepped for surgery. The bill came to more than $12,000. However, the delay in seeking medical care almost cost him dearly—his surgery was more extensive, and there were additional complications because of the delay. Robert nearly died. His recovery was compromised and took far longer than he could have imagined.

The surgery required Robert to take a significant amount of time off work because he could not do the heavy lifting and physical work required in his construction job. The family received unemployment benefits, but they were only a fraction of his earnings and were of limited duration. At the urging of his friends from work, Robert investigated whether he would be eligible for other benefits, such as disability pay, but he was not eligible because he was not certified as "disabled." He looked for odd jobs to supplement their income, and found some, but most were only temporary and paid near minimum wage, at $5.15 an hour. Their family was now stretched financially far beyond its means. Robert assumed he would be ready to go back into construction within a year, but how would the family live in the meantime? They both knew that Maria would have to find a job, although it took them a while to admit it to one another. She was very busy taking care of four young children, and she wondered how she would fit a job into her schedule.

I didn't really want to work, you know, with four young kids and all. I envisioned my life as a homemaker, not a breadwinner. But there was no choice, really. Robert was trying to find work, but mostly all he could get was just a few bucks. He's a hard worker, but even most of the temporary jobs want him to lift and carry and he just can't. Not yet. We can't risk it because it will injure him.

Maria's license to practice cosmetology had expired and renewing it took additional time and money. She did not have the time to develop a large client base, so she went to work at a styling shop in the nearby mall where customers dropped in without an appointment and received the first stylist available. She first worked part-time and then boosted her hours to nearly full-time when an opening emerged, and she became the primary breadwinner. However, her earnings were low. At $6.00 an hour, plus tips of $20 to $25 a day, her family of six was now living in poverty and was swamped by medical debt.

The two oldest children were in school, but with Robert working odd jobs when he could find them and Maria working nearly full-time, they needed someone to help them care for their twins, Levi and Jake. First, they asked relatives, and although a few could help out a day or two a week, none were available on a full-time basis. Maria cried as she browsed through the telephone book for daycare centers. Of the first 15 she called, all were full, and she could not have afforded their fees of $700 a month *per child* anyway. She looked through the want ads and found a woman living about a mile away who would watch the twins for $6.00 an hour. Maria and Robert quickly did the math and decided that, at three days a week, it would run about $600 a month for their two sons. They felt they could eke that out of the budget, if they could rely upon their families for the other two days. On days that Robert was home, he could watch the children. So they began to patch together childcare for their sons that varied from week to week. Their previously stable and predictable lives were now in a constant state of chaos. Said Maria:

> Let's see, it's Tuesday, so where are Levi and Jake today? That's about how it was, every day they were someplace else. Daddy has them today, the babysitter tomorrow, Auntie El has them the next day, or wait, does she have them the day after? It just tore at my heart, you know, that's not what we had planned for our family.

Their extended families offered assistance as they could. Although no one had a lot of money, they offered services. Robert's brother fixed their washing machine when it went out. His sister and nieces babysat when needed. His nephews helped clean out the garage. Other relatives donated children's clothes. Maria's parents generously offered to pay to continue Sarah and Adrian's orthodontic care from their retirement savings, a significant gift given their limited financial means.

Despite this assistance, it was not enough. Robert and Maria's income was reduced to less than $1,500 a month, half of what it had been a few years earlier, with significant bills to pay. They thought of filing bankruptcy, but they did not want to further hurt their credit rating. They thought of selling the house, but they questioned where the six of them could realistically live. Moreover, they believed that their poverty was only temporary and that things would soon be better.

Unfortunately, their bout with poverty was longer than expected. When Robert's doctor finally certified that he was ready to resume demanding construction work, Robert found that someone else had filled his position. He was angry, but recognized that it would have been difficult for his boss to hold his position for more than a year. Robert looked for a new job, but it took him three months to find another one. Moreover, the pay in his new job was half of what he earned before, and although it provided health insurance for his family, it was very limited coverage and would only insure them after he had been at the job for six months. Nonetheless, he gratefully accepted the job.

What Can We Learn From Robert and Maria?

Robert and Maria do not fit our stereotypical image of the poor. They are a two-parent family, they are hardworking, and they have marketable skills. Moreover, their poverty is short-term and caused by a specific crisis—an illness—rather than a chronic condition. Yet, despite the stereotypes, many poor families fit squarely into this pattern.

Poverty is not always long-term. Sociologist Mark Rank suggests that we reconceptualize the poverty experience because most Americans will experience poverty and will turn to some form of public assistance at some point during their lives. Using national longitudinal data to estimate the likelihood of poverty spells over the life course, he found that by the time Americans have reached age 75, 59 percent would have spent at least a year below the poverty line during their adulthood. Moreover, approximately two-thirds would have received public assistance as adults for at least one year (Rank 2003).

These facts suggest that we must depart from the "we" versus "they" dichotomy that is such a strong feature of American life. Unlike western Europeans, Americans are quick to suggest that poverty is a personal failing, and that people are poor because of their own laziness and personal shortcomings (Cozzarelli, Wilkinson, and Tagler 2001; Hancock 2004; Feagin 1975; Seccombe 2007). Americans believe that individuals are largely responsible for their own economic position in society and that opportunities are available to all who are willing to work hard and who are sufficiently motivated. One recent study of 112 undergraduates at a Midwestern university found that respondents who believed that the world is largely a just place tended to have negative attitudes toward the poor, while participants who believed the world is unjust had more positive attitudes toward the poor (Coryn 2002). Tales of Horatio Alger types abound—the "rags to riches stories"—the moral being that anyone can pull themselves up by their bootstraps with hard work, sweat, and motivation.

The case of Robert and Maria also highlights the importance of health insurance for the financial well-being of families. According to data from the U.S. Census Bureau, 47 million Americans, or 16 percent of the population, were without health insurance in 2005 (DeNavas-Walt, Proctor, and Lee 2006). Eleven percent of children were uninsured, including 19 percent of those living in poverty.

Why is health insurance of such concern? It is estimated that both adults and children who do not have health insurance use the healthcare system less often than those with insurance. They are less likely to have a regular source of healthcare and are more likely to rely on emergency rooms for treatment (Hadley 2003; Kaiser Commission on Medicaid and the Uninsured 2003). Uninsured children are less likely to get routine well-child care, and they use medical and dental services less frequently than do insured children, causing unnecessary suffering. In an extensive review of research published over the past 25 years, it was estimated that having health insurance could reduce the mortality rate of the uninsured by at least 4 percent, and possibly by 25 percent (Hadley 2003).

Health insurance is a family affair because medical costs risk a family's entire economic viability. When even one member is uninsured, all family members become at risk. The costs of healthcare are far outpacing inflation, and many families have trouble paying medical bills. Attempts to finance healthcare are a leading cause of debt and personal bankruptcy, and concern over costs of healthcare benefits are a leading cause of workers' strikes. Preexisting conditions can be used to deny a person healthcare benefits, thereby endangering the financial well-being of not only the individual but also his or her entire family (Doty, Edwards, and Holmgren 2005; Sered and Fernandopulle 2005; Committee on the Consequences of Uninsurance 2002). The healthcare system is recognized as being in "crisis" largely because no one is exempt from vulnerability. The total number of uninsured Americans grew even during years of economic prosperity (Holahan and Kim 2000).

Health insurance is a critical dimension of social and economic well-being, is vital to understanding American patterns of social stratification, and deserves a prominent place in our study of the relationship between socioeconomic status, social conditions, and mortality (Link and Phelan 1995; Phelan et al. 2004). While all persons, rich and poor, are vulnerable, families at the bottom of our economic and occupational structure are particularly close to an impending crisis. Robert, Maria, and their children represent some of the victims.

Poverty Is a Structural Problem

This chapter presents several case studies to illustrate the diversity among poor families. Despite popular opinion, not all poor families are on welfare, are single mothers, are minorities, or have lots of children. Many poor families are hard working. Others have physical or mental health conditions that prevent them from working. Most are white. Moreover, many are poor for only short spells because some particular incident propelled them into poverty, such as a divorce, a job loss, or an illness, and they need time to amass their resources to lift them back out of impoverishment.

This book explores many dimensions of families living in poverty. It examines who is poor, with what consequences, and how families ended up this way. It also looks at what can be done to prevent families from slipping into poverty or to help those who are already there.

Dee, Kate, Robert, and Maria reveal an important, but hidden fact about poverty. Most families are poor because of structural conditions, not because of their own laziness or lack of motivation. The first theme of this book is that *poverty is a structural problem, not merely a personal one.* Sociologist C. Wright Mills stressed the importance of understanding the relationship between individuals and the society in which they live, calling this the **sociological imagination** (Mills 1959). He suggested that problems such as poverty, unemployment, work-family stress, or finding adequate childcare and affordable housing, are more than just personal troubles experienced in isolation by a few people. They are issues that affect large numbers of people and originate in the institutional arrangements of society. They are rooted in our social structure, including our social institutions, such as our economic system of capitalism that has a primary goal of profit; our healthcare system that leaves millions uninsured and unable to access healthcare; and our government policies that leave families largely to fend for themselves to find childcare or affordable housing.

These problems are also rooted in our social positions and their accompanying roles, including sex and race. For example, the feminization of poverty is well documented, and is due in part to the lower wages paid to women in virtually every job category (U.S. Department of Labor 2005a). Women who are employed full-time earn only about 81 percent of the wages paid to men (U.S. Department of Labor 2006c). Likewise, racial discrimination continues to be widespread—one study reported that as recently as 1990, a substantial portion of whites saw Blacks, Hispanics, and to a somewhat lesser degree Asians, as unintelligent, lazy, and prone to violence. For example, 29 percent of whites claimed that most Blacks are unintelligent, 44 percent reported that most Blacks are lazy, and 56 percent claimed that most Blacks prefer welfare to work (Davis and Smith 1990).

If poverty is generally a structural problem rooted in our social arrangements, social positions, and their accompanying roles, then the second theme of this book is that *the solutions to poverty are also largely structural in nature.* It is not enough to try to motivate people to get out of poverty with a variety of individual inducements or punishments. Instead, the solutions that will have the largest impact on poverty are those that will amend our social institutions and social statuses so that equality, fairness, and social support are key values. Social policies should support children, and support parents as they raise them. Our economic system should ensure living wages; accessing the healthcare system should be a right rather than a privilege and be provided to all in need regardless of ability to pay; and government should pass proactive policies to assist all families struggling to raise healthy, happy, intelligent, and socially responsible children. If poverty is a social problem rather than simply a series of personal shortcomings, then the primary solutions must address the root of the social problems rather than focus on individuals.

The stories of Dee, Kate, Robert, and Maria reveal the complexities and challenges experienced by many Americans who are struggling to feed, clothe, house, and care for their families. We can question certain points—why would someone get involved with an abusive partner, why would someone have four children, why would someone have children before their job skills were fully developed, why would someone continue working in a job without health insurance—but the answers to these questions are also complex. Blaming individuals for the choices they make will never really answer questions about the causes of poverty, its consequences, or its remedies. Instead, their struggles reveal that a true understanding of the nature of poverty requires us to look at the social factors that enable people to slip through the cracks of our society, and examine how the structure of our safety net limits their abilities to thrive.

Conclusion and Organization

This book draws upon recent quantitative and qualitative data to describe the trends in poverty in the United States; to define how poverty is measured and provide a critique of various measures; to describe the consequences of poverty on children and adults; and to offer and analyze several explanations for poverty from the structural, economic, and individualistic perspectives. It discusses labor market issues such as unemployment, the minimum wage, and employer-sponsored fringe benefits; describes and critiques programs in the United States designed to eliminate or reduce the incidence of poverty or its effects on families (e.g., food stamps, Medicaid, Head Start); discusses the evolution of the 1996 welfare reform legislation and the Temporary Assistance to Needy Families (TANF) program; describes and evaluates the effects of welfare reforms; and compares and contrasts our family antipoverty policies with those of other industrialized nations. The goals are to bring together the best and most recent quantitative and qualitative data to better understand the extent of poverty among families in the United States, the problems poor families face, and ultimately, to argue that poverty is not insurmountable and that real solutions do exist.

Chapter 2 addresses two questions: what is poverty and who is poor? This chapter describes the extent of poverty across specific subgroups in our population, and it examines who makes up "the poor." It also describes how poverty is defined and measured, illustrating how the political climate of the 1960s influenced the development of the federal government's official poverty thresholds. It critiques the official method and describes alternative measures.

Poverty has many deleterious effects on families. *Chapter 3* describes the ways that poverty affects children and adults, including physical and mental health, social capital, educational achievement, hunger and food insecurity, access to healthcare, teenage pregnancy and parenthood, inadequate housing, job and economic opportunities, and neighborhood problems such as crime and violence.

People commonly blame individuals for their poverty because it is easier to assign poverty to personal attributes, failings, or just plain bad luck than to something as obscure as "society." *Chapter 4* discusses several specific theories of poverty, including individualistic, structural, subcultural, and fatalistic explanations, and analyzes why some explanations are more popular than others.

Chapter 5 describes how the Personal Responsibility and Work Opportunity Reconciliation Act of 1996 (PRWORA, P. L. 104-93) altered the context in which poor families can receive cash assistance. With the passage of the PRWORA, the federal government replaced Aid to Families with Dependent Children (AFDC) with TANF. Although it turned over many of the specific details of welfare law to states, it imposed time limits and implemented work requirements. It reduced support for education and human capital development, and it allowed states to cap benefits if a woman had another child while receiving assistance. This chapter will describe this legislation and its consequences. Are families better off after leaving TANF?

What programs and policies are needed to build stronger families? Many programs have been created and policies enacted over the past 40 years, particularly since the War on Poverty, to ameliorate the effects of poverty. *Chapter 6* discusses several of the more prominent programs, including Medicare and Medicaid, food stamps, and Head Start. It also describes two important financial programs: the Earned Income Tax Credit and Social Security.

Chapter 7 shows how researchers make comparisons of poverty between the United States and other industrialized countries. All measures show a similar pattern: the U.S. poverty rate exceeds those of other comparable countries. This chapter will describe why the United States—the wealthiest nation in the world—has relatively high rates of poverty. The primary reason for this discrepancy is that most industrialized nations have an interrelated set of proactive and universal programs to help families escape poverty.

Critical Thinking Questions:

1. How do these three case studies confirm or conflict with your own personal idea of who is poor and the reasons for their poverty?

2. The author suggests that poverty is a structural problem. But are not individuals responsible for their own economic plight? Why or why not?

3. What are you doing in your own life to ensure your life circumstances are different than those of Dee, Kate, Robert, and Maria? Can individuals really prevent poverty?

2

WHO ARE THE POOR, AND WHAT EXACTLY IS POVERTY, ANYWAY?

DURING THE PAST 15 YEARS, the U.S. economy has been on a roller coaster ride. The 1990s were boom years, with incomes and spending up, unemployment low, and poverty rates in decline. The mood was exuberant and people were genuinely optimistic about the future. Likewise, at the turn of this century, the U.S. Census Bureau reported seemingly good news about the new millennium: median income was up, and poverty rates among families, single adults, and children were down. "Every racial and ethnic group experienced a drop in both the number of poor and the percentage in poverty, as did children, the elderly and people ages 25 to 44. . . . And on the income side, this was the fifth consecutive year that households experienced a real annual increase in income," hailed Daniel Weinberg, chief of the Census Bureau's Housing and Household Economic Statistics Division (U.S. Census Bureau Public Information Office 2001b). Poverty rates declined more than 15 percent between 1990 and 2000, although most of this decline occurred in only two years—between 1998 and 2000.

However, that exuberance and optimism was short-lived. By the next year, the booming economy began to fade. In the recession of the early 2000s, jobs were lost, wages were stunted, and important benefits, such as health insurance, were eroded or had disappeared. Safety nets were inadequate to meet the demands of a growing number of people who needed assistance meeting basic, yet critical, needs for food, shelter, and clothing. The number of families living in poverty began to rise significantly.

How Many Are Poor?

After falling for most of the 1990s to near-record lows, poverty began to increase after 2000. By 2005, 37 million Americans, or 12.6 percent, lived below the poverty line. The poverty rate reached 10.8 percent among all persons living in families and 31.1 percent among those living in families with female-headed households without men, as shown in Figure 2.1 (DeNavas-Walt, Proctor, and Lee 2006). All groups, including children, adults, the elderly, whites, Blacks, Hispanics, and Asians experienced an increasing likelihood of living in poverty.

Race, Ethnicity, and Poverty

Blacks and Hispanics have the highest rates of poverty, at 24.7 percent and 21.8 in 2005, respectively, as shown in Figure 2.2. In contrast, 8.3 percent of non-Hispanic whites and 10.9 percent of Asians live in poverty. However, while poverty among all race and ethnic groups increased between 2000 and 2005, the proportional

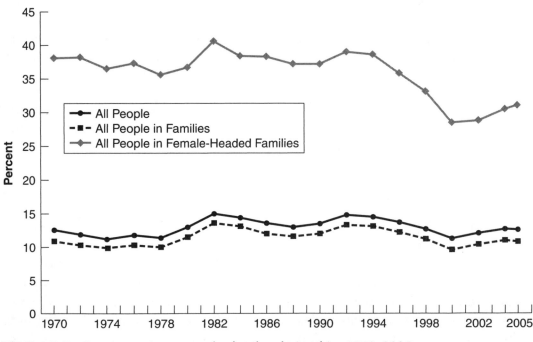

Figure 2.1 Percentage in poverty by family relationship: 1970–2005
Source: DeNavas-Walt, Proctor, and Lee 2006, Table B-1, pp. 46–51.

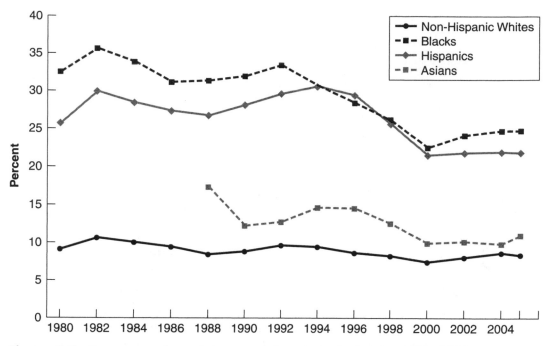

Figure 2.2 Percentage of people in poverty by race and ethnicity: 1980–2005
Source: DeNavas-Walt, Proctor, and Lee 2006, Table B-2, pp. 46–51.

increase is largest among whites and Asians, the two groups with the lowest rates overall (DeNavas-Walt, Proctor, and Lee 2006).

The Census Bureau collapses race and ethnic categories, such as "Hispanic" or "Asian." Nonetheless, it is important to recognize the cultural and economic diversity among minority groups. For example, not all Hispanic groups have high poverty rates. Although Mexican Americans and Puerto Ricans have high rates, the rate among Cuban Americans is very close to that of whites. Likewise, Chinese and Japanese Americans have very low rates of poverty, while Vietnamese Americans are somewhat more likely to be impoverished. The broad race and ethnic classifications used by the Census Bureau can mask tremendous differences within these groups.

Children in Poverty

Of all impoverished groups, perhaps the one that tugs the hearts of most people is children. Child poverty has increased about 10 percent since 2000, touching the lives of an additional 1.3 million children. This increase is alarming because a childhood spent in poverty can have negative repercussions on an individual's

Table 2.1   Percentage of People in Poverty by Age: 1980–2005

	Children Under 18	Adults 18–64	Elderly 65 and Over
1980	18.3	10.1	15.7
1990	20.6	10.7	12.2
2000	16.2	9.6	9.9
2005	17.6	11.1	10.1

Source: DeNavas-Walt, Proctor, and Lee 2006, Table B-2, pp. 52–57.

entire life. By 2005, about 18 percent of children were impoverished, as shown in Table 2.1. Moreover, children under the age of six are more likely than older children to live below the poverty line (20 percent versus 16 percent, respectively in 2005).

Children in female-headed families and minority children are particularly vulnerable. About 43 percent of children in female-headed families are poor, in contrast to less than 9 percent of children living in married couple families. With respect to race and ethnicity, one in three Black children, almost three in ten Hispanic children, slightly more than one in ten white (non-Hispanic) children, and one in ten Asian children were poor (Children's Defense Fund 2005b; U.S. Department of Commerce 2005; Child Trends Database 2005; DeNavas-Walt, Proctor, and Lee 2006).

Even more disturbing than the rise in poverty is the marked increase in the number of people, especially children, who live in **extreme poverty.** Extreme poverty is defined as living below one-half of the poverty level. This measure translates into a family of three having to support itself on about $7,500 a year, or on no more than $20 a day (Children's Defense Fund 2005b). Census data reveals that nearly 8 percent of children, or 5.6 million young people under the age of 18, live in households with earnings less than one-half of the poverty line (DeNavas-Walt, Proctor, and Lee 2006). For every five children who have fallen into poverty since 2000, more than three of these children fell into extreme poverty. Their lives are seriously compromised.

Other Parts of the Story

However, increasing rates of poverty reveal only part of the story. Several other indicators also have emerged, revealing that many families are truly vulnerable and live on the economic margins of our society.

- Inequality in income and wealth (a total economic package including stocks, real estate, and other assets in addition to income) has steadily increased, and the gap between rich and poor is the largest in recent history.
- The purchasing power represented by the poverty line has been steadily eroded.
- Families leaving welfare for work earn wages averaging only $7.50 per hour—far below what is needed to lift them out of poverty.
- Unemployment rates rose to their highest levels in decades. Minority group members and teens were particularly hard-hit by unemployment.
- The percentage of poor children who are "food insecure" (i.e., have difficulty obtaining enough food, have reduced quality of diets, report anxiety about their food supply, or experience moderate to severe hunger) has increased.
- Approximately 47 million Americans have no health insurance whatsoever. Millions more have health insurance that is woefully inadequate to meet their needs.

Pearl's Family: Living in Extreme Poverty

I interviewed a family living in extreme poverty in Florida (Seccombe 2007). When I interviewed Pearl, she was receiving cash assistance welfare for herself and four sons aged 9, 12, 14, and 17 years. She also has three older children who do not live at home, aged 18, 26, and 28. Pearl looked significantly older than her 48 years. She had no teeth, was extremely thin with sunken eyes, and looked exhausted.

Pearl was raising her children alone. She divorced her husband because she was tired of his repeated infidelities that placed her at risk for sexually transmitted diseases. She and her children live in an apartment in a run-down housing project, although she made an obvious attempt to keep her apartment neat and clean, and had planted and tended to several beautiful plants outside her front door.

Pearl's life is very difficult, and it has always been difficult. She left school in the eighth grade to help support her family by picking vegetables. Poverty has plagued her most of her life despite hard work in agriculture. The pay usually amounted to minimum wage, but combining her income with her ex-husband's, their family managed to get by. She also has worked as a maid in hotels and has cleaned houses.

Today, however, is a different story. The extreme poverty and the stress of taking care of seven children virtually on her own with so few resources have taken a serious toll on her mental and physical health. These health problems further exacerbate her family's poverty by limiting her capabilities for work.

I have a lot of pressure. It's like a bruise, you know, all my life. By staying down and worrying about the kids. I've had to raise them all myself. Stress. I've been under a lot of stress for a long time. They put me on Prozac. Sometimes I have so much pressure, sometimes I don't take them. I just sit there and let the pressure worry me. I had fainting spells, and the doctor said, "I can't see anything, just get it together." Like I want to. But I tried, but with the kids, it was like, throw me back. It's hard being with such pressure all the time. I let myself go down by worrying about them.

What has life been like for her children? None of them has had an easy life, and all have been in trouble with the law one way or another. Her two eldest sons, who live elsewhere, have been in and out of jail repeatedly. Living in a run-down housing project, her children are looking for escape and are surrounded by temptations for "easy money" from selling and using drugs.

You know, in this neighborhood, they get with other kids, and they are doing drugs, so they want to do the same thing... I've been trying to get money to get out of here. I want to move far out of the projects. There is too much drugs. They're messing everywhere you go. Lots of drug dealers in this neighborhood. Those drug dealers put ideas of easy money into their heads...

From her sons' perspectives, why not sell drugs? It is portrayed as glamorous, easy, and profitable work. She told me that she has tried to teach them the value of a dollar, and she suggested that if they worked in the fields on Saturdays, she would let them keep all of the money earned and put it toward the high-priced sneakers or clothing they beg for. They laughed at the idea of working in the fields, only to make minimum wage at the end of the day.

None of her children has graduated from high school; all dropped out in the ninth or tenth grade. At the time of the interview, her 12-year-old son was home because he had been suspended from school for two weeks because of a sex-related offense, of which he claimed innocence. Her 14-year-old son was home watching TV because of a "cough," though I did not hear him cough once during the 90 minutes that I was there. Her children rarely help her with household chores.

I wash clothes 24 hours a day, hang them up, fold them, and put them in the room. I mop the floor and clean up the house all the time. . . . They don't want to do nothing like that. If you don't have any money, your children don't want to help you nowadays. I feel so much pressure that I can't go to sleep at night.

Pearl acknowledged that she loves her children fiercely, but she has little control over them. Trying to keep them out of drugs and in school, and cleaning up after them is more than a full-time job itself. It is more than she can manage on many days.

It was unclear what type of job Pearl could realistically get, and whether she could hold one down. Her health problems, lack of job skills, and her age pose formidable barriers.

Do all children living in extreme poverty have such despondent lives? Of course not. Yet, the lifelong risks associated with impoverishment are clearly established. Compared to the more affluent, children living in poverty are less likely to graduate from school, are more likely to become pregnant or impregnate someone as teens, and are exposed to inadequate healthcare, substandard housing, and poor nutrition. As adults, their incomes are low, and they are more likely to raise their own children in poverty (Children's Defense Fund 2005b; Seccombe 2000).

How Is Poverty Measured?

Counting the number of poor among us is done with an air of authority, but exactly how are these numbers determined? Is there some standard, fool-proof formula? Not really. It is important to note that there are many different ways to measure poverty, each with a different set of assumptions, results, and interpretations (Roosa et al. 2005). The federal government and U.S. census reports use one standardized method, and this approach receives the most attention in the literature. However, it is not the only approach available.

Absolute measures of poverty focus on the amount of money required to have basic needs met (e.g., food or shelter). Persons or families living below this amount are counted as poor (Iceland 2003). The focus is on the ability to purchase the necessities to sustain life and these measures do not account for subjective and changing perceptions about poverty. In contrast, **relative measures** are more subjective and assume that poverty exists only relative to a society's level of economic and social advancement (Iceland 2003). Someone we consider poor in the United States may be considered quite well off in parts of Ethiopia, Bangladesh, or India, because the American likely has food to eat, clothes to wear, and a home to live in. He or she has gone to school and may even own items like a car or television set. Likewise, American standards of living are constantly changing, and what once was considered a normative standard of living would now be seen as signs of impoverishment—a lack of indoor plumbing or crowded living conditions, for example. As incomes and expectations rise, so do the perceptions of what a family minimally needs to survive.

Absolute Measures

Of these two approaches, the United States tends to rely on absolute measures of poverty. The federal **poverty thresholds (or poverty lines)** were established by the Social Security Administration in 1964 as a way to measure the number of people living in poverty, and they are the most common way that poverty is measured today (Dalaker 2005; Fisher 1997; Orshansky 1965). Mollie Orshansky, an analyst at the Social Security Administration, developed a set of poverty thresholds in the early 1960s that focused on family food consumption because, as she wrote, "... there is no generally accepted standard of adequacy for essentials of living except food" (Orshansky 1965). Survey data in the 1950s indicated that families spent approximately one-third of their after-tax income on food. Therefore, she reasoned that a poverty threshold could be obtained if she calculated a reasonable food budget and multiplied it by three.

What is a reasonable food budget? Dieticians with the U.S. Department of Agriculture (USDA), using complex procedures, had already developed several food plans designed to meet basic nutritional requirements. Within each food plan, dollar amounts, and thus food choices, varied. The Social Security Administration elected to use the most stringent of these food plans, "The Economy Food Plan," as it was then called, which was developed as a very low cost food budget and designated "for temporary and emergency use when funds are low" (cited in Fisher 1997:1). Orshansky then multiplied this minimalist food budget by a factor of three, which results in the nonfood items in a family's budget also being reduced sharply. However, she assumed that the nonfood portion of a poor family's budget also would be minimal, but adequate.

Since families' food budgets vary by family size and composition, she developed 124 different poverty thresholds to take these factors into account. For example, four-person families have larger food budgets than do three-person families, and therefore, the poverty threshold is higher as a result. She adjusted the thresholds of one- and two-person families by slightly higher factors because she reasoned that those families likely had higher fixed costs. She also differentiated her thresholds by farm/nonfarm status, by the sex of the family head, by the number of family members who were children, and by aged/nonaged status, arguing that these types of families may spend more or less than one-third of their income on food, thereby adjusting her multiplier somewhat. For example, it was decided to set farm poverty thresholds at 70 percent of the corresponding nonfarm thresholds (because those on farms can grow some of their own food).

With a number of recent modifications to streamline poverty thresholds (e.g., eliminating the farm/nonfarm and female-/male-headed families distinctions), and updated by the Consumer Price Index for the cost of food, this method for calculating poverty thresholds continues today (Committee on Ways and Means 1996). The food budget parallels the current "Thrifty Food Plan," which forms the basis of food stamp benefits and continues to be the least expensive food plan developed by the USDA (Family Economics and Nutrition Review 1997). It provides far below the amount most middle-class families spend on food. Individuals or families with annual incomes below this established threshold are counted as "poor."

Table 2.2 illustrates the poverty threshold by family size. Presented here are averages; thresholds continue to vary by whether the individuals are over or under age 65, and whether a person lives in the 48 contiguous states or Alaska and Hawaii, because food costs are expected to differ for these various groups. It is revised yearly based on inflationary changes in the Consumer Price Index. The average 2005 poverty thresholds are $15,577 for a family of three, and $19,971 for a family of four (DeNavas-Walt, Proctor, and Lee 2006). Therefore, only families living on less than these thresholds are counted in the federal poverty statistics. Meanwhile, other families who are living on incomes only slightly above the poverty thresholds are still teetering on the margins and struggling to make ends meet, but they are not counted in official government statistics.

How easy or difficult is it to live on a poverty-level budget? The 2005 poverty threshold for a family of three comes to about $1,300 a month before taxes. This means that a family with three people (e.g., a single mother and two children, or two parents and one child) are only counted as poor if they live on about $1,300 a month or less. If they live on more than this amount, they are not counted as poor. Could your family of three live on this amount?

Let's find out by examining a sample budget. The figures we use here will be drawn from government data estimating annual costs of basic needs in 2005. These data include reports by the USDA, the Center on Budget and Policy Priorities, and other consumer expenditure reports estimating the price of a "low-cost"

Table 2.2 Weighted Average Poverty Thresholds in 2005, by Size of Family

One person	$9,973
Two people	$12,755
Three people	$15,577
Four people	$19,971
Five people	$23,613
Six people	$26,683
Seven people	$30,249
Eight people	$33,610
Nine people or more	$40,288

Source: DeNavas-Walt, Proctor, and Lee 2006

food plan, the fair market rent for a two-bedroom apartment, the cost estimate for childcare, and other expenditures. The cost of living varies somewhat from one community to another, so you may quibble over the cost of specific items in this budget. For example, maybe rents are higher (or lower) where you live than the estimate provided below. These numbers are just sample estimates based on national averages. Plug in your own figures that better represent costs in your community if you believe that these are inadequate. The question is: Is it reasonable to assume that a family of three in the United States can live on $1,300 a month? Keep in mind that someone who works full-time, year round, at approximately $7.40 an hour would earn this amount. Many full-time workers earn considerably less. In 2006, the national minimum wage was $5.15 per hour.

The following example is based on a single parent earning minimum wage, working full-time and raising two children, ages four and seven, and is adapted from a model assembled by the Children's Defense Fund (Children's Defense Fund 2004).

Sample Expenses

Housing (2 bedroom apartment and utilities):	$800
Food:	$425
Childcare:	$620
Healthcare:	$ 65
Clothing:	$ 60
Transportation:	$416
Miscellaneous:	$100
TOTAL	**$2,486/month or $29,832/year**

Already we have gone significantly over the budget. What can we cut back on?

- A cheaper apartment or one in a less desirable part of town? Do not forget that two children live here.
- Reduce the food budget? It is already based on a USDA low-cost food plan.
- Lower the utility bill by keeping the house colder? Inadequate heat is one reason why poor children are more frequently sick.
- Eliminate the telephone? This decision could be dangerous in times of an emergency.
- Cut back on toiletries? Toilet paper, shampoo, and tampons are basic needs.
- Eliminate car maintenance? How will the family get to work and school, or run errands?

Even this revised budget assumes that the family already has a household set up. There is no money included to buy furniture, a car, or household items like towels or dishes. In other words, even $2,486 a month is unrealistically low for three people to live on. As you can see, the poverty line is an inadequate measure of poverty. For all practical purposes, a family of three living on less than $2,500 a month, or $30,000 a year, remains in jeopardy. Yet this is about two times the federal poverty threshold.

How can people survive living below the federal poverty line? Stephanie is a divorced mother living in poverty with her 7-year-old daughter, and they typify a young family living on a poverty budget but determined to have a better life. She has not seen or heard from her ex-husband in four years, and he has not paid any child support. She is a student at a university majoring in nursing, and when I met her, she was one year away from graduation. Supporting herself and her daughter on a university financial aid budget was a challenge, but she trudged on, knowing that a brighter future would someday be within her grasp. Stephanie discussed what it means to try to make it day-to-day without enough money to afford life's basic necessities, including a respectable place to live (Seccombe 2007:171–72):

> . . . is something going to come out and bite me? This is the equivalent of the Black Plague, with all the rats. How can anyone grow up normal, intelligent, and become a productive member of society living like that? I don't understand. And when you're hungry at night or when your child goes to bed cold, how can you expect them to go to school the next morning and learn anything? You know, Maslow's hierarchy of needs. If you don't meet the very bottom ones, how are you supposed to be anything on top? We're humans and will resort to survival skills. And I'm sure that's what many people are doing. Just surviving. I've known a lot of women who live in these villages [student family housing at the university] who are not as fortunate as I am. I mean, I had a house full of stuff when I moved in here because I already had a house. I mean, how can any child grow up and be stimulated in an environment where they may or may not be able to heat the house, or be able to afford the extra $20 or $30 that I had left over at the end of the month to buy food? Or they may not be able to go out and buy the clothing that their child needs when they outgrow it, or the shoes. Most of the time I can swing it. But, like I said, if it wasn't for family housing and living on campus, and my financial aid, there would be no way.

Poverty Threshold (Lines) vs. Poverty Guidelines

To complicate matters a bit, programs that serve the poor, such as food stamps, school lunch programs, educational programs such as Head Start, or cash welfare such as Temporary Assistance to Needy Families (TANF), may use a somewhat different set of criteria to define poverty levels. The **poverty guidelines** are a simplified version of the federal poverty thresholds and are used for administrative purposes—for instance, determining financial eligibility for certain federal programs. They are issued each year in the *Federal Register* by the U.S. Department of Health and Human Services (DHHS). They are calculated somewhat differently, and end up being slightly higher than the federal thresholds. For example, although the federal poverty threshold (or line) for an average family of three in 2005 was $15,577, the federal poverty guideline was $16,090 (U.S. Department of Health and Human Services 2005a). As is the case with the official poverty thresholds, the poverty guidelines are also adjusted for family size, and are adjusted annually for inflation. By 2006, the poverty guidelines for a family of three were adjusted to $16,600.

In addition to the federal thresholds and guidelines previously described, there are other absolute measures that are used in limited contexts. For example, some researchers use participation in a state or federal antipoverty program as an indicator of whether a person or family is living in poverty. This indicator is not an official U.S.-sanctioned measure, because eligibility requirements vary state by state (or even community by community), and some persons may be systematically excluded from programs (e.g., illegal immigrants). Therefore, although the goal of this measure is to broaden the scope and more realistically measure the true extent of impoverishment, it may actually be biased and exclude large numbers of the poor.

Criticisms of the U.S. Poverty Thresholds (and Guidelines)

Is there a better and more accurate way to measure poverty? This question has received significant attention (Brady 2003; Dalaker 2005; Iceland 2003; Roosa et al. 2005; U.S. Department of Commerce 2005). Discerning poverty rates is important because they measure the country's economic well-being, and they allow us to assess trends over time. Absolute poverty measures, such as the thresholds used by the United States, appeal to many people because of their objectivity, simplicity, and ease. Poverty thresholds can be uniformly applied in all states, and distinct lines can be drawn distinguishing the poor from the nonpoor. Comparisons can be made over time based on the assumption that, regardless of rising incomes, there is some specific dollar amount that signals deprivation.

The official poverty threshold measures also have been severely criticized for other reasons, most pointing one way or another to the fact that the measure is highly political. The use of an extremely low food budget, which was designed for temporary and emergency use only, was used as a deliberate strategy to keep the poverty count low to avoid government spending on antipoverty programs (Betson and Warlick 1998).

Another criticism is that the cost of living throughout the United States is highly variable, and the official measure does not take this into account with the exception of Alaska and Hawaii. However, the difference in the cost of housing between New York City or San Francisco and a small town in Alabama is huge.

Related to this point, the poverty threshold does not reflect the increasing cost of nonfood items within a budget, such as home heating, rent, or transportation costs, relative to food expenditures. Food may no longer constitute one-third of a poor family's budget, but realistically constitute one-fourth or one-fifth of a budget. Again, these numbers may vary across the country. Raising poverty thresholds from the current three times the cost of a minimal diet to more than five times the cost of such a diet would increase the poverty threshold by 70 percent for a family of four (Ruggles 1990).

Another criticism is that the poverty threshold does not reflect important changes in our economic and social policies since the 1960s, when it was created. In 2005, 54 percent of mothers with children under age 3, and 63 percent of mothers with children under age 6 were employed for pay (U.S. Department of Labor April 27, 2006). Who will take care of these children, and at what cost? Childcare bills consume about a quarter of a poor family's budget at $67 per week (Johnson 2005). On average, costs in a daycare facility can be more than $10,000 a year per child (Schulman 2000). Likewise, the cost of healthcare has skyrocketed since the 1960s, and the working poor and low-income workers are overrepresented among the 47 million uninsured Americans (DeNavas-Walt, Proctor, and Lee 2006). Yet, the rising costs of childcare and healthcare are not factored into the poverty threshold formulas.

Finally, in-kind benefits, such as food stamps, Medicaid, or subsidized housing, are not calculated as income, and therefore, some critics argue that the measure actually overestimates the number of poor. Also, because the official measure uses pretax income, policies such as the Earned Income Tax Credit, which greatly reduces the tax burden of low-income families, significantly increase the real earnings families can keep (Dalaker 2005). Theoretically, if a family received all forms of assistance, would they truly be poor?

The method used to calculate poverty can dramatically influence the number (and percentage) of persons counted as poor. Some people suggest that the current measure is woefully underestimating poverty, while others suggest that the current measure overestimates the numbers of poor. Because there is little agreement and the results of changes will be politically charged (i.e., does any president really want to be known for significantly increasing poverty?), the United States continues to use the measure devised more than 40 years ago, despite its limitations.

Relative Measures

Another way to assess the numbers and social cost of poverty is to explore it as a **relative measure** rather than in absolute terms—how are the poorest households doing relative to others? Have the lowest groups made gains or experienced losses over time compared to the middle class and wealthy? In other words, have income disparities increased or decreased over time? A comparative assessment shows us how the poorest in our nation are doing relative to everyone else, and it is another mechanism for measuring the economic well-being of our most vulnerable.

Relative measures are more subjective and take into consideration peoples' feelings about poverty. They also reflect historical conditions, such as the rising standard of living. For example, surveys may ask respondents what they believe is a minimal household budget. Alternatively, measures may be based on a percentage of the median income for a given year, such as one-half of the median income. For example, if the median household income were $60,000 one year, rising to $62,000 the next year, the poverty lines could be set at $30,000 and $31,000, respectively.

Generally, relative measures use cut-offs for poverty that are significantly higher than the official measure. Although the U.S. government measures such as the poverty thresholds or poverty guidelines approximate less than one-third of the median income, relative measures usually range between 40 percent and 60 percent of the median income (Iceland 2003). The median income for a four-person family in the United States is about $65,000 per year (U.S. Census Bureau 2005), yet the poverty threshold for a family of four averaged only $19,971 in 2005. If we used the relative measure of 40 percent of the median income, the new poverty threshold would be $26,000. If we used 60 percent of median income for our measure, the new poverty threshold would be $39,000, thereby drastically increasing the number of people counted as poor and likely eligible for various antipoverty programs and services. Millions of families would be affected by the change in how poverty was counted.

Relative measures have several advantages. They reflect changing perceptions about poverty and rising standards of living, and they are grounded in national and historical contexts (Townsend 1980). They also can be compared internationally; for example, the European Union defines poverty as an income less than 60 percent of the median income (Glennerster 2000).

However, although some may applaud the subjectivity of relative measures, others claim it is their weakness. Some people consider relative measures unscientific and too complicated to be of real use. Relative measures also fall prey to some of the same criticism as absolute measures—they may fail to take into account the tremendous variation within the United States. For example, although the median income of a family of four is about $82,000 in Massachusetts, it is only $47,000 in Mississippi (U.S. Census Bureau 2005). Using a nationwide average will mask these differences, possibly underestimating poverty in some states, and overestimating it in others.

Inequality in Wealth and Income

There are more families living in poverty today despite continued growth in our society's material resources. Another way of conceptualizing poverty is to focus on the degree of inequality found in society, because inequality may be a better predictor of many dimensions of health and well-being than simply looking at poverty rates. Our growing national wealth is not being shared by all.

It comes as no surprise to hear that income and wealth are unequally distributed in the United States. What may be more surprising is that disparities have grown in the past several decades. The rich are getting richer, and the poor are getting poorer. The magnitude in the inequality and the size of its growth are startling, given the strong economy during the 1990s. Inequality continued to grow during the more depressed economy of the early 2000s and continues today.

Income refers to wages or earnings from employment or investments, while **wealth** is the total value of money and other assets, minus any outstanding debts. Wealth may include such items as stocks, bonds, or real estate.

Data released by the U.S. Census Bureau, the Internal Revenue Service (IRS), the Congressional Budget Office, and the Center on Budget and Policy Priorities show dramatic increases in disparities in income over time (Shapiro 17 October 2005; U.S. Census Bureau 6 October 2004; Congressional Budget Office 2005). These agencies assess changes by dividing wage earners, households, or families into five groups with an equal number in each, called **quintiles.** They then examine the share of aggregate income of the lowest fifth, second fifth, middle fifth, fourth fifth, and highest fifth groups. They also look at the share of income held by the top 5 percent. Because organizations have been tracking this information for decades, we can examine changes in economic inequality.

Even after taxes and tax changes designed to support lower-income workers, the lowest income groups have experienced only very small increases in income over time, while the wealthiest groups have made tremendous gains. The poorest fifth of all wage earners had an after-tax increase of only 4.5 percent between 1979 and 2002, amounting to just $600 (after inflation), while the income of the top fifth increased by nearly 50 percent, amounting to more than $42,000 during this period. Moreover, the income of the top 1 percent of wage earners increased by 111 percent during this period (Shapiro 17 October 2005).

Because income grew fastest among the most affluent, their share of the total national income grew as well. The top 1 percent of the population received 11.4 percent of all national after-tax income in 2002, up from 7.5 percent in 1979. This 4 percent change translates into hundreds of millions of dollars. In contrast, the share of national income received by the middle fifth declined from 16.5 percent in 1979 to 15.8 percent in 2002. The poorest fifth received 6.8 percent of such income in 1979, but only 5.1 percent in 2002. These data indicate that economic inequality is increasing (Shapiro 17 October 2005).

Wealth is even more unequally distributed than is income in the United States. Families earning at least $100,000 per year have a median net worth of $510,000, and a mean net worth of $1,728,000. In comparison, families earning less than $10,000 have a median net worth of only $3,600, and a mean net worth of $40,000. (The mean is skewed upward because of the significant wealth of a few.) This difference in net worth obviously translates into very different spending and consumption patterns.

What is it like to be part of the poorest fifth of Americans? What kind of work do they do? Many adults work in jobs that service the rest of us, and earn less than $7.00 an hour for their efforts. Barbara Ehrenreich holds a Ph.D. in biology and is a noted author. She decided to ask and answer these questions, and she wrote about her experience in the book *Nickel and Dimed: On Not Getting By in America*. She went undercover as a poorly educated, inexperienced, job-seeking homemaker to see if it is really possible to live on minimum-wage work. Her idea was to visit three different cities (in Florida, Maine, and Minnesota) with some money (around $1,000) plus a car, and see if it would be possible to get a job and make enough to stay on the next month. The jobs she took included waitress, house cleaner, hotel maid, and Wal-Mart clerk. In most cases, she made around $6 or $7 per hour and had no benefits. Ehrenreich takes us on a journey inside a desperate world where few middle-class persons have ventured, except for perhaps brief stints while in college. Although she cheats a bit (e.g., she does not start out totally broke, she rents a car, she always has an ATM card to fall back on if she runs out of money for food or housing, she has no children, and she can walk away anytime she wants) she vividly describes the demeaning and dangerous work that millions of women and men do every day. For example, while working for the Merry Maid company, she experiences firsthand the toll on the body: she learned to scrub all floors on her hands and knees, and to strap vacuum cleaners on her back. "Merry Maids" spend their day bending, squatting, reaching, lifting, and scrubbing away grime, dirt, and feces. Nonetheless, little attention is paid to germs. The maids' focus is on mere cosmetics, and so maids may use the same wet rag on the toilet as they do on the kitchen countertops. The work is demeaning. Maids are not allowed to eat, drink, or use the bathroom for hours. When a fellow maid sprains her ankle, the boss demands, "Work through the pain!" Homeowners treat the maids no better. Ehrenreich learns to keep a steady supply of aspirin available to combat the pain and muscle fatigue.

What does her two-year journey into the lives of the working poor reveal? She itemizes the wages she made at each job, along with her living expenses. With each job, her take-home pay minus expenses left her with less than $10 a week for savings or miscellaneous spending. Housing costs consumed most of her pay. There was virtually no money left for the investment needed to "pull herself up by her bootstraps." Instead, many people who work in these jobs must take a second low-paying and demeaning job if they have any realistic hope of improving their circumstances even slightly. Ehrenreich's main reason for carrying out the experiment was to see if her income could match her expenses "as the truly poor attempt to do each day" (Ehrenreich 2001:6). She demonstrates that it cannot be done, and she shows us the economic, physical, and emotional vulnerability experienced by low-wage workers (Ehrenreich 2001).

Inequalities in wealth and income are dramatic in the United States. The trends in inequality are further exacerbated by the explosion in the average compensation of chief executive officers (CEOs). The Economic Policy Institute reveals that the average CEO compensation in 2003 was 185 times that of the typical worker, compared to 24 times as much in 1965 (Mishel, Bernstein, and Allegretto 2005). CEOs of major companies received an average of nearly $10 million in total compensation, or more than $38,000 for each day of work (Geller 2005).

Moreover, an increasing share of total national income has been going toward corporate profits rather than to wages. The *Financial Times* reported that by the end of 2004, profits of U.S. companies soared to a record $1.27 trillion, or 10.6 percent of the GDP—a level surpassed only once since 1968 (March 31, 2005). Meanwhile, low-income workers receive a smaller share of the shrinking dollars that go to employee wages.

While the *share* of national income that goes to those in the middle and bottom groups has declined, so has its *real value*. After peaking in 1999, median household incomes have continued to fall (DeNavas-Walt, Proctor, and Lee 2006). Despite a slight increase in 2005 of about 1 percent, median income remains less than that of 1999, controling for inflation. Low-income families in particular, are seeing the gains made in the 1990s evaporate. Median incomes have dropped to about $36,000 for Hispanic households and $31,000 for Black households—73 percent and 63 percent of white household income, respectively.

Social Class

Finally, another way to conceptualize poverty is to think of it in the context of social classes in society. **Social class** is an obscure concept (compared to sex, race or ethnicity) because social class groups in the United States are not easily defined. Nor can we readily identify which people belong to which class. Social class boundaries are theoretically open so that people who gain schooling, skills, or income may experience a change in their social class position. However, we do know that social classes exist in a hierarchy, and they are based on income and wealth most apparently, but also on other resources, such as occupational prestige and educational level. Using this conception of poverty allows us to examine the lifestyles and consumptive patterns of different social strata in society. It also allows us to distinguish between the "working poor," who hold jobs with low earnings, and the "underclass," who do not or cannot work and whose lives are particularly bleak.

For Karl Marx, a German economist and philosopher in the nineteenth century, one's social class resulted from one's relationship to the means of production. The capitalist class, or the **bourgeoisie**, owns the means of production. They own the land and money needed to operate factories and businesses, for example. Meanwhile, the **proletariat** consists of those individuals who must sell their labor to the owners to earn enough money to survive.

German sociologist Max Weber, in contrast, developed a multidimensional approach, emphasizing (1) **wealth**, which, as mentioned, is the value of all of a person's or a family's economic assets—income, real estate, stocks, bonds, and other items of economic worth—minus debt; (2) **prestige**, defined as the esteem or respect a person is afforded; and (3) **power**, defined as the ability to achieve goals even in the face of opposition from others (Weber 1925).

These differing views show us the complexity in defining social class with keen precision. It also is not clear how many social classes exist in the United States. Although it might be safest to think of class as a continuum, for practical purposes most people tend to think of classes as categories. Today, people often define class as some combination of education, occupation, and income, and we sometimes call this measure **socioeconomic status (or SES)**. Dennis Gilbert and Joseph A. Kahl have developed a widely used model of social class based on SES (1993). Their model includes six categories: (1) the upper class; (2) the upper middle class; (3) the middle class; (4) the working class; (5) the working poor; and (6) the underclass.

The Upper Class

This category is made up of the wealthiest and most powerful social class in the United States, and consists of about 5 percent of the population. Although this class is small in number, they have a tremendous influence upon the economy and the rest of society. Their members may have very high incomes, but more importantly, they own substantial wealth. They may be entrepreneurs, sit on the boards of major corporations, or get involved in politics by either running for office or by serving in key policy positions.

Some families have been wealthy for generations. Family names like Rockefeller, Kennedy, and DuPont come to mind. These individuals and their families have been nicknamed "old money" or "bluebloods." They may belong to the exclusive *Social Register*, an annual listing of elites that has been published since the late 1800s, and they may prefer to socialize only with their peers. They belong to exclusive clubs, and their children attend private prep schools and Ivy League colleges, where applicants are carefully screened. There is very little mixing with other social classes; a debutante ball, which brings together unmarried young men and women to meet and socialize, carefully controls even dating. Researcher Susan Ostrander interviewed members of the upper class and asked them how they perceived their class position. One respondent told her, "I hate to use the word *class*. We are responsible, fortunate people, old families, the people who have something." Another respondent revealed, "I hate *upper class*. It's so non–upper class to use it. I just call it 'all of us,' those who are wellborn" (Ostrander 1980:78–79).

Other members of the upper class, sometimes nicknamed "new money," have acquired their great wealth within one generation. They earned their money in business, entertainment, or sports. Despite their vast material positions, which may be ostentatiously displayed, they lack the prestige of "bluebloods." Wealthy businessman Bill Gates, entertainer Oprah Winfrey, and real estate developer Donald Trump are examples of persons who have amassed great wealth within one generation.

The Upper Middle Class

Approximately 20 percent of the U.S. population is categorized as "upper middle class." Persons in this group are often highly educated professionals who have built careers as physicians, dentists, lawyers, college professors, or business executives. Household income may be in the range of $100,000 to $200,000, and perhaps even more if two adults are employed. These families generally have accumulated some wealth, have nice homes in well-respected neighborhoods within the community, and play important roles in local political affairs. Education is strongly valued for their children: The vast majority of upper-middle-class children go on to college, and many continue into post-graduate education as their parents did.

The Middle Class

With incomes roughly between $40,000 and $100,000 a year, 35 percent of the U.S. population can be thought of as "middle class." They are truly in the "middle," because the median household income in the United States is approximately $46,000 a year; $57,000 for **all family** households, and $66,000 for all **married-couple** households (DeNavas-Walt, Proctor, and Lee 2006), falling squarely in this category. Members of the middle class work in occupations that may or may not require a college education and they tend to be less prestigious on average than their upper-middle-class counterparts. Some middle-class occupations are classified as "white collar" jobs, such as nursing, lower-level management, and other semiprofessional positions. Other middle-class occupations include highly skilled blue-collar jobs, such as electronics and building construction. Traditionally, middle-class jobs have been secure and have provided a variety of opportunities for advancement; however, with corporate downsizing, escalating housing costs, and a generally rising cost of living, many middle-class families find their lives considerably more tenuous than in the past. Young middle-class families may find it difficult to purchase their first home in many cities around the country, and older middle-class families find that saving for both retirement and their children's college bills stretch their budget beyond its means. Consequently, it is increasingly common for both husband and wife in two-parent families to be employed outside the home.

The Working Class

Members of the working class earn less than do middle-class families, and their lives are more vulnerable as a result. Approximately 25 percent of the U.S. population falls into this group. Some working-class occupations may include those that require a short period of on-the-job training. Others require little more than basic literacy skills. Specific working-class jobs may include sales clerks, factory jobs, custodial positions, and semi-skilled or unskilled labor. Members of the working class report less satisfaction in their jobs than do those in higher social classes, and they experience less social mobility. The average income of working-class families may be around $20,000 to $40,000 a year, which is below the national average. Their income figures may be somewhat higher if two adults are employed. But generally, these families live in modest neighborhoods and have difficulty sending their children to college, although many would like to. Family members must budget carefully to pay their monthly bills, because unexpected doctor bills or car repair bills can wreak havoc on the family budget.

The Working Poor

The working poor account for approximately 10 percent of the U.S. population. They are employed in minimum or near–minimum wage jobs, such as lower-paid factory jobs, seasonal migrant labor, or as service workers in the fast-food or retail industry. Their wages are low, hovering around or only slightly above the poverty line, up to about $20,000 a year. Many workers receive no fringe benefits, such as health insurance or sick pay. The working poor live month-to-month and are unable to save money for the unforeseen, but inevitable emergency. Unemployment is common. Single mothers and their children represent a sizable component of the working poor. Some of these women intersperse work with bouts of welfare (Berrick 1995; Edin and Lein 1997; Seccombe 2007). It is a vicious cycle: they work in a variety of low-wage jobs, but then quit because the low wages and lack of benefits leave their families exceedingly vulnerable. They then seek the safety of welfare, where at least they can get their families' basic needs taken care of, such as food, shelter, and medical care. Then, faced with the stigma and hardship of day-to-day living on welfare, they once again seek work. They begin their jobs with hopes for a better life, but they soon find that their health and welfare benefits have been reduced or eliminated, and their families are poor once more. Then, again, they may turn to welfare for help.

The Underclass

This group, perhaps 3–5 percent of the U.S. population, has been defined by Gilbert and Kahl (1993) as extremely poor and often unemployed. Some cannot work because of disability or age. Others face difficult employment prospects because they lack education and job skills. Many reside in the inner cities, where job prospects are few because factories and businesses have moved across town or overseas. Some, but not all, members of the underclass receive assistance from governmental welfare programs, perhaps drawing upon them for extended periods of time to live and survive. Their circumstances are bleak and may be exacerbated by racial or ethnic discrimination. Sociologist William Julius Wilson (1987) refers to these individuals as a "truly disadvantaged" underclass in America.

How Does Social Class Affect Our Lives?

Consider the following profiles of Tommy Johnson and Randall Simmons (Seccombe and Warner 2004):

PROFILE 1:
Name: Tommy Johnson
Age: 29
Father's Occupation: Janitor
Mother's Occupation: Housecleaner, part-time
Community When Growing Up: Miami, Florida

Principal Caretakers when a Child: Grandmother, neighbor, older sister

Number of Siblings: Two brothers and one sister

Education: Large public elementary and secondary schools in inner city Miami. Emphasis on rote learning of basic skills. Security guards patrolled school. Occasional church camp during the summer. Classmates included sons and daughters of domestics, sales clerks, factory workers, service workers.

After School Activities: Hanging out in the neighborhood with friends, watching TV

Family Activities as a Child: Church, television, visiting with family members

First Job: Age 16, short-order cook at a fast-food restaurant in Miami. Earned minimum wage. Worked 15–25 hours per week while in high school.

College Attended: Nearby community college. Quit after one semester to take a full-time job.

First Full-time Job: Age 19. Sales clerk at auto parts store in Miami

Current Job and Earnings: Assistant muffler installer at a small shop that is devoted to installing mufflers and brakes. Has been with the company for three years. Works Tuesday through Saturday, with occasional overtime, averaging 40–45 hours per week. Annual earnings approximate $22,000 a year. Limited health insurance coverage and other benefits, and these were only available after 12 months of employment.

Hobbies: Working on cars

Marital Status: Married at age 20 to Renee, who is a full-time homemaker

Children: Together, Tommy and Renee have three children, aged 5, 2, and 9 months

Family Activities: Bowling, church, watching television, city league baseball, visiting with relatives

Current Residence: Owns a small three-bedroom mobile home located in a trailer park in a lower-income Miami suburb. Comfortably furnished with older and well-worn furniture and appliances. Has two cars—a Ford Escort, and a minivan—both of which are more than eight years old.

Goals: To someday manage his own auto parts store; to send children to vocational college to learn a "good trade," and to be a good father and provider to his family

PROFILE 2:

Name: Randall Simmons

Age: 29

Father's Occupation: Real estate attorney

Mother's Occupation: Homemaker and community volunteer

Principal Caretakers when a Child: Mother and governess

Number of Siblings: One sister

Community When Growing Up: Beverly Hills, California

Education: Private elementary and secondary college preparatory schools devoted to liberal and creative arts. Small student-teacher ratio. Fellow students are the sons and daughters of business leaders, physicians, and ambassadors. Spent summers in camps devoted to educational enrichment, including athletics and riding lessons.

After School Activities: Supplemental tutoring in French, piano, clarinet; horseback riding

Family Activities as a Child: Riding horses, theater, summer vacations in Europe, winter vacations at a condo in the Caribbean. His parents made generous donations to the performing arts community, and were, therefore, granted season tickets for the family to music and dance events at the community theater.

First Job: Age 26. Attorney in large and prestigious law firm in West Los Angeles. Initial salary of $125,000.

College Attended: Bachelor of arts degree at small, elite private college. Active in a campus fraternity and the college debate team. Attended law school at Yale University, where father, grandfather, and uncle are alumni.

First Full-time Job: Age 26. Attorney in large and prestigious law firm in West Los Angeles—the same job as above.

Current Job and Earnings: Attorney in the same law firm. Works approximately 50 hours per week. Annual salary approximates $175,000 a year. Generous health insurance package and full benefits. Also receives dividends of $150,000 a year from stocks and trust funds established by his wife's parents.

Hobbies: Riding horses (owns two horses, which are boarded approximately 35 miles from home), golf, gourmet cooking

Marital Status: Married at age 27. Wife, Susan, is a community volunteer. She has a Bachelor of arts degree in music from the same college as her husband Randall.

Children: No children, but would like to have a baby within two or three years. Ideal family size is three children.

Family Activities: International travel, theater, riding horses, golf at the country club

Current Residence: A 3,000-square-foot home in the Pacific Palisades area of Los Angeles, located five blocks from a private beach on the Pacific Ocean. Parents helped with the down payment. Interior was professionally designed and furnished. He has two cars, a late-model BMW and a new Mercedes Benz.

Goals: To make partner in law firm where he is currently employed within next 5–7 years, and to have children.

Tommy Johnson and Randall Simmons, two young men who live in large metropolitan areas, could not have more different lives. The lifestyle of one reflects economic privilege; the lifestyle of the other reflects the working class. Tommy, his wife, and children live near poverty, despite Tommy's full-time job. Although both men work long hours and are highly motivated, the social class in which each was born has substantially shaped their opportunities, goals, achievements, and constraints.

As these cases show, although theoretically Americans can be anything they want to be, in reality there is little substantial upward **social mobility**, or upward movement from one social class to another. People usually live out their lives in the same social class from which they come because of the norms that are learned, and the constraints and privileges they experience. Tommy's parents were poor or nearly so, and therefore, not surprisingly, so is Tommy. In contrast, Randall grew up in a family that was able to lavish him with expensive trips and top-notch educational opportunities. He lived in a posh neighborhood. He received a wide variety of opportunities that were unavailable to Tommy, such as travel, and music and riding lessons. Randall did not have to quit college to support himself; instead he received extensive parental financial support that enabled him to attend an elite private university, to participate in extracurricular activities, and to graduate and further his education by attending law school. His family provided considerable social capital on which he could draw. As expected, these opportunities have shaped his personal and family life and continue to influence him as an adult. They influenced his hobbies, his choice of mate, his choice of an occupation, and his type of residence.

Tommy and Randall reveal that economic standing influences life opportunities in myriad ways. Economics can also influence health and well-being, as revealed in Chapter 3. Poverty, however measured, touches our lives to the core, as does affluence.

Critical Thinking Questions:

1. Speculate on the direction of Pearl's life today. Do you think she found a job? Is her employment helping her take better care of her family?

2. Evaluate the official federal poverty measure. What do you see as its strengths and weaknesses? How would you design a "better" measure?

3. The author reports that there is little substantial upward social mobility; people usually live out their lives in the same social class from which they came because of the norms learned, and the constraints and privileges they experience. What norms have you personally learned, and what constraints and privileges have you experienced?

3

LIVING POORLY: POVERTY'S EFFECTS ON CHILDREN AND THEIR PARENTS

❧

TODAY, NEARLY ONE CHILD in five lives in a family officially designated as poor and struggles to meet the most fundamental needs. Food may be of poor quality and perhaps scarce at the end of the month, housing may be inadequate, and clothing is likely secondhand and in worn condition. Poor families are forced to make choices that are beyond the comprehension of most people—having to choose between buying food and paying the rent, for example. Children's lives are particularly at risk, as their bodies and spirits need special nourishment to thrive. Yet, children are dependent on others, and they cannot alter family conditions by themselves.

What does living in poverty mean to these children, and how does it influence their lives? Similarly, how do adults in poor families fare? This chapter will explore these emotional questions. The literature is clear: impoverished families face a higher degree of stress, disorganization, and other problems compared to more affluent families. Yet, poverty is not simply about money. The effects of poverty are witnessed in stresses associated with the daily struggle to meet basic needs. The effects can be far-reaching and devastating within a variety of realms, including work, family, home, health, schools, and the neighborhood. There are multiple pathways through which poverty operates, and it takes a heavy toll on fragile families.

Carlos

Carlos, now 15 years old, is one of the millions of children who know what it is like to be poor. He and his mother live in a cramped one-bedroom apartment "on the other side of the tracks." The complex is run-down, on a busy street, and in a neighborhood plagued with crime. Several neighbors or their guests use drugs, and the walkways are frequently littered with needles, other drug paraphernalia, or used condoms. Gunshots are heard frequently. Carlos and his mother live there because it is one of the few affordable apartments in town. Because of the safety risk, Carlos spent most of his childhood indoors, often watching television. He credits television with teaching him English, because his mother speaks primarily Spanish at home.

Carlos' parents never married. He sees his father only sporadically and his father does not contribute financially to his support. Carlos and his mother lived on welfare when he was young, augmented by her sporadic entries into the labor market. However, his mother never made much more than minimum wage at any of her jobs, and the financial and emotional stresses of low-wage work usually led her back to welfare. They found that they were generally worse off financially when she worked because of the new costs associated with transportation, child-care, and keeping her uniform neat and clean. However, because of the current welfare policy emphasis on work rather than cash assistance, his mother now holds a full-time job in a factory, for which she earns $7.25 an hour.

Carlos has always been embarrassed by his family's poverty. Most children at his school are not poor, and therefore, he feels like he stands out among them. His clothes are old and less fashionable than those of his peers because his mother buys them from the thrift store. He wonders if one of his school friends will recognize a shirt as theirs, and he shudders to think of it. His pants are too short, the sleeves of his jacket are too long, and his shoes are scuffed far beyond any fashionable sense.

Carlos also knows hunger. Although he has received food stamps all of his life, at less than $300 a month for the two of them, the aid runs out at the end of every month. His mother tries to get creative with food—her specialty is "surprise" casserole—but the reality is that he often goes to bed hungry at the end of every month. The gnawing in his stomach sometimes makes it difficult to sleep at night. He is thankful for the free breakfast and lunch he receives at school during the school year. He dreams about oatmeal, muffins, eggs, and cereal. The warm summer months when school is not in session are always rougher. Carlos and his mother often resort to using food banks or other charities, which they both detest doing.

Carlos was a sickly child, and he continues to be ill often today. He ingested lead paint that was peeling off the wall near his crib when he was only a toddler.

The doctors explained to his mother that his lead levels are several times higher than normal, and this condition likely explains some of his illnesses, hearing loss, stunted growth, and his inability to focus and concentrate in school. When working, his mother usually does not have health insurance, so he can rarely go to the doctor when he is sick. Instead, he generally just stays home from school, feeling very lethargic.

Other than the free meals, school has never had much appeal to Carlos. His poor health has caused him to miss many days of school, and he has fallen behind in his learning. His fellow students now tease him not only for his worn-out clothes, his short stature, and because of where he lives, but they sometimes now call him "stupid." These comments affect his school attendance even further—who wants to go to school and be teased? Consequently, he cuts classes with increasing frequency and hangs out at home. He sometimes forges notes from his mother excusing his absences. She would be upset if she knew about this situation because she wants him to do well in school and she sees education as a ticket to a better life than the one that they have. She pleads for him to take school seriously. However, she is at work all day and does not know the extent of his absences from school.

Although typically a bit of a loner, last year Carlos began to meet up with a group of young men and women who were also truant or who had officially dropped out of school. They meet in the afternoon at an adjacent apartment to smoke, watch television, play cards, and sometimes drink beer when one of the friends can get his older brother to buy it for them. One of his new friends has a car, and they go cruising when they can afford to fill the gas tank. A young woman who joins the group a couple of days a week—Tessa, who is also 15 years old—has caught his eye. They have recently begun having sex, one of the only couples to do so, bolstering Carlos' social position within the group. However, Tessa recently told him, in tears, that she is pregnant.

Carlos' situation reveals how a relative lack of income may have repercussions for virtually all aspects of life. Hundreds of studies have examined the effects of poverty on children; collectively, they reveal that poverty injures the body and the spirit (Brooks-Gunn and Duncan 1997; Seccombe 2000). Income is associated with such factors as children's physical health, mental and emotional well-being, cognitive abilities, school achievement, and teen pregnancy rates. Moreover, the earlier a child is exposed to poverty, and the longer the poverty experience, the more harmful are the consequences (Duncan et al. 1998; Korenman, Miller, and Sjaastad 1995).

However, despite the volume of research showing the deleterious effects of poverty, many studies lack the precision necessary to isolate *whether it is really poverty per se that causes these outcomes rather than some other factor or set of factors.* In the example of Carlos, is poverty responsible for his truancy, low school achievement, drug use, and involvement in a teen pregnancy, or is some other factor the real culprit, such as living in a single-parent household or his mother's level of education? At first glance all these factors seem to be interrelated, but what precisely are the effects of income? Answering this question requires us to disentangle poverty from other related variables so we can isolate the specific effects that poverty itself may contribute to outcomes. Researchers do this statistically by "controlling for the effects" of other possibly related variables, such as marital status, maternal education, ethnicity, and any other seemingly relevant variables. Understanding the true causal relationships between these variables is necessary to design effective policies to ameliorate poverty and other social problems (Duncan and Brooks-Gunn 1997).

The following discussion focuses primarily on those large-scale studies that use national longitudinal data sources to estimate the specific effects of income on children's lives. Naturally, some of these conditions are more relevant for some age groups than others (e.g., school achievement is particularly relevant for children over the age of 5). These studies have collected data over multiple years and at different stages of children's lives. Taken together, they not only reveal the effects of income on child outcomes, but they can specify how the timing and duration of poverty may affect the outcomes as well.

Physical Health

Research is unequivocal about the relationship between poverty and health regardless of health indicators (Children's Defense Fund 2005b; Isaacs and Schroeder 2004; Seguin et al. 2003). In terms of general measures, only 70 percent of children in families below the poverty line were reported by their parents to be in very good or excellent health in the National Health Interview Survey (NHIS), compared with 90 percent of families with incomes at least 200 percent of poverty (Dey and Bloom 2005). Moreover, 5 percent of poor children were described by their parents as having only fair or poor health, compared to just 0.6 percent of upper-income children. Poor children continue to suffer from a variety of ailments at higher rates than do more affluent children. For example, they are more than three times as likely to be iron deficient, 1.5 times more likely to have frequent diarrhea or colitis, twice as likely to suffer from severe asthma, and 1.5 times more likely to suffer partial or complete blindness or deafness (Children's Defense Fund 1994).

Poverty puts the health of children at risk in several ways, including increasing the frequency of low-birth-weight babies and undernutrition, which in turn increases their likelihood of serious chronic and acute illness. Children living in poverty have a higher risk of infant mortality because of biological factors, such as low birth weight or birth defects, and environmental hazards during the fragile first year of life. Also, poor mothers often receive inadequate prenatal care.

Birth Outcomes

The foundations for children's physical, mental, and emotional health begin prior to birth, and are in large part dependent upon maternal health behaviors and prenatal health. Prenatal care is critical not only because it can identify immediate health problems, but also because it can identify risky behaviors, such as smoking or drinking, that can impede fetal development and lead to infant mortality or low birth weight.

Low birth weight, defined as 2,500 grams (about 5.51 pounds) or less, is a key indicator of child health because it increases the likelihood of subsequent illness, infant mortality, and cognitive and emotional problems that can plague children throughout their lives. For example, children born with low birth weight are about 50 percent more likely to score below average on measures of reading and mathematics (Breslau, Paneth, and Lucia 2004), and a low-birth-weight child is twice as likely as a normal-weight child to have clinically significant behavior problems, such as hyperactivity (Gray, Indurkhya, and McCormick 2004).

However, estimating the impact of poverty alone on birth outcomes can be complicated because so many other factors also come into play—low birth weight is more common to women with low levels of education, single women, and Blacks, all of whom also have high rates of poverty. For example, Black infants are almost twice as likely to be born with low birth weight as white infants (13.4 vs. 6.9 percent). However, one study using data from the National Longitudinal Study of Youth, a large nationally representative sample, controlled for such factors as mothers' age, education, marital status, and smoking status. It found that poor white women were still more than three times as likely to have a baby with low birth weight as a nonpoor white woman. In contrast, among Blacks, poverty itself did not have any significant independent effects on birth weight after the other variables were controlled for (Starfield et al. 1991).

Lead Paint Poisoning

Troccora Nicholson lives in Duncan, Mississippi, with her five children. Their home is a dilapidated trailer that should be condemned. Parts of the wall are falling down; a section of the plywood from the wall fell and hit her son in the head. The sky can be seen through a hole in the ceiling. Rain gets into the trailer, which is now filled with mold. In the bathroom, there is a gap in the floor covered with plywood because it is large enough for snakes to enter. Troccora's unsafe home is the reason that one of her youngest sons has lead paint poisoning and RSV (Respiratory Syncytial Virus). She receives Medicaid and other public assistance for her children, but she cannot move out of the trailer because she is currently unemployed and has no way of traveling to a job. (*Children's Defense Fund Action Council 2005:38*)

Although most people are not aware of it, lead poisoning is one of the most serious and common environmental health hazards that threaten children. Almost 900,000 children have elevated blood levels (Centers for Disease Control and Prevention 2006). Although all children are at potential risk of lead exposure, the risk is greater for low-income and minority children. For example, low-income children (below 200 percent of poverty) are more than five times as likely to have elevated blood lead levels of at least 5 micrograms per deciliter (mg/dL) as higher-income children, and 16 percent of lower-income children living in older housing have lead poisoning, compared with 4 percent of all children (Parker and Malone 5 April 2004; Centers for Disease Control and Prevention 2006).

Lead paint exposure is harmful to children even in small doses. Lead exposure can lead to stunted growth, hearing loss, learning disabilities, developmental delays, behavioral problems, vitamin D metabolism damage, impaired blood production, and toxic effects on the kidneys (Markowitz 2000; Parker and Malone 5 April 2004; Centers for Disease Control and Prevention 2006). Despite the benefits of early testing, only one in five children enrolled in Medicaid, a group at high risk for elevated blood lead levels, is screened (U.S. General Accounting Office 15 January 1999).

Where do young children come into contact with lead paint? Surprisingly, they find it in their own homes and their own bedrooms. The U.S. Department of Housing and Urban Development (HUD) estimates that 64 million homes in the United States still contain lead paint, and it has identified 5 to 15 million of these homes as being "very hazardous" (Parker and Malone 5 April 2004). Much toxic paint remains on the walls of old dilapidated housing. As it peels, children breathe the lead dust and eat the sweet-tasting paint chips. Millions of poor children may be at risk of impaired physical and mental development related to ingesting the lead-based paint flaking off the walls in older homes (Needleman et al. 1990). Lead-based paint is also found in many older schools, where it was used until it was banned in 1978. A 1998 study by the California Department of Health Services found detectable levels of lead in 95 percent of the elementary schools they tested (California Department of Health Services 15 April 1998).

Food Insecurity and Hunger

Most Americans find some comfort in knowing that the type of hunger and malnutrition occurring in developing nations is not found in the United States.

Nonetheless, many poor Americans do suffer from hunger and face critical nutritional deficits, and their numbers are rising (Chilton and Giardino 2004; Furness, Simon, and Wold 2004; Nord, Andrews, and Carlson 2005). The U.S. Department of Agriculture (USDA) estimates that more than 38 million Americans, including 14 million children, are **food insecure.** The USDA defines food insecurity as not having access to enough food at all times for active, healthy living. Of these children, 540,000 experience **food insecurity with hunger** (Nord, Andrews, and Carlson 2005). They do not have enough nourishing food available to them on a regular basis. They live in households with limited or uncertain access to food and sometimes go without food at some point every month, suffering the immediate pain of hunger, and the more long-term consequences of malnutrition. Food hardships are most pronounced among poor and minority children: 47 percent of poor children and 30 percent of Black and Hispanic children live in households that are food insecure, and do not have access to diets nutritionally adequate for an active, healthy life (Nord, Andrews, and Carlson 2005).

Most food-insecure households avoid hunger by limiting the types of food they buy and relying on public or private food charities. However, according to the USDA, in about one-third of food-insecure households, one or more household members are hungry at times, having the uneasy or painful sensation caused by a lack of food. Sometimes these are children (Nord, Andrews, and Carlson 2005).

Without proper nutrition, children are in a weakened state. They run the risk of more frequent colds, ear infections and other infectious diseases, impaired brain function, and stunted growth, and they are more vulnerable to lead and other environmental toxins. One study based on caregivers of more than 11,000 children in five states and Washington, D.C. reported that, after controlling for relevant confounding variables, food-insecure children were twice as likely to be in only fair or poor health, and were one-third more likely to have been hospitalized since birth (Cook et al. 2004).

Children with inadequate nutrition also are more likely to show signs of iron deficiency, a major cause of anemia, which is a strong predictor of learning and behavioral problems in later life. They have higher levels of aggression, hyperactivity, anxiety, and passivity. Hungry and malnourished children do not perform as well in school. In a national study, kindergarteners from food-insecure homes scored lower on math tests taken at the beginning of the school year. They also learned less over the year (Winicki and Jemison 2003). Hungry and malnourished children miss more days from school, are more likely to be tardy, are more likely to have repeated a grade, and are almost twice as likely to be suspended from school (Murphy et al. 1998; Alaimo, Olson, and Frongillo 2001; U.S. Conference of Mayors 2004; Children's Defense Fund 2 June 2005).

Access to Healthcare

Children (and adults) living in poor families are not only at a higher risk for serious medical problems, but often these problems go untreated. The chance of being uninsured is increasing for most Americans, as employers attempt to cut the costs of doing business by reducing eligibility for health insurance benefits (Gilmer and Kronick 2005). By 2005, nearly 47 million Americans, amounting to 16 percent of the population, were without health insurance, which is the primary ticket for accessing the healthcare system (DeNavas-Walt, Proctor, and Lee 2006).

Some poor families have **Medicaid,** the government-sponsored insurance program for specific low-income persons who qualify, or **State Children's Health Insurance Program (SCHIP),** which is designed to cover low-income children. SCHIP has had some positive results; the number of children without health insurance declined slightly between 2000 and 2005, from 8.6 to 8.3 million children (DeNavas-Walt, Proctor, and Lee 2006). However, this means that 11.2 percent of children still lack insurance, and for whatever reasons, are not enrolled in SCHIP (Children's Defense Fund 2005b). Not surprisingly, many of these children are likely to be poor. Sixteen percent of **poor** children under age 19 remain uninsured, compared to only 5 percent of nonpoor children (Cohen and Bloom 2005), and they are particularly disadvantaged with respect to getting the healthcare they need. Vivian is one of these poor children.

> Janice's husband makes about $550 every week plus commissions delivering linens. He works hard, often doing overtime, but his job doesn't provide health insurance. Until recently, their 2-year-old daughter Vivian was enrolled in SCHIP and urgently needed that health coverage when she was hospitalized for a week with serious pneumonia. Some of her medications cost $100 per prescription, and her parents never could have afforded them without health insurance. But now, because of the new way that income is being calculated, the family makes $37 above the limit to qualify for SCHIP and cannot afford the $500–$600 a month it costs to pay for private health insurance, which for them would be an entire paycheck. A month after losing SCHIP coverage, Vivian fell and her parents feared she had broken her arm. Fortunately, there was no serious physical damage but the financial issues are grave: Vivian's family is now faced with an $800 emergency room bill and does not know how they will pay it. (*Children's Defense Fund 2005b:*7)

Data from the NHIS reveals that, compared to children living at more than 200 percent of poverty, poor children were nearly three times as likely to have gone at least five years without seeing a health professional and more than twice as likely to have an unmet medical need (Dey and Bloom 2005). They also were more than four times as likely to have no usual place that they received care, thereby receiving less follow-up care. Instead, they are more likely to rely on emergency rooms as their source of treatment (Dey and Bloom 2005).

Access to dental care may be the most elusive of all healthcare treatments. Tooth decay (dental caries) is one of the most common chronic diseases affecting children in the United States; by age 8, more than 50 percent of children have experienced decay (Centers for Disease Control 2004). Poor children are significantly more likely to be without dental insurance than their more affluent counterparts, and therefore, visit the dentist far less often. Sixty-six percent of children living in households over 200 percent of the poverty line have seen a dentist over the past six months, compared to only 43 percent of poor children, while in contrast, poor children are 50 percent more likely than nonpoor children to have gone more than five years without seeing a dentist. Not surprisingly, they are nearly three times as likely to have an unmet dental need (Dey and Bloom 2005). Even children with Medicaid may have trouble accessing dental care because most providers are hesitant to accept public-paying patients because of low reimbursements and burdensome paperwork—only 10 percent of dentists nationally accept Medicaid patients (Mouradian, Wehr, and Crall 2000; U.S. General Accounting Office 2000).

Chris is a woman with three children living in Portland, Oregon, who recently left welfare for work, and who illustrates how a lack of health insurance can make it difficult to get needed healthcare (Seccombe et al. 2005). All of her children have had recurrent health problems, including middle ear infections and dental problems. Prior to leaving welfare for work, Chris was covered by Medicaid, which met virtually all the health needs of her family. She felt secure knowing her children could see a doctor, receive medicines, and even be hospitalized if needed. However, once Chris left welfare for employment, she, like millions of other women and men leaving Temporary Assistance to Needy Families (TANF), found that Medicaid would only continue for one year. After this brief period, her transitional benefits expired, and it is her responsibility to find health insurance for her family. Although Chris found a job, she is very worried because her employer does not offer health insurance.

> My main priority was getting as much work as I can to keep a roof over my head. Now they hire more temps. I know I've proven myself. I feel like I'm being used right now through my work. . . . I was willing to give up part of my pay, to be permanent and have medical. I don't care about vacation or sick leave. What have I got to fall back on? What have my kids got to fall back on?

All three of Chris' children need medical care. Due to a serious dental condition, her daughter's needs are immediate. Chris described their recent situation:

What she needed was a crown to be put on there permanently. I couldn't afford a crown, so that's why the temporary was placed in there. It shouldn't be in there as long as it has, or it's going to affect her gum and rot it out, and the teeth are going to be rotten. I couldn't afford the crown so the doc has to hold off until I figure out something.

Chris continued:

It's been terrible. We never got our dental work done. I finally got my boys in to have their teeth cleaned and that's all we got because my medical stopped, so we never got our other appointments. I've got letters saying you have to finish your appointments, yet I don't have the coverage. When I call and say I need some help with my kids to get them insured, I want somebody to get it in motion, not send me somewhere else or refer me, give these people a call. I'm asking for help.

During the interview, Chris began to cry. In tears she explained that in the past, she had Medicaid to fall back on, but now she does not, and the stress is overwhelming. The bottom line is that her children go without getting care.

I've always had medical coverage, at least through Medicaid. So I've never really thought about it. I could have gone the rest of my life without the feeling I go through, the stress and worry about what I'm going to do. . . . I wasn't given no suggestions on where to go for help. They say they got all these funds out there. I'm just asking for one time to help my daughter. It's not like it's just to milk them. I believe that I should have a chance.

Cognitive Abilities and School Achievement

Children living below the poverty level are more likely to suffer cognitively and academically than are children who are not poor (Duncan and Brooks-Gunn 1997). Overall, poor children receive lower grades, receive lower scores on standardized tests, are more likely to experience learning disabilities and developmental delays, are less likely to finish high school, and are less likely to attend or graduate from college than are nonpoor youth (Downey 1994; Teachman et al. 1997; Duncan et al. 1998; National Institute of Child Health and Human Development (NICHD) Early Child Care Research Network 2005; Dey and Bloom

2005). Education is important because, on average, each year of education increases a worker's hourly wages by 10 percent (Schweke 2004). The U.S. Census Bureau reports that adult workers with a bachelor's degree earn an average of $51,206 a year, compared to $18,734 for those without a high school diploma (Bergman 28 March 2005).

Specifically, Smith, Brooks-Gunn, and Klebanov (1997) examined the consequences of poverty upon young children's cognitive and verbal ability, and their early school achievement (Smith, Brooks-Gunn, and Klebanov 1997). They used three different types of assessment: intellectual quotient (IQ), verbal ability, and achievement tests. They found that the duration of poverty had a significantly negative effect on all three assessment tests. Children in families with incomes less than one-half of the poverty line scored between 6 and 13 points lower on various standardized tests than did children in families with incomes between 1.5 and 2.0 times the poverty line, enough to make the difference in being placed in a special education class. In all cases the differences were statistically significant. Children living in families whose incomes were higher, but still below the poverty line, also did significantly worse on a majority of tests than the higher reference group. Economic conditions in early childhood, particularly ages 3 to 8, seem to have the biggest impact on achievement levels, whereas the effects of poverty during adolescence on cognitive ability are more moderate (Peters and Mullis 1997). Moreover, the duration and degree of poverty also affected children's scores. For example, children who lived in persistently poor families—defined as poor over a four-year period—had scores that were six to nine points lower than nonpoor children on the various assessments.

Researchers also have found that children in poverty complete fewer years of school and are more likely to drop out of school. However, much of the observed relationship is related to other confounding factors such as parental education or occupation, family structure, and neighborhood characteristics rather than poverty *per se* (Haveman and Wolfe 1994; Haveman and Wolfe 1995; Brooks-Gunn and Duncan 1997). After statistically controlling for the effects of these other variables, the independent effects of poverty on school achievement are relatively small. This means that, although the poor do indeed complete fewer years in school and are more likely to drop out, the effects are likely due to reasons other than poverty itself. For example, 93 percent of nonpoor students use computers, compared to 80 percent of poor students (DeBell 2003). The "digital divide" is significant because greater access to technology correlates with greater educational attainment and future income. However, this outcome may also be explained by parental education level, and other sociodemographic factors such as race and ethnicity, or language.

These data lead to an interesting irony—why do the strong effects of poverty on cognitive ability not necessarily lead to reduced schooling? The answer is unclear, but Brooks-Gunn and Duncan (1997) speculate that one reason may be that extrafamily environments, such as schools and neighborhoods, matter as much or more for children once they reach school age. A second possible reason is that the timing of poverty may be crucial for school achievement. One study found that poverty from birth to age 5 had a far more powerful effect on the number of school years a child completes than does family income between ages 5 and 10 or between ages 11 and 15 (Duncan et al. 1998). Apparently the seeds for educational achievement are planted at young ages.

Children's Mental Health, Social Adjustment, and Well-being

Children living in poverty have more emotional and behavioral problems than do more affluent children. They are more likely to suffer from internalizing behavior, such as depression and social withdrawal, and to have peer relationship difficulties and low self-esteem. They also are likely to have more externalizing behavior, such as aggression, fighting, and other conduct disorders (Conger, Conger, and Elder 1997; Children's Defense Fund 2005b; Evans et al. 2005; NICHD Early Child Care Research Network 2005). These findings persist even when the effects of other potentially confounding variables are controlled.

For example, Takeuchi, Williams, and Adair (1991) found that children on welfare or families that experience financial stress are more likely to exhibit impulsive, antisocial, and depressive behaviors. However, they noted that children from families experiencing stress at two different points in time, separated by five years, did not differ from children whose families were under financial stress at only one point in time.

Likewise, a study using data from the National Longitudinal Study of Youth (NLSY) reported that children living in long-term poverty (defined by the ratio of family income to the poverty level averaged over 13 years) ranked 3 to 7 percentile points higher on a behavior problem index than did nonpoor children, indicating more difficulties. Interestingly, the study also found that children who experienced only one year of poverty had more behavioral problems than children who had lived in long-term poverty (Korenman, Miller, and Sjaastad 1995).

Other researchers have found that longer poverty spells are more damaging to children. McLeod and Shanahan (1993; 1996) examined children's mental health and found that "the mental health disadvantages that poor children face increase with the length of time that their families are poor" (McLeod and Shanahan 1996:207). Children who suffered long-term poverty had higher rates of depression than did children whose poverty was of shorter duration. Research by Dubow and Ippolito (1994) also reveals that the years spent in poverty predicted marked increases in antisocial behavior in children.

Weinger (1998) conducted a qualitative survey to hear directly from children themselves how they are affected emotionally by poverty. She found that poor children have a very difficult time holding on to positive self-images. They view poverty as a deprivation, and hear messages in society that are highly critical of the poor. She found that they internalize many of these negative messages.

One behavioral issue of particular policy interest because of its long-term consequences is teenage childbearing. The birthrate among teenagers has been declining for the past 15 years, and today stands at about 41.2 births per 1,000 women 15–19 years old (Hamilton, et al. 2005 October). This rate is more than 25 percent lower than the peak rate of nearly 62 births per 1,000 teenage women reached in 1991 (The Alan Guttmacher Institute 19 February 2004). The declines are evident among all racial and ethnic groups. Yet, the media coverage of teenage pregnancy and birth is extensive because the potentially harmful consequences of teen pregnancy and childbearing to the mother and child are so well documented (Fergusson and Woodward 2000; Hofferth, Reid, and Mott 2001). Teenage mothers are more likely to die in childbirth compared to older mothers, their infants are more likely to have low birth weight, and the babies are more likely to die within the first month of life. Teen mothers are more likely to drop out of high school than are other teens, are considerably poorer, and are more likely to receive welfare. Adolescent mothers also are less knowledgeable about child development than are other mothers, are less prepared for childrearing, and are more likely to be depressed.

The data suggest that poor children are more likely to become pregnant or impregnate others than are nonpoor children, but once again, is poverty the casual variable? The evidence is inconsistent. It appears that income is significant, but not poverty *per se.* That is, it makes little difference in teen pregnancy and birth rates if a child lives in poverty or has an income only somewhat above it. Significant reductions in teen pregnancy and childbearing tend to occur only when a family is living at an income of at least twice the poverty level (Haveman, Wolfe, and Wilson 1997).

Consequences for Adults

Although this chapter has so far focused on children, the potentially harmful health effects of poverty on adults are numerous as well. Poor adults arc in worse health than others, and therefore, health insurance is of critical concern (Wood et al. 2002; Corcoran, Danziger, and Tolman 2003; Levin-Epstein 2003; Centers for Disease Control (CDC) 2004). For example, using a common single-item measure that asks respondents to evaluate their health as poor, fair, good, very good, or excellent, only one-third of adults who recently left welfare for work in Oregon rated their health as excellent or very good, compared with two-thirds of the general population aged 18–64 (CDC 2004; Seccombe et al. 2005). Moreover, about one-quarter of the Oregon respondents evaluated their health as only fair or poor, compared to about 10 percent in nationwide samples (CDC 2004). Another study found nearly one-third of low-income women in the four counties that were part of the Manpower Demonstration Research Corporation's Urban Change Project had low physical well-being scores, compared to one-tenth of adults nationally (London, Martinez, and Polit 2001). Poor adults are more likely to work in dangerous occupations and live in unsafe neighborhoods, and their homes are more likely to be located near toxic sites. A review of virtually any medical sociology textbook will reveal that income is highly correlated with health and disease, using both objective measures (e.g., incidence of specific diseases) and subjective measures (e.g., self-rated health) (Cockerham 2001; Weitz 2001).

Poverty also affects adults in other ways. One issue with far-reaching consequences for families is that poor men and women are less likely to marry (White and Rogers 2000; Edin and Kefalas 2005). Poverty undermines economic security and makes men less attractive marriage partners. For example, William Julius Wilson suggests that a key factor in explaining the falling marriage rate among inner-city Blacks is their declining employment opportunities as jobs move to the suburbs or overseas (Wilson 1987; Wilson 1996). Few low-skilled or semi-skilled jobs remain in the inner city core, and the local men cannot find jobs. Unemployed or underemployed men are not deemed to be good marriage prospects. Indeed, in another study based on in-depth interviews with young unmarried mothers, it was found that neither the young mother nor her parents supported marriage to a man who was not employed (Farber 1990).

Poverty (as well as other forms of economic hardship) also undermines marital stability (Vinokur, Price, and Caplan 1996; Conger, Rueter, and Elder Jr. 1999). Poor economic conditions are associated with lower levels of marital happiness and greater marital conflict because of the higher degree of stress involved in such a situation. Conger, Ge, and Lorenz (1994) suggest that poverty and economic hardship can lead to greater levels of depression, which can then lead to hostile marital interactions such as anger, resentment, and hostility between partners These feelings then lower marital quality. As one wife, in a study of distressed rural families, put it:

I . . . highly resent my husband's debt and selfishness. I would like a better home and to be able to be rewarded for my hard work instead of being limited by his failures and debts. I'm tired of his bills always being a pressure. (*Conger, Ge, and Lorenz 1994:188*)

Pathways

Our review reveals that living in poverty has many detrimental effects on the lives of children and adults; however, what are the *pathways* by which poverty exerts its influence? If we are serious in our desire to reduce the harmful effects of poverty, it is critical that we understand not only the effects of poverty but also the pathways or mechanisms through which poverty operates. Interventions can then be targeted to these pathways.

In this section, six potential pathways are discussed and illustrated in Figure 3.1: (1) health and nutrition, (2) quality of the home environment, (3) parental stress and mental health, (4) fewer resources for learning, (5) housing problems, and (6) poor quality neighborhood. This model draws upon those of Brooks-Gunn and Duncan (1997) and the Children's Defense Fund (1994) that identified critical pathways through which poverty operates and touches the lives of its victims. Their models differ somewhat in their degree of emphasis, and the following is an attempt at a synthesis. Although their focus is primarily on children, the model also applies to adults.

Health and Nutrition

Although health was previously discussed as an "effect" of poverty, it is also a pathway through which poverty influences other outcomes. Poor children, who may have low birth weight or elevated blood lead levels, or who are without health insurance, experience a variety of problems. These can include reduced cognitive abilities, IQ, school achievement, and social adjustment and well-being. These problems can affect their ability to thrive over the long run. One study reported that cumulative poverty-related health factors such as anemia, recurrent ear infections, low birth weight, and elevated blood lead levels may account for as much as 13 to 20 percent of the difference in IQ scores between poor and nonpoor 4-year-olds (Goldstein 1990).

Adults who experience health problems or have children with serious health problems also face a myriad of issues that can pull them into poverty or make it difficult to improve their financial circumstances. They may have trouble finding and maintaining steady work, which may further affect their choice of housing or the neighborhood in which they can afford to live and their ability to secure health insurance, and which may lead to subsequent depression.

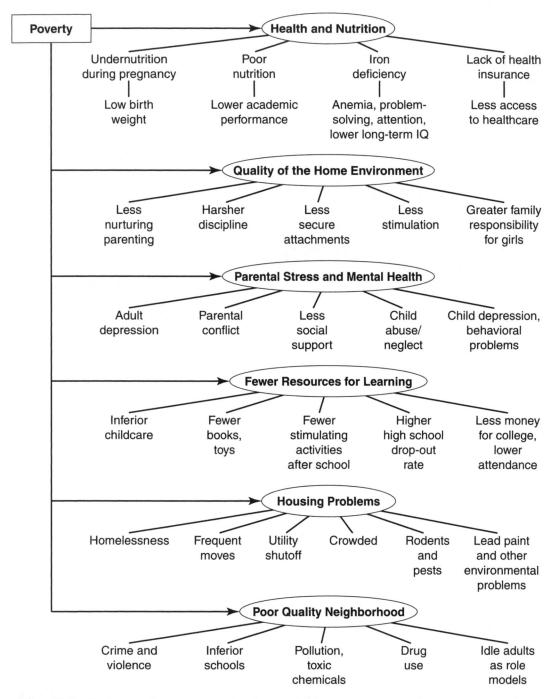

Figure 3.1 Pathways from poverty to adverse child outcomes
Source: Adapted from Children's Defense Fund 1994; Brooks-Gunn and Duncan 1997.

Sarah's case reveals how having a child with health problems exacerbates financial problems and severely compromises the ability to thrive after leaving welfare for work (Seccombe et al. 2005). Sarah, age 32, was living in the basement of her parents' home to save expenses and to have occasional babysitting assistance for her 8-year-old son, Jake. Before we undertook the "business" of the interview, it was clearly important to Sarah that we meet Jake and have an understanding of his situation.

Sarah carefully and lovingly presented her son, who was lying on a blanket on the floor of his grandparents' cramped living room. Due to the heat, he wore nothing but a diaper. Jake's skin looked as though he had never been exposed to sunlight and he was surrounded by toys of all description. Though he is the size of a normal child his age, Jake is in all other respects an infant, due to a severe case of cerebral palsy and developmental delays that were likely caused by complications during pregnancy. Sarah had placenta previa, which occurs when the placenta tears from the uterus, so her son was without proper oxygen and food when she was approximately six months pregnant. Sarah cares for her son by herself, in conjunction with his school. She receives a little babysitting help from her mother, but Jake's father is not a part of his life. In our interview, she described the heartache of caring for a child who is seriously disabled, the struggles she faces in doing this on a near-poverty budget, her confusion over insurance procedures, and anxiety about this lifelong commitment that she is undertaking virtually alone.

Sarah described her pregnancy and the birth of her son:

> We did an ultrasound the week before he was born, and the most they could see was that he was small in size and [there was] not a lot of amniotic fluid around him. If a child doesn't have a lot of nourishment coming, they have a tendency to use their bladder because, even though it's waste, you can reuse that. The amniotic fluid is the baby's waste, so he was trying to hold onto that to try and reuse it, and that's a sure sign of lack of food and lack of oxygen too. A week later we went in for another ultrasound and they could see the placenta was tearing, and so I had a cesarean done and they lost his heartbeat. So when he was born, he was basically not breathing. He was clinically dead for three minutes. They revived him because they figured he had potential. So the cerebral palsy came from when I was pregnant, and the rest of it kicked in because of the lack of oxygen when he was born. That's where the seizures started because his brain would hemorrhage.

Sarah went on to describe what life had been like for her since Jake's birth. Because he is so deeply dependent on Sarah, all of her own needs, desires, and aspirations take a backseat to his daily survival. Eight years later, what is her son Jake like?

He's 8 years old. He doesn't talk. He makes sounds, more or less to indicate what he needs . . . He's in a wheelchair because he doesn't walk. So it's basically like having a 3-month-old child that cries whenever it needs anything, and as a mom you do the same thing any mother would. You go down a little checklist: you've just eaten, you've had your diaper changed, so it's a matter of a guessing game of what he needs or wants. Sometimes you can see the frustration in his eyes because he can't communicate what he wants. His favorite sound is 'uh,' which sometimes means he wants a drink of water. But 'uh' also means he can't reach his toy, 'uh' means you're watching TV and not feeding me . . . My child is 8 years old and the plain fact [is], he's 8 years old, and he can't do anything for himself, except play with his toys and his newspaper. He can't verbally communicate with me. He basically can't do anything for himself. If I set him here on the floor, he stays in this vicinity, he falls over to his side, he rolls on his tummy, he turns himself around a little bit, but he's subject to this part of the house because that's where I put him. Other than crying, I could leave him here all day long if I so desired and that would just have to work; there's nothing he could do about it. Not that I would, and let me tell you, that boy's got a great set of lungs.

Sarah is currently uninsured. She does not receive insurance from her employer, even though it is offered for $160 a month. She does not complain about the cost of insurance, which she feels is reasonable despite her near poverty–level budget. Like so many others, Sarah falls through the safety net because of failing to complete the paperwork that would have secured her insurance. Some people may be tempted to blame this situation on Sarah herself. After all, she could have had insurance for herself and her son if she had paid attention and filled out the forms on time. However, my interviews reveal that Sarah is not alone—a high number of families are confused about the rules and procedures needed to secure health insurance. Why is this? Their lives are turbulent. In Sarah's case, at the time she was supposed to be following through on the insurance forms, her father died, her mother was out of the country, and she worked full-time while caring for her son by herself. In addition, she was in the midst of moving. She was unaware of the procedure for getting insurance coverage started and simply forgot to follow up on it. She is paying a high price for her forgetfulness.

By the time I realized what was going on, it dawned on me that I didn't have confirmation that I had insurance. It's one of those stupid things—you never think you have to have insurance until you have to have insurance.

Currently Sarah relies on Jake's school to provide the assistance and equipment that he needs. However, his school does not go year-round, and unless she secures insurance quickly, she may not be able to meet all of his needs. Sarah fears for her son and his future. She dreads the day when she is no longer able to physically care for Jake, who is still growing, as would a normal 8-year-old. Additionally, she is deeply concerned that people he meets in his everyday life will mistreat him or ignore his needs, and she does not have the money to buy the care he really needs and the security she craves.

> You can't have somebody come over and baby-sit at your house for five dollars. You're not talking about a kid who can say, "I'm tired, I want to go to bed," or "Can we watch this movie?" Or "I'm hungry now." My fear of having any other sort of daycare take care of him is because of the fact he doesn't complain about things. Does that mean he's going to sit in the corner for an hour and a half? There's no way of knowing, and in this day and age, God knows, he can't tell me if someone is doing anything unmentionable to him. I just pray to God every time he leaves the house that the person I'm sending him to school with is dependable and not some weirdo. Nowadays you hear about all that stuff on TV about how a child was molested in daycare. Good God, you're paying these people to do nasty things to your children.

Sarah's case reveals the depths of the struggle that every parent of a sick child faces. How can I help my child? Parents of children with chronic conditions face additional burdens knowing that their child will never truly get well; they can only hope that their child's suffering, and their own, will somehow be lessened over time. The burden of repeated emotional struggles and difficult decisions is exacerbated further when a mother is on a near poverty–level budget, without help from the child's father, and without a lifeline of social support. Sarah must provide an inordinate amount of care to her son, and this extra labor surely affects her ability to pull herself out of poverty.

Quality of the Home Environment

A child's home environment has profound effects on his or her cognitive and behavioral outcomes. Warm and loving relationships with parents, opportunities for learning, and the physical condition of the home help children to thrive. Poverty affects the home environment, and it influences how parents interact with their children. For example, researchers found that the average child between 13 and 36 months of age on welfare hears half as many words per hour as the average working-class child, and less than one-third of the average of a typical child in a professional family. Why? Parents cannot teach their children what they themselves have not been taught (Children's Defense Fund 2005b).

The **Home Observation of the Measurement of the Environment (HOME)** is a widely used and detailed interview and observation scale of parent-child interaction and household resources. It measures maternal warmth, discipline, and other parental practices, as well as learning experiences provided to the child. The research shows that family income and poverty have significant effects on the quality and stimulation of the home environment, even after controlling for the effects of other variables (Garrett, N Ng'andu, and Ferron 1994; Duncan et al. 1998). Poor families have fewer toys, books, and other stimulating activities. The HOME scale also reveals that poor parents are less nurturing toward their children, display less warmth, and use harsher forms of discipline, including spanking. Improvements in family income had strong effects on improving the overall quality of the home environment for children who were born to a poor family.

However, an important question begs to be answered. Which cause the most problems for poor children—the relatively fewer stimulating toys, books, and activities, or the harsher and less nurturing parenting practices? One study of 753 children between the ages of 3 and 5 investigated precisely how family income matters to young children (Yeung, Linver, and Brooks-Gunn 2002). The researchers found that two sets of mediating factors were key to understanding the relationship between income and child outcomes—much of the association between poverty and lower achievement test scores was attributable to the family's difficulty or inability to provide a stimulating learning environment with educational toys or books. In contrast, the relationship between poverty and behavior problems was primarily attributed to maternal stress and depression, parenting practices such as spanking or other punitive parenting practices, and less warmth and social interaction between parent and child. Thus, it appears that both of these negative aspects of the home environment disadvantage poor children in different ways.

As children grow, they continue to have differing family experiences across income levels. For example, as parents in low-income and welfare-to-work families search for affordable daycare and household help, they often rely on the oldest daughter to help to keep the family together by taking over the responsibilities of caring for younger children, housework, and cooking as a substitute for the mom who is unavailable to do it all. These young girls have been nicknamed "mini-moms" (Dodson and Dickert 2004).

Researchers examined how low-wage families survive and how youth in high schools prepare for economic survival. They identified the role of the daughter who, of necessity, takes on the role of childcare provider and assistant housekeeper. "An important, consistent, and unexpected finding in this research is the amount of girls' family labor," states Dodson, the study co-author. "The upside is that girls, mothers, and some teachers identified some strengths in children taking on family obligations. Low-income families with mini-moms may be more bonded and more loyal, and the girls much more mature about social responsibilities than adolescents in higher-income families" (Dodson and Dickert 2004).

However, the researchers also found a downside to these girls' responsible family roles. Their commitments to their homes and to younger siblings undermine their education and social development outside the family and may even encourage early marriage and pregnancy. The heavy responsibilities at home impede the girls' chance to focus on their own development, and as a result, they are more likely to carry poverty into the next generation (Dodson and Dickert 2004).

Parental Stress and Mental Health

Data indicate that parents are less nurturing, more authoritarian, and use less consistent and harsher physical discipline as a family's economic situation worsens (McLoyd 1990). Moreover, although child abuse occurs in many different types of households, poor children have a higher probability of being abused, neglected, and injured more severely by the abuse than do their more affluent peers (Gelles 1992; Children's Defense Fund 1994). As Gelles reports:

> Abusive violence is more likely to occur in poor homes. Specific social and demographic characteristics increase the likelihood that poverty will lead to abuse. Poor young parents who are raising young children have an elevated risk of using the most abusive forms of violence toward their children, as do poor single mothers. (*Gelles 1992:271*)

What is it about an impoverished family environment that increases the likelihood of negative outcomes for children? One likely culprit is that parents who are living in poor conditions have a high level of stress related to their situation. Parents with low and unstable incomes experience more emotional distress, depression, and see themselves as less effective parents than do parents with higher incomes (McLoyd 1990; Conger, Conger, and Elder 1997).

Increased social support from family and friends reduces the amount of stress poor families experience. This then reduces the degree of violence or harsh discipline poor children may experience, and fosters improved self-esteem and the ability on the part of the child to overcome adversity (Hashima and Amato 1994; Bowen and Chapman 1996). However, some of the most vulnerable poor families, such as those who are homeless, tend to have very little social support.

Fewer Resources for Learning

On average, poor children have fewer resources for learning in the home. Therefore, high-quality childcare and preschool programs are necessary to provide them with the extra advantages needed to overcome their home environments. Unfortunately, poverty also affects the resources available for learning outside the family.

With increasing numbers of mothers turning to employment over the past several decades, many children are spending substantial amounts of time in the care of someone other than their parents. Forty-two percent of children under age 5 with employed mothers spent at least 35 hours a week in childcare in 2002. Among families in which the mother works full-time, 50 percent of children are in full-time care (Capizzano and Main 2005). The quality of this childcare should be of public concern.

Most researchers have established that higher-quality childcare is associated with better developmental outcomes, and lower-quality care with poorer developmental outcomes in children. There are two primary components to quality. *Process quality* refers to children's interactions with caregivers and other children, activities to enhance language stimulation, and attention to health and safety measures. *Structural characteristics* of the childcare setting include attention to the child-adult ratios, the size of each group of children, and the education and training of the caregivers (Vandell and Wolfe 2000). These two sets of indicators are related. Higher-quality childcare tends to be characterized by lower child-adult ratios, and therefore, caregivers can offer more stimulating and supportive care. The caregivers are more highly trained and children's activities tend to be of higher quality. They also are likely to have better health and safety practices, which result in fewer illnesses and injuries among children (St. Sauver et al. 1998; NICHD Early Child Care Research Network 2000).

There is important evidence that the quality of childcare experienced during the preschool years has both immediate and long-term effects on the child. For example, poor process quality predicts increased behavior problems, whereas children in higher process quality environments have closer and more secure attachments, and they perform better on standardized cognitive and language tests (Peisner-Feinberg and Burchinal 1997; NICHD Early Child Care Research Network 2000).

However, given the costs of childcare noted in Chapter 2, should we be surprised that low-income families cannot afford the highest quality care? More than one in four families with young children earn less than $25,000 per year (Children's Defense Fund 2001); therefore, most forms of formal childcare remain out of their reach without some sort of public subsidy. Instead, poor families are often forced to leave their children in substandard, unlicensed, and unregulated care.

The quality of childcare is only one of many ways in which poor children are disadvantaged with respect to resources for learning. Because they live in poorer neighborhoods, their public schools may be inadequately funded with far fewer resources than schools in wealthier neighborhoods (Kozol 1992). In a moving account, Kozol reveals the consequences of grossly understaffed and underfunded schools in the inner cities and less affluent suburbs, and he juxtaposes these schools with neighboring schools in wealthier communities. He describes a two-tier system in which poor and minority children have so shamefully few resources for learning that their hopes for the future are immediately dashed. Should we be surprised then that poor children are less likely to finish high school, and less likely to attend college?

Housing Problems

Shelter is considered one of the basic necessities of life. How much does "decent" housing cost, and who makes these decisions? One way to evaluate the cost of housing is to refer to the **fair market rent (FMR)** standards established by the U.S. Department of Housing and Urban Development (HUD). These standards, adjusted for regional differences and updated annually, are the amount that would be needed to pay the gross rent (shelter rent plus utilities of privately owned, decent, and safe rental housing of a modest [nonluxury] nature with suitable amenities (HUD 2003; National Low Income Housing Coalition 2005). These FMRs are used to determine payment standard amounts for voucher and subsidized housing programs. Sample 2007 FMRs for a two-bedroom apartment include $854 in Seattle, $782 in Phoenix, $935 in Chicago, $768 in Houston, and $817 in Tampa, Florida (HUD 2006).

The United States currently faces a severely limited supply of affordable housing units, most of which continue to deteriorate (Children's Defense Fund 2005b). More than 14 million households spend more than 50 percent of their income on rent, and three-quarters of these households are poor. Even full-time minimum wage workers cannot afford to pay fair market value in any jurisdiction across the country (Joint Center for Housing Studies 2003). To afford a modest two-bedroom unit in 2005, a worker needed to earn $15.78 an hour, which is three times the federal minimum wage of $5.15 an hour, and more than the mean wage of renters at $12.22 an hour (National Low Income Housing Coalition 2005).

Poor families cannot afford to pay FMR, and instead, many must live in damp, dirty, crowded, dangerous, and disease-ridden housing that may lack proper cooking or sanitation facilities (Joint Center for Housing Studies 2003). Poor children are 3.6 times more likely to have signs of rats or mice in their homes; are 3.4 times more likely to have family members sharing bedrooms; and are 2.7 times more likely to have spent time in a house that was considered by a parent or other survey respondent as "too cold" (Children's Defense Fund 1994). Exposure to rodents, crowding, and cold can seriously compromise a family's health and well-being. For example, manifestations of rats and mice, in addition to the more obvious concern associated with bites, can contribute to asthma and other respiratory problems by filling the air with rodent urinary proteins (Swanson, Agarwal, and

Reed 1985). A study that summarized 100 anecdotes and articles in medical journals from doctors, nurses, and social workers, estimates that nearly 18,000 children are hospitalized each year because of asthma complications from cockroaches, rats, and mold. Another 1,400 are hospitalized due to contact with exposed radiators. Where children live can have a tremendous effect on their health, the authors conclude (*Gainesville Sun* 1998).

One of the most rapidly growing segments of the homeless population is families with children. A recent survey of 27 U.S. cities found that in 2004 families with children accounted for 40 percent of the homeless population (U.S. Conference of Mayors 2004; National Coalition for the Homeless 2005). Homelessness severely affects the health and well-being of all family members. In particular, homeless children suffer more physical health problems than do children with homes (e.g., asthma, ear infections, stomach problems), and more mental health problems (e.g., anxiety, depression, withdrawal). They are also more likely to experience hunger, and they often have delayed development (National Coalition for the Homeless 2005). Jenna and Francie are two young children who have direct experience with homelessness.

> Jenna is a slight 5-year-old girl with big brown eyes, a shy smile, and the determination of a mountaineer scaling Everest. Her parents are homeless, forced to abandon their Section 8 apartment in fear for their children's health. Their landlord, despite court orders, refused to make repairs to their apartment, which had holes in the floor, a broken toilet, no heat or hot water for two winters, and, most disastrously, dangerously high levels of lead. As a result, Jenna suffered lead poisoning that caused brain damage and developmental delays. This is most noticeable in her almost unintelligible speech. Jenna explains herself over and over again in an attempt to communicate her needs and thoughts. Often tears squeeze out in frustration. Her older sister, Felicia, 8, keeps a close eye, piping up to translate Jenna's muddled words when someone does not understand.
>
> Nine-year-old Francie is very quiet and shy and still peers anxiously out from her blankets each morning. She remembers when rats were everywhere, burrowing in the walls and running freely through her apartment at night. She and her family became homeless after a rat attacked her foot, biting through her skin. Francie's family has applied for (subsidized) housing and is awaiting approval along with a very long list of others in New York City. (*Children's Defense Fund 2005b:6–7*)

Poor Quality Neighborhoods

Poor children are increasingly isolated from the nonpoor in their neighborhoods and communities and live in inner cities where violence, crime, truancy, loitering, and a sense of despair predominate (Kotlowitz 1992; Massey and Denton 1993;

O'Hare 1995; Ross 2000; Selis 2003). Between 1979 and 2002, guns killed almost 96,000 American children and teens, and guns wounded another 480,000 (Children's Defense Fund 2005c). Homicide is the third leading cause of death among children ages 1–4, the fifth leading cause among children ages 5–14, and the second leading cause among teenagers ages 15–19. It is the leading cause of death among young Blacks ages 15–34.

In his bestselling book *There are No Children Here,* author and journalist Alex Kotlowitz describes the lives of two brothers, Lafayette and Pharoah Rivers, who are growing up in the violence-ridden public housing projects of Chicago. In this true story, Kotlowitz takes the reader on a journey into a neighborhood where murders and shootings frequently occur, and introduces the reader to two young boys who are trying to survive their childhood despite the odds against them. Although gun violence has never been, and is not now a primarily Black or inner-city problem (about half of victims are white), it remains that many young children live in crime-ridden neighborhoods and shootings are all too common (Children's Defense Fund 2005c).

Analyzing data from a survey of nearly 2,500 Illinois residents, Ross found that residents of disadvantaged neighborhoods—characterized by a high percentage of poor, mother-only households—had higher levels of depression than residents living in less disadvantaged neighborhoods (Ross 2000). More than half of this depression could be accounted for by the greater numbers of disadvantaged residents, such as the poor, unemployed, and women, all of whom are known to have higher depression levels than their counterparts. However, Ross also found that disadvantaged neighborhoods exert their own impact on residents' mental health, above and beyond the characteristics of their residents, through the breakdown of social control and order. "In disadvantaged neighborhoods, residents are more likely to report that there are too many people hanging around on the streets, using drugs, and drinking; that there is a lot of crime, graffiti, and vandalism; and that their neighborhood is not safe. These signs of disorder are distressing," says Ross (2000:1).

Some findings suggest that those neighborhoods characterized by "poverty, excessive numbers of children per adult resident, population turnover, and the concentration of female-headed families are at highest risk for maltreatment" (Coulton et al. 1995:1,262). Drake and Pandey (1995) found a positive relationship between neighborhood poverty and three types of maltreatment—neglect, physical abuse, and sexual abuse—with the strongest relationship appearing between neglect and neighborhood poverty (Drake and Pandey 1995). Of course, this finding does not mean that these types of acts only occur in lower-income communities, but rather, it means that they are *more likely* to occur there than in higher-income communities.

Bowen and Chapman (1996) surveyed 207 middle and high school students in communities within Florida and North Carolina (Bowen and Chapman 1996). They found that low-income youth were significantly more likely to report such neighborhood dangers as gunshots, murders, gang-related fights or selling illegal drugs during the past 30 days than were their more affluent peers. Although these dangers were not frequent occurrences among either group, it remains that low-income youth did not feel as safe in their neighborhoods as did others.

Low-income neighborhoods are less likely to offer after–school programs for children and teens, and they are less likely to have parks or recreational facilities within them. Moreover, poor families are less able to afford the costs associated with extracurricular activities, such as uniforms or dues. Children in middle- and upper-middle-class families are two to three times more likely than low-income children to be enrolled in extracurricular activities such as sports, clubs, or lessons (Fields et al. 2001). Poor families cannot afford them, and are instead forced to find ways to entice their children to stay at home and out of trouble.

Marissa, a mother living in Florida, is concerned about her neighborhood, and she is typical in the way she likes to keep her children occupied. She has four children, the oldest of whom is 12 years old. They live in a house in a notoriously poor section of town, plagued with a high crime rate. The children all have extensive chores around the house every day after school and on weekends. Her goal is to keep them busy and out of trouble.

> There is nothing out in the streets but trouble. I talk to my children a lot, and I say, "Look, you see how people hang out in the street? It's not good for you." Because there are so many young kids hanging out on the streets. You walk down this main road, and that's all you see is young kids. Hanging out in the streets, I can't handle that. My daughter has a 14-year-old girl going to her school right now and she's pregnant. And it's like, man, I'm not risking that. (*Seccombe 2007:129*)

This chapter reveals many of the ways that poverty touches the lives of children and their parents, including their physical and mental health, and social well-being. It also illustrates the pathways that link poverty to adverse outcomes. The research is becoming increasingly clear: poverty has many direct deleterious effects on families. Impoverished families face a higher degree of stress, disorganization, and other problems compared to others. Yet, poverty is not simply about money; it contributes to a way of life that can erode the spirit and dim the chances for a full and rewarding life.

Critical Thinking Questions:

1. If we assume that many of the deleterious consequences of poverty originate in the home environment, how should we improve child outcomes? Should we

focus on giving poor children a boost from policies or programs outside the family, such as expanding Head Start programs or developing similar programs? Or should we intervene in the home environment in some way? What could be done in the home, and how controversial would such programs or policies be?

2. If poor children like Carlos get a significant amount of their food and nutritional requirements met at school through subsidized school breakfast and lunch programs, what happens to them in the summer when school is not in session? Where would you turn if you did not have enough food to eat?

3. Whose responsibility is it to take care of poor children? Is it the personal responsibility of their parents? Or is it the responsibility of society? Who is "society," and is "society" willing or able to pay these costs? What evidence do you have to support your answers?

4

HOW AMERICANS VIEW POVERTY: WHY ARE SO MANY FAMILIES POOR?

❧

AMERICANS ARE NOT THINKING MUCH ABOUT poverty these days. Unless forced to think about it, people see other social issues as more significant, such as terrorism, healthcare, education, or the economy. A survey conducted in English and Spanish by National Public Radio (NPR), the Kaiser Family Foundation, and Harvard University's Kennedy School of Government with a representative sample of 1,952 adults found that only 10 percent rated poverty, welfare, or something similar as one of the top two issues that government should address (NPR Online 2001). However, when they were asked directly about poverty, 55 percent claimed that it is a big problem in society, 33 percent reported that it is somewhat of a problem, and only 10 percent claimed it was a small problem or not a problem at all. As might be expected, opinions varied by income, with higher-income groups reporting poverty to be a less serious problem than lower-income groups (NPR Online 2001). So, although not at the front of American minds, it does seem that most see poverty as a social problem.

The trouble is, most people do not know how poverty is defined or where poverty thresholds lie. When asked what income level makes a family poor, most survey respondents gave a wrong answer. They used income thresholds that were significantly higher than the official federal government's definition. For example, in 2001 when the survey was conducted, the government's threshold for poverty for a family of four was around $17,000 a year. However, nearly two thirds said that a family of four with an income of $20,000 was poor, and 42 percent believed that a family of four earning $25,000 was poor. Likewise, 50 percent reported that a family of four could not get by on $20,000 per year, and 29 percent said that a family of four could not get by on $25,000 per year (NPR Online 2001). Thus, it may be safe to assume that even more people would consider poverty a serious problem if they knew more precisely how poverty was measured and tabulated, and how low the poverty thresholds actually are.

Yet, despite Americans' concern about poverty in general, their views about *poor people* tend to be more mixed. Many people are not very sympathetic toward the poor. Likewise, Americans' views toward welfare and other antipoverty programs are also deeply divided. It appears that although people think poverty is a problem, many attribute poverty to personal failings or shortcomings (NPR Online 2001; Rector 2004; Seccombe 2007). This attribution is especially apparent among those who view their own financial status as excellent or good— 51 percent of persons with incomes at least twice the poverty line say that the primary cause of poverty is that poor people lack motivation, and 50 percent of this group say that poor people have it easy because they can get so many government benefits without doing anything in return (NPR Online 2001). Rhonda, a poor single mother, told me that she frequently hears these views.

> I've heard one girl was going to quit working because all the taxes come to us. Plus, you know, they downgrade us in every kind of way there is. They say we look like slobs, we keep our houses this way and that way. And our children, depending on the way they're dressed, we're like bad parents and all sorts of things like that. (*Seccombe 2007:55*)

This chapter explores in depth how Americans view poverty and the impoverished. It provides a historical view and current theories about why a country as wealthy as the United States has significant numbers of families living in poverty.

Historical Views About Poverty

Today's opinions about poverty and the impoverished do not exist in a vacuum; they are derived from age-old questions and answers about poverty and the distribution of wealth more generally. They reflect our views about human nature, about the importance of hard work and our dislike of idleness, and our longstanding questions about if, how, and under what circumstances we should care for others who do not seem able to care for themselves.

Colonial America

The United States has a strong history of rugged individualism, a spirit of Calvinism, and the idea that hard work will reap tangible results. A common assumption as early as the colonial period was that the roots of poverty lay primarily not in structural economic causes but in individual misbehavior. Borrowing from the **Poor Laws** of England, the United States distinguished early on between the "worthy poor" (e.g., the disabled, the aged), and the "nonworthy poor" (e.g., the able-bodied). In 1619, the Virginia assembly ordered that idle able-bodied persons should be bound over to compulsory labor. Likewise, in 1633, the General Court of Massachusetts decreed harsh punishment for those who spent their time "idly or unprofitably" (Iceland 2003).

Poor people were very visible because there were few social programs in which they could hide. Social programs were generally not very popular because most people had a dim view of people who sought assistance. Unless they fell into one of the "worthy" categories, the poor were stigmatized and labeled "dependent," "defective," or "delinquent" (Iceland 2003). These arguments were further fueled by Social Darwinists who tried to legitimize the competitive struggle to secure one's economic status by allowing the "fittest" to win out over others. Government should not hamper this competitive struggle, many reasoned, because benefits would also trickle to the "unworthy" poor, and thereby reduce their incentive to work and better their own economic circumstances. Our social welfare system developed within this framework of duality, and it continues to operate in this fashion today. Our system has been described as "reluctant," indicating our generosity toward the worthy poor, while demonstrating callous disregard for others (Jansson 1988). Thus, current decisions about who constitutes the worthy poor, and at what level they should be taken care of, reflect these longstanding debates. The most consistent part of our evolving antipoverty policy is to reinforce the work ethic. We are cautious about giving assistance because we fear that people will no longer want to work if they are given something for free.

The Nineteenth Century

The nineteenth century saw the growth of poorhouses, also known as "indoor relief," as a method of dealing with the poor (Trattner 1999; Iceland 2003). By the 1830s, state governments began to write laws mandating that counties build institutions to house the poor. These institutions were called **poor farms** or **poorhouses.** Life in the poor farms and poorhouses was harsh; their purpose was to deter everyone but the most desperate from applying for help. Conditions were unsanitary, crowded, and often unsafe. "Inmates" were expected to work as a form of punishment, moral training, education, and reform (Iceland 2003).

Rural poverty was easier to ignore than poverty that arose in cities as the United States began to industrialize and urbanize. The large waves of immigration provided the labor fueling industrialization, and these immigrants resided in the rapidly growing urban regions. Millions of Irish, German, English, Scandinavian, and other Northern European immigrants came to the United States in the mid-1800s, encouraged by the prospect of a better life. By the late nineteenth and early twentieth century, millions more had come primarily from Southern and Eastern Europe, including Greeks, Poles, Italians, Russians, and other Slavic groups. Other groups from Asia, such as the Chinese, later immigrated to work primarily in certain industries. Between 1830 and 1930, more than 30 million immigrants came to the United States.

Immigrants were an important component of the changing economy, and they were employed in a number of key industries. A survey of 20 major mining and manufacturing industries found that more than half of the workers were foreign-born. In clothing factories, the figure was more than three-quarters. In packing-houses, steel mills, textile mills, coal mines, and a host of other industries, nearly half of the workers were immigrants to the United States (Steinberg 1981).

Most immigrants were members of the poor or working class. Women were preferred over men in certain industries because they could be paid significantly less, and they were considered to be more docile and obedient. Many jobs became categorized and separated by sex. Men did the heavy manual labor. Women toiled in tedious and repetitive jobs, and jobs that corresponded with their domestic skills, such as seamstresses, laundresses, or domestic servants to the rich. Men and women's wages were low, and consequently children also often worked fulltime, sometimes side by side with their parents in the growing industries.

Weatherford, in her 1986 book *Foreign and Female: Immigrant Women in America, 1840–1930*, describes the appalling conditions in which many immigrant families lived. Housing was crowded, substandard, and often lacked appropriate sanitation facilities. Raw sewage was strewn about, causing rampant epidemics of disease in the neighborhoods in which immigrants congregated. Upton Sinclair also describes the harrowing plight of immigrants in his bestselling novel *The Jungle*, originally published in 1906. It is a story about an immigrant family from Lithuania. In describing some of the dreadful conditions in the family's neighborhood, he wrote of raw sewage and cesspools drawing flies and rodents where children played. Working conditions were often dangerous, unsanitary, and inhumane. His book was influential in creating many new laws during the "progressive era" of the early 1900s to protect workers' health and safety. Sinclair describes the dangers of working in the meatpacking plants in Chicago:

> Of the butchers and floorsmen, the beef-boners and trimmers, and all those who used knives, you could scarcely find a person who had the use of his thumb; time and time again the base of it had been slashed, till it was a mere lump of flesh . . . The hands of these men would be criss-crossed with cuts, until you could no longer pretend to count them or to trace them. They would have no nails—they had worn

them off pulling hides; their knuckles were swollen so that their fingers spread out like a fan. There were men who worked in the cooking rooms, in the midst of steam and sickening odors, by artificial light; in these rooms the germs of tuberculosis might live for two years, but the supply was renewed every hour. There were the beef-luggers, who carried two-hundred pound quarters into the refrigerator cars; a fearful kind of work, that began at four o'clock in the morning, and that wore out the most powerful men in a few years. There were those who worked in the chilling rooms, and whose special disease was rheumatism; the time limit that a man could work in the chilling rooms was said to be five years. There were the wool-pluckers, whose hands went to pieces even sooner than the hands of the pickle men; for the pelts of the sheep had to be painted with acid to loosen the wool, and then the pluckers had to pull out this wool with their bare hands, till the acid had eaten their fingers off. (1981:98)

The strain of family life under these working and living conditions was severe and took its toll. Alcoholism, violence, crime, and other social problems stemming from demoralization plagued many families. Yet, immigrants continued to crowd the cities in search of work because they hoped that it would eventually lead to a better life. Many immigrants hoped that if they simply worked hard enough, they would soon join the ranks of the middle and upper classes, although few saw this dream come true.

How prevalent was poverty during the late nineteenth century? There was no official measure during this period, and therefore, estimates vary widely. Robert Hunter, in his 1904 book *Poverty*, estimated that at least 10 million people were poor, which represented about 13 percent of the American population in 1900. In contrast, Katz (1986) ventures that perhaps half the population of typical nineteenth century cities was poor.

Black Americans, Native Americans, Mexicans, and other immigrants were among the most vulnerable, although they were not necessarily deemed "worthy" of any assistance because of the racist sentiment of the time. These groups were seen as inferior to whites, and therefore assistance was often unavailable to them or came with heavy strings attached. For example, to be eligible for early welfare assistance, foreign-born women were urged to assimilate and to adopt white, middle-class values (Abramovitz 1996a).

Black Americans

The first Africans brought to the United States were enslaved for a specified amount of time, and then they were free to purchase their own land. But by 1790, the slave trade was well underway with at least 750,000 Africans captured. Thousands more died on the long, grueling ship ride to the United States where food, water, and sanitary conditions were abysmal. Although not all whites in the South owned slaves, the southern agrarian economy supported the importation, selling, breeding, and horrendous living conditions of slaves (McLemore and Romo 2004; Parrillo 2005).

Although the vast majority of Black Americans living in the United States were slaves, prior to the Civil War there were an estimated 150,000 free Blacks living in the south, and another 100,000 living in the northern part of the United States. They were allowed to work for wages (Mintz and Kellogg 1989), yet, even "free" Blacks were not necessarily allowed to vote or attend white schools and churches. Whites treated even free Black Americans as grossly inferior. Jobs were difficult to come by. Consequently, many free Blacks were poor, had high levels of unemployment, and were barely literate. Women had an easier time than did men in finding employment because whites sought them out as domestic servants.

Moreover, the number of free women outnumbered free men in urban areas. Together, the high rates of poverty and the sex imbalance of free Black Americans challenged their ability to marry and raise children. It is therefore not surprising that many children were reared in female-headed households. One study indicated that when property holdings, a key measure of income, were held constant, the higher incidence of one-parent families among Black Americans largely disappeared (Mintz and Kellogg 1989).

Black Americans continued to face severe poverty after the Civil War, when they were freed from slavery. They were barred by law or custom from almost all full-time jobs, and most worked in agriculture in the southern United States or as domestic servants or laborers in the northern regions. Their economic outlooks continued to be grim because opportunities for promotion and advancement were virtually nonexistent for African Americans in these positions. Racism remained an unfortunate fact of life.

Overall, due to the effects of slavery and continued racism, Black families have historically had different family patterns from those of white families. They are less likely to be married, they have more children, and they are more likely to have close extended family relationships. They also are more likely to be poor, with many significant repercussions. Family scholars and policymakers have often interpreted these differences as "problematic" (Moynihan 1965). In New York Senator Moynihan's book *The Negro Family: The Case for National Action*, published in 1965, he suggested that the repercussions of slavery, racism, failing social institutions, and decaying urban structural conditions were destructive and destabilizing forces to Black families. Although his book focused on structural features, it has often been seen as criticizing Black families and individualizing their plight. He spoke of their high rates of poverty, which he believed caused men to leave their families, encouraged mothers to become "matriarchs," and led to high rates of delinquency, illegitimacy, alcoholism, and school dropout.

More recent scholars point out that Black families have many strengths (Ladner 1998; Hill 1999). Billingsley (1968) pointed out that the structure of Black families was not the cause of social problems, but was actually an adaptive response to a racist culture (Billingsley 1968). He suggested that rather than considering the Black family as deteriorating, we should see it as showing resilience in the face of economic and social difficulties. Another scholar, Charles Willie, believes one of the greatest gifts of Black Americans to the culture of the nation has been the egalitarian family model in which neither the husband nor the wife is always in charge (Willie 1983; Willie and Reddick 2003). He suggests that the idea of matriarchal families in which Black men play little part is a myth.

Mexican Americans

The labels "Hispanic" and "Latino" cover groups so diverse that it makes almost no sense to combine them. The largest Hispanic group in the United States is made up of Mexican Americans, who have a rich history drawn from the contributions of Native American and Spanish heritage (Meier and Ribera 1994; McLemore and Romo 2004; Parrillo 2005).

After decades of war with Mexico, the United States annexed Mexican territory in 1848. Although the Treaty of Guadalupe Hidalgo guaranteed Mexicans the retention of their property, most landowners had their land confiscated and old land grants were no longer effective. Consequently, many Mexican families who were secure and had some degree of wealth prior to annexation became impoverished laborers on land owned by others.

Mexicans, including those men and women who had done skilled work in Mexico, were hired to do the physical labor that whites choose not to do. During the nineteenth century, employers hired women and children as domestics, laundresses, cooks, and farm laborers (alongside their husbands and sons). Men were hired to work on the railroads or in mining, along with farm laboring. Their pay was little, far below what whites typically earned, and consequently multiple family members were often employed—husband, wife, and children—so that they could feed themselves and keep a roof over their heads.

Despite the economic hardships, Mexican Americans were quite successful at preserving their traditional family structure. Family relationships were paramount and took precedence over individual needs or wants, a characteristic known as **familism** (Williams 1990). Women usually worked outside the home because of economic necessity, but they defined their primary role as wives and mothers. Families often contained several generations living together or near one another and pooling resources (Mindel 1980). Individual family members may have earned poverty or near-poverty wages, but collectively, families could raise their standard of living.

Poverty among most Hispanic groups remains high—Cuban Americans are the notable exception. For example, Hispanic households have less than 10 cents for every dollar of wealth owned by white households (Kochhar 2004). There remains a high degree of prejudice and discrimination against Hispanics, contributing to their high rates of poverty. A study of 3,000 Hispanics living in California, Texas, New York, Florida, and New Jersey found that about 30 percent reported that they, a family member, or a close friend had experienced prejudice during the past five years because of their racial or ethnic background. Similar percentages also reported receiving poorer service than other people at restaurants or stores (41 percent), being called names or insulted (30 percent), or not being hired or promoted for a job (14 percent) because of their race or ethnic background (The Pew Hispanic Center and Kaiser Family Foundation, 2004 March).

In the past, the growth in the Hispanic population was primarily due to immigration, with large numbers of people migrating to the United States from Mexico, Central America, Cuba, and other regions. Although immigration is at the forefront of political and media discussions (The Economist 2006), now, their population growth is fueled more by a high fertility rate. In other words, the Hispanic population in the United States is now expanding not solely due to immigration, but because of children born to those immigrants. This change poses many new and intriguing questions. How will the lives of the second generation be different from the first? Will the second generation do better economically? What will be their degree of assimilation? Will they retain their Spanish language and culture? What type of prejudice and discrimination do Hispanics face, and how might the dynamics of this change in the coming years as increasing numbers are born here rather than elsewhere (Brodie et al. 2002)?

Even though immigration is not the sole cause of Hispanic population growth in the United States, Americans are increasingly concerned about illegal immigration and focus primarily on Hispanic immigrants, although illegal immigrants come from around the world. A March 2006 survey conducted by the Pew Hispanic Research Center with 2,000 adults throughout the United States, and 4,000 adults living in Phoenix, Las Vegas, Chicago, Raleigh-Durham, and Washington, D.C.—illustrates this growing concern, but also demonstrates the lack of consensus about the problem and its solutions. The survey found that 52 percent of respondents believe that immigrants are a burden, taking jobs and housing (up from 38 percent in 2000), and only 41 percent believe that immigrants strengthen the United States with their hard work and talents (down from 50 percent in 2000)

(The Pew Research Center and the Pew Hispanic Center 2006). Yet, the study found that the public is nearly evenly divided among their support for three main approaches for dealing with illegal immigrants: 32 percent think it should be possible for illegal immigrants to stay permanently; 32 percent believe some should be allowed to stay under a temporary worker program under the condition that they leave eventually; and 27 percent think that illegal immigrants should be required to leave the country. Attitudes about immigrants likely contribute to the ambivalent attitudes toward immigration. For example, on one hand, 80 percent of respondents believe that Hispanic immigrants work very hard, up from 63 percent in 1997. Eighty percent believe that Hispanic immigrants have strong family values, also an increase from a decade ago. But not all attitudes are favorable. One-third believe that Hispanic immigrants often end up on welfare or significantly increase the crime rate. Survey respondents also express concerns that illegal immigrants do not learn English quickly enough and are less willing to assimilate than immigrants who came to this country in the early 1900s (The Pew Research Center and the Pew Hispanic Center 2006).

Native Americans

When European settlers arrived in the so-called "new world," they found that it was already inhabited. It is estimated that there were nearly 18 million natives who had diverse customs and who spoke an estimated 300 different languages (John 1988). Most Native Americans lived in tribal societies based on lineages, and these ranged from simple hunting-gathering groups to larger groups who used sophisticated horticultural methods. Kinship was an important component of political organization and provided the primary basis for tribe governance. Whether matrilineal or patrilineal, kinship was the basis for political power and status.

Tremendous diversity existed among Native American groups, and conflict or wars sometimes erupted among them; however, nothing prepared them for the scale of massive destruction they experienced in the nineteenth century (McLemore and Romo 2004; Parrillo 2005). Often under the guise of religion, "progress," or sheer economic greed, Native American groups experienced slaughter and enslavement, and they were forcibly removed from their land and put onto reservations by white European settlers and their descendants. There were numerous conflicts between whites and Native Americans, along with attempts to virtually obliterate Native American groups. For example, exposure to smallpox (deliberately or unwittingly), for which Native Americans had built no immunity, killed millions of adults and children. Many of their traditions were difficult or impossible to maintain under these circumstances, and many Native Americans suffered extreme poverty and hardship (McLemore and Romo 2004; Parrillo 2005).

By the early twentieth century, only an estimated 240,000 Native Americans remained, although their numbers have increased in recent years (Wells 1982; U.S. Census Bureau 6 October 2004). Native Americans continue to face difficulties. Infant mortality rates are high and life expectancy is low, particularly on reservations. Poverty rates are nearly triple those of other Americans and unemployment is even higher. High school dropout rates are high. Many Native Americans live in substandard housing. For example, approximately 10 percent of housing on reservations lacks indoor plumbing.

Part of the difficulty is that most Americans know little about Native American culture, and social programs may not be culturally sensitive. Consequently, tribal leaders in recent years have implemented numerous strategies of their own to improve social and economic conditions, such as developing alcohol awareness programs and opening tribally controlled colleges to educate young adults. Native American tribes are developing strategies to raise significant funds for these endeavors, including building gambling establishments on tribal lands.

Our quick analysis of history reveals that Americans' values and beliefs reflect the ideas that individuals are primarily responsible for their own economic conditions; that the world can be divided up into worthy poor and unworthy poor; that work is good and idleness is a vice; and that social services are likely to dull initiative and hard work. Moreover, many Americans fail to acknowledge the connections between the historical exploitation of minority groups and their higher-than-average poverty rates. As a result of these values and beliefs, American antipoverty programs were specifically designed to stigmatize those who receive assistance to minimize the likelihood that those currently receiving aid would get too comfortable, and to make a statement to onlookers that aid comes at an emotionally expensive price.

Current Views About Poverty

In a country of vast wealth, it remains that nearly 37 million families live in poverty today (DeNavas-Walt, Proctor, and Lee 2006). How do Americans see poverty and the impoverished today? What are the root causes of poverty? Understanding the causes of poverty is critical because it can then guide us to the appropriate solutions.

Here I introduce several frameworks that attempt to explain the existence of poverty, including (1) **Individualism**; (2) **Social Structuralism**; (3) **Culture of Poverty**; and (4) **Fatalism**. If we think of these perspectives as residing upon a continuum, Individualism and Social Structuralism are at each end. The Individual perspective focuses on the achievement of the individual, arguing that we are ultimately responsible for our own economic positions, both poor and wealthy. In contrast, Social Structuralism identifies the primary source of poverty as the inequality found in social institutions, such as the labor market, families, and government, that affect our economic positions. Other perspectives, such as the Culture of Poverty or Fatalism, combine features of the first two perspectives to explain the ways in which our social structure shapes individual action. The Culture of Poverty argues that the poor have developed a unique subculture as an adaptation to the structural barriers they encounter, and this subculture has the unintended consequence of perpetuating their poverty. Fatalism attributes poverty primarily to quirks of fate that people cannot generally control.

Individualism

The Individualistic perspective is reflected in our country's response to the poor throughout most of our history. Tales of Horatio Alger types abound—the "rags to riches stories"—with the moral that anyone can pull themselves up by their bootstraps with hard work, sweat, and motivation. The poor, and particularly welfare recipients, are blatant examples of those who have failed to "make it." Reasons abound, but the Individualistic perspective suggests that, at best, the poor are uneducated and untrained; at worst, they are lazy and unmotivated. Either way, the poor, like the affluent, are held largely responsible for their own economic plight.

Is this a popular perspective today? The Heritage Foundation, a large conservative American think-tank, expresses the individualist perspective as they denigrate poor families:

> Rather than being materially poor, American's "poor" suffer from the effects of behavioral poverty, meaning a breakdown in the values and conduct that leads to the formation of healthy families, stable personalities, and self-sufficiency. This includes eroded work ethic and dependency, lack of educational aspirations and achievement, inability or unwillingness to control one's children, increased single parenthood and illegitimacy, criminal activity, and drug and alcohol abuse. (*Rector 2004:2*)

The Heritage Foundation, and others who support Individualism, suggest that the poor lack moral values, have an eroded work ethic, lack aspirations, and are poor parents.

Likewise, a recent letter to the editor published in the magazine *Brain, Child*, was highly critical of an article in the magazine about the "mothers' movement," a movement to promote social programs and policies to help mothers and their families. Although less vicious than the Heritage Foundation's criticism of poor families, the author of the letter spoke for many people as she pleaded for increased personal responsibility and failed to see family concerns as social issues requiring social solutions.

> You have missed the obvious reason that mothers, such as myself, are not jumping on your version of a "mothers' movement." What you are proposing—universal after-school care, universal preschool, paid leave, giving tax credits and subsidies for income that was not earned—is socialism. Many of us know that socialism rots a society from the inside out; therefore we would never jump onto your mothers' movement bandwagon . . . Instead of urging women to stand for a socialist agenda, why not educate women about saving and fiscal responsibility, long-term investing, and finding excellent daycares? Why don't you encourage mothers to take the responsibility and thus claim the power over their choices in life rather than turning to Uncle Sam? (*Donnelly 2006:4*)

How representative are these views? Studies conducted over the past several decades show the persistent popularity of the Individualistic perspective in the United States. Although there are important gender, race, and income variations, generally individualism is a highly popular explanation of inequality by women and men, Blacks and whites, and the affluent and poor (Feagin 1975; Smith and Stone 1989; Hunt 1996; Seccombe, James, and Battle-Walters 1998; NPR Online 2001; Hancock 2004).

A study conducted in 1969, a time ripe with social change, reported similar sentiments. Sociologist Joe Feagin conducted a survey with 1,017 randomly selected adults from all regions of the United States that illustrated how deeply rooted the Individualistic perspective is (Feagin 1975). More than half of the sample believed a lack of thrift, laziness, and lack of effort, along with a lack of ability and talent, were very important reasons for poverty. Nearly 90 percent said that these were at least somewhat important explanations of poverty. Only 18 percent suggested that poverty was due to poor people being taken advantage of by rich people (Feagin 1975:97). Those persons most likely to espouse Individualistic explanations were white Protestants and Catholics, residents of the south and north central regions of the United States, persons over age 50, middle-income groups, and those with moderate levels of education.

Additionally, Feagin found little tolerance for welfare recipients, with most respondents indicating a high degree of suspicion and distrust of them. Eighty-four percent of respondents agreed with the statement that "there are too many people receiving welfare who should be working," 71 percent agreed that "many people getting welfare are not honest about their need," and 61 percent felt that "many women getting welfare money are having illegitimate babies to increase the money they get" (Feagin 1975:103).

A recent poll by the Joint Center for Political and Economic Studies noted that in response to a national survey evaluating the welfare system and its biggest problems, there was little difference among Blacks, whites, and Hispanics. Seventy-two percent of Blacks reported that fraud and abuse by welfare recipients is a problem, as did 70 percent of whites and 79 percent of Hispanics. Likewise, 70 percent of Blacks felt that welfare encouraged poor women to have babies out of wedlock by giving cash assistance for children, as did 74 percent of whites and 70 percent of Hispanics (Hancock 2004). This sentiment was expressed repeatedly in my interviews with families on welfare (Seccombe 2007).

The poll conducted by NPR, the Kaiser Family Foundation, and Harvard University (described in the opening of this chapter), asked its respondents whether the biggest cause of poverty today is that people are not doing enough to help themselves out of poverty, or is it that circumstances beyond their control cause them to be poor. The answer? Nearly half of the survey respondents (48 percent) claimed that people were not doing enough, and a slightly smaller number (45 percent) claimed circumstances. The remainder said that they did not know. As might be expected, answers were somewhat dependent on such things as income, race or ethnic background, and political affiliation. Thirty-nine percent of people living in poverty claimed that the biggest cause of poverty is that people are not doing enough, compared to 50 percent of persons living at an income of 200 percent of the poverty line. Thirty-six percent of Blacks blamed poverty primarily on individuals not doing enough, compared to 49 percent of whites. Likewise, 37 percent of Democrats gave "people not doing enough" as the primary cause of poverty, compared to 63 percent of Republicans and 48 percent of Independents (NPR Online 2001).

When probed further, and asked about the specific major causes of poverty, low-income Americans were significantly more likely than other Americans to name drug abuse, medical bills, too few jobs (or too many being part-time or low-wage), too many single-parent families, and too many immigrants, as shown in Table 4.1. Opinions about poverty and welfare recipients reflect deeply held beliefs that the poor are largely responsible for their own economic circumstances because of laziness, lack of thrift, or lack of talent. Most Americans are relatively unconcerned about poverty and do not see the increasing inequality as a problem for the country. In fact, one out of five Americans thinks there are too *few* rich people (Zimmerman 2001).

But perhaps what is most interesting in these data is *the degree of similarity* across income groups. In fact, low-income groups are actually *more likely* than higher-income groups to blame poverty on a lack of motivation or a decline in moral values, and they are nearly equally likely to blame the welfare system for poverty.

Table 4.1 Is (ITEM) a major cause of poverty, a minor cause of poverty, or not a cause at all? (Percentage saying major cause)

	>200%	100%–200%	<100%
Drug abuse	68	76	74
Medical bills	54	68	71
Too many jobs being part-time or low-wage	50	61	70
Too many single-parent families	52	59	64
A shortage of jobs	27	47	62
Too many immigrants	27	38	42
The welfare system	47	44	46
Poor people lacking motivation	51	56	55
A decline in moral values	56	59	57
Poor quality public schools	47	47	45

"200%" references poverty level, so >200% represents those making more than twice the poverty level, and <100% represents those making less than the poverty level.
Source: NPR Online 2001.

These findings support other studies that indicate that the poor denigrate others in poverty. My study of welfare recipients revealed that they, too, blame the poverty of other welfare recipients on those recipients' own behavior, yet see themselves as exceptions to the general trend (Seccombe 2007). I interviewed a woman named Janie, a 19-year-old mother of a 2-year-old child, who characterizes the Individualistic perspective. She lives in an apartment that is not subsidized and has a roommate to share expenses. The apartment is in good condition, although her furnishings are modest and sparse. Despite being only 19, Janie has been living virtually on her own for years. She ran away from home as a young teenager, lived on the streets for a period of time, stayed in shelters, and more recently has shared apartments with one or two other people. Janie was gang raped several years ago, and she became pregnant as a result. She decided to keep the baby and turned to welfare for help. Janie has received welfare since her daughter was born two years ago, but, like others I interviewed, is convinced that welfare is just a temporary step in her otherwise busy, confused, and complicated life. She hopes to be off the system within a year or two, after she pays off her bills and "gets established." But she feels that many others who receive assistance are far less motivated than she is.

> There are some people on welfare who don't need to be on welfare. They can go out
> and get a job. They have nothing better to do than to live off of welfare and to live
> off the system. I'm sorry. I have no sympathy. Look at all the signs on the road,
> "will work for food". Go down to Day Labor, for crying out loud. They'll pay you
> more money than you can make in a regular day. It's by choice. Either (a) they don't
> want to work, (b) they are being supported by others, or (c) they don't give a damn
> about themselves. (*Seccombe 2007:66–67*)

Likewise, Sheri is a 27-year-old with three children who had been on welfare
for seven years. She believed that people on welfare are lazy, but she clearly did not
include herself in this category, despite the fact that outsiders may be concerned
over her supposed long-term welfare "dependency."

> I think a lot of them are on it just to be on it. Lazy. Don't want to do nothing. Lot of
> them on it 'cause a lot of them are on drugs. Keep having kids to get more money,
> more food stamps. Now that's abusing the system. And a lot of women are abusing
> the system. (*Seccombe 2007:67*)

Sheri, like other women on welfare, distanced herself from other recipients
physically and emotionally. Clear distinctions were drawn between "me" and
"them." Many women believe that other women do not deserve to receive welfare,
are bad mothers who neglect their children, or in other ways commit fraud or
deliberately abuse the system.

Welfare recipients are perhaps the most stigmatized subset of the poor. We
assume that they should be able to improve their economic circumstances easily,
yet we ignore that the vast majority of welfare recipients are unmarried women
with dependent children. Given their daily parental responsibilities, tasks, and time
constraints, they do not have the same opportunities to "pull themselves up by
their bootstraps" as do other adults who are without children (e.g., poor men). To
ignore the emotional and time commitment involved in taking care of dependent
children, and to fail to recognize the ways in which caretaking can inhibit women's
ability to be socially mobile, is to ignore the reality of many women's existence. It
is unfair to assume that unmarried women who stay home to take care of their
dependent children are lazy, lacking in thrift, or have little or no talent.

The argument behind Individualism is that we need to change the individual
and increase her or his motivation and level of human capital to be competitive for
jobs. Little attention is given to features of our social structure, such as the growing number of service-sector jobs that generally pay sub-poverty level minimum
wage. Yet, what proponents of this perspective fail to ask themselves is, if the bulk
of new jobs are being created in the low-paying service sector, can we really train

people out of poverty? Will not someone else then occupy these roles? Poverty may be transferred to someone else, but it will not be eliminated.

Social Structuralism

A social structuralist perspective, in contrast, assumes that poverty is a result of economic or social imbalances within our social structure that restrict opportunities for some people. Social structure is defined as the social institutions, organizations, groups, statuses and roles, values, and norms that exist in our culture.

Another letter to the editor in the magazine *Brain, Child* illustrates a structural approach to viewing poverty. The author compares the benefits available to families in Hungary to those in the United States. She writes:

> ... I live in Hungary, where the benefits for families surpass those of any other country I've heard about. Maternity leave is three years. Daycare and preschool are free. Elementary school starts at eight a.m. and runs until two p.m., with optional aftercare. Most schools also offer ballet, music lessons, computer clubs, soccer, etc., in the afternoon. We all receive a monthly family supplement grant, which increases with each child and lasts until the child turns eighteen. When the child hits school age, we get an additional lump sum at the beginning of each school year amounting to about $100 per child to cover school supplies. All children have medical coverage through the age of eighteen—longer if they are in college—and pediatricians make house calls. If you have a child with a disability, you may stay home with the child for the rest of his/her life and receive the minimum wage. ... There is no question that the United States needs more generous benefits for families. I am an American (my husband is Hungarian) and our choice to move to Hungary to have kids was a very conscious one. When I feel pangs of homesickness, I think of my overworked, stressed-out friends with kids back home and think: No way. I feel like I've got a balance in my life I would have a difficult time achieving in the States. I wish that all American parents had the same opportunities we've got here in Hungary to make life easier for families. (*Strong-Jekely 2006:2*)

Her point is that families need programs and policies in place to remain socially and economically healthy. Families without these checks in place are more likely to slip into poverty.

Three distinct themes exist under a broad Social Structualist perspective: (1) a concern with capitalism, (2) a focus on a changing economy, and (3) a concern that the welfare system itself exacerbates poverty. Social conservatives seeking to dismantle the welfare system have often invoked this last theme.

Concerning the first theme, some in our society contend that poverty is an inherent feature of capitalism (Marx and Engels, cited in 1968), and the subsequent control over other social structures, such as education and the polity, is designed to serve the interests and maintain the dominance of the wealthy class. Karl Marx's early writings draw attention to the exploitative relationships found within capitalistic societies. They feature a greater division of labor, where workers do not work for themselves but sell their labor for wages to capitalists. Marx argued that workers are not paid wages that reflect their true worth (e.g., their output). Instead, capitalists prefer to keep wages low, pocketing the remainder as profit. Producing more goods, with fewer workers, especially when they are not paid wages equivalent to their output, ensures higher profits. Capitalism thrives on a reserve labor force; people who are available to work in times of booming economic expansion or union busting. This reserve labor force is expendable, and many workers are discarded when the boom subsides. Consequently, their poverty is an inevitable feature of capitalism.

Second, other structuralists point to the features of a changing economy, such as the growth in low-paying service sector jobs, the erosion of the minimum wage, and the relocation of jobs from inner cities (Wilson 1987; Wilson 1996). For example, dual labor market theory posits that the economy can be divided into at least two sectors: primary and secondary. Workers' location in one or the other sector systematically affects their earnings, bargaining power, and likelihood of fringe benefits such as health insurance, even when workers have similar levels of education, training, job tenure, other skills, or human capital. Furthermore, there is little mobility, and workers tend to become trapped in one sector or the other. Job characteristics vary dramatically in these two sectors. Jobs in the primary sector tend to offer positions possessing higher wages, better working conditions, more opportunities for advancement, greater employment stability, and generous fringe benefits. The secondary sector, in comparison, offers lower wages, fewer possibilities for promotion, higher turnover rates or seasonal employment, and fewer critical fringe benefits.

At $5.15 an hour in 2006, the national minimum wage has been criticized as being far too low to support a family. Many families earning minimum wage are living below the poverty line, and they need programs such as food stamps to make ends meet. A worker earning $5.15 an hour earns $10,712 a year, several thousand dollars below the poverty line for a family of even two or three. Likewise, the purchasing power of the minimum wage has eroded over the past several decades and is no longer sufficient to support even a small family.

In response to this concern, the living wage movement has gained a significant foothold in at least 60 local governments, including New York City, Baltimore, Portland, Chicago, Minneapolis, and many other cities. A typical **living wage** ordinance requires contractors and businesses receiving governmental financial assistance to pay a minimum wage that is deemed a "livable wage" in that community. Only a specific set of workers is covered by living wage ordinances, usually workers employed by businesses that have a contract with a city or county government or those who receive economic development subsidies from the locality. The rationale behind the ordinance is that city and county governments should not contract with or subsidize employers who pay poverty-level wages. Pay should provide a wage that a family can reasonably expect to live on, and this income will ultimately decrease the number of persons who will be dependent on social programs. Living wage movements also have expanded their goals to include health benefits, vacation days, and other benefits. Usually wages range from 150 percent to 225 percent of the minimum wage.

Critics of living wage legislation claim that these laws actually harm those people they are intended to help by reducing their work opportunities. Critics charge that as the price of labor increases, a loss of jobs will result, and people will be even worse off than before. Some living wage critics argue that the living wage will create a "hostile business climate." However, the costs of the living wage ordinance will have a very small impact on the profits of the small number of firms affected by the law. The profit margins for firms affected by the living wage are estimated to range from 10 to 20 percent of production costs. In comparison, the wage increases from living wage ordinances are estimated to be 2 percent of production costs (Economic Policy Institute 2002). Yet, opponents suggest that a better alternative is a targeted wage subsidy that lifts the income of those most in need without raising labor costs to employers. Wage subsidies are usually administered as federal tax credits. This strategy would, in essence, shift much of the financial burden from the local governments to the federal government, which is supposedly better able to absorb these costs. An example of a wage subsidy, or tax credit for low-income persons, is the Earned Income Tax Credit (EITC), discussed in Chapter 6.

The third structural approach suggests that social programs and welfare policies themselves contribute to poverty and exacerbate welfare use by trapping people into poverty and welfare dependency instead of helping them escape. The welfare system is accused of encouraging dependency and discouraging work incentives. This theory is popular with social conservatives and welfare critics and is used as an argument favoring a dismantling of welfare programs (Anderson 1978; Murray 1984; Murray 1988). They claim, as did De Tocqueville more than a hundred years ago, that people are inherently lazy and will lose motivation and incentive if they know that governmental programs are there to take care of them. For example, people will snub work at low-paying jobs, and will instead rely upon the free money of welfare if given the opportunity. They argue that eliminating or drastically reducing welfare is a critical first step to curbing poverty. Reducing aid significantly will keep people from getting too comfortable with the system. In the recent NPR study discussed earlier, 46 percent of respondents believe that the welfare system is a major cause of poverty, and another 37 percent believe the welfare system is a minor cause of poverty (NPR Online 2001).

Ironically, there may be some merit to the argument that the welfare system can breed dependence, but the cause of that dependence is that aid is too little, not too generous. In a study of welfare families, I found that the majority of women claimed that the welfare system had built-in disincentives or penalties for work (Seccombe 2007). Working, especially at minimum-wage jobs that usually lack health insurance and other important benefits, would not achieve their goals of self-sufficiency, and in fact would jeopardize the health and well-being of their children because they would lose critically needed benefits. Moreover, taking great pride in motherhood, they said they would never want to jeopardize their children's well-being. From these interviews, it became clear that without continued assistance with (1) health insurance, (2) childcare, (3) transportation, (4) food stamps, and (5) subsidized housing, working not only becomes prohibitive, but also sometimes is seen as downright dangerous. Many women I spoke with claimed that they want to work, or that they could find a job, or even that they had a job previously, but felt compelled to quit because working, along with the automatic reduction in their welfare benefits, actually lowered their standard of living or jeopardized their children's health. They expressed frustration that the welfare system, as currently structured, actually discourages them from working by raising their rent, eliminating Medicaid, and cutting them off from needed social services before they have a chance to establish themselves. Jo Lynn, a mother of two young children, claimed

I've had a job before, and I know I can get a job. It's just really hard. It's like, I got a job at Hardee's [fast-food franchise] and I had a friend take me back and forth. I was paying her 20 dollars a week for gas. I got off the system. I was honest about it and told them I had a job. They took my assistance away, and they raised my rent $200. And they said they weren't going to give me any Medicaid either, and I didn't have any health insurance. I had a baby at the time, and she was only a year old. She had to go to the periodic appointments and stuff, and I was like, "Okay, well I'm going to try to do it." And I had to work there six months to a year to get health insurance. I was really scared, like, what am I going to do? But I'm gonna do it. So I started doing it, and then I started realizing that, you know, that after about two months, I was under the welfare level. I mean, by making minimum wage I couldn't keep my bills up, and I could never afford to take her to the doctor. It wasn't getting me ahead. I was being penalized for trying to get off the system, and it's happened to all my friends that are on welfare. It's like a trap, and they don't help. (*Seccombe 2007:96*)

Jo Lynn did what our society wants welfare mothers to do—she found a job. But with that job, her financial picture became even bleaker. She told me it caused her to be "under the welfare level." Jo Lynn's situation was not an isolated case. The welfare system offers too little, not too much, and therefore, curtails many families' opportunities for independence.

Culture of Poverty

The Culture of Poverty perspective blends features of the preceding two perspectives. It suggests that a subcultural set of values, traits, and expectations has developed as a direct result of the structural constraints associated with living in isolated pockets of poverty. People in poverty are said to live in a subculture with a weak family structure and present-time orientation, and they display a helplessness and resignation toward work (Burton 1992).

Although there is a wide range of opinion regarding the specific antecedents, features, and consequences of the subculture (Moynihan 1965; Lewis 1966; Valentine 1968; Gilder 1981; Wilson 1987; Mead 1992), there is concern about the transmission of these values from parents to children. The question of whether poverty and welfare use are intergenerational—that is, are they passed on from parents to their children—is an enduring theme in the poverty literature.

Donna is one woman who lived in a culture of poverty, but her story reveals the structural constraints that shape these traits (Jean 2005). Donna, a petite white woman with blonde hair, was born the child of migrant farm laborers. Her family followed the fruits of the field, picking cotton and cherries. No one in her family was educated beyond the eighth grade. For generations, the family survived on low-wage employment and migrant farm work. They worked hard, but were constantly evicted from their home, hungry, and struggling with poverty. When Donna did not have a home to stay in, the cherry field was her bed sometimes, or if she was lucky, a car.

Donna was in and out of schools, never the same one for an entire year. Her school experiences were not fun or exciting. They were stressful. "You had to be clean and have the right clothing, the right shoes, and the right lunch to fit in. You had to be on time and you had to finish all your homework to stay out of trouble." The latter was particularly difficult. Cherry fields do not usually come with desks, and hunger will not sharpen the mind or a pencil.

Her educational experiences hold memories of violence, humiliation, and fear, she explains, so she dropped out of school, got married, and worked in a foam rubber factory as a laborer, and in other low-wage jobs. She worked long hours for little pay. Eventually she had children, and she loved them as dearly as her own parents loved her.

At 26, she had been homeless most of her life, and it was a lifestyle that she, as a single mother, was unwittingly passing down to her own children. For 26 years that was her world, and there seemed no escape. Things just are the way they are sometimes, she reasoned.

One day, as she passed by a fast-food restaurant looking for work, she realized things had to change, even if she did not know how or what to do. The family's utilities had been shut off, and as she contemplated yet another job at a fast-food restaurant, she knew it would not fix anything. It would not be enough money to make ends meet, and it would take her away from her children for long periods of time.

A few days earlier, she had been given a card for someone at a community action agency with assurances that this person could help her. Reluctantly, she went, expecting only help with utilities. While there, someone not even affiliated with the agency told her of a program that could ultimately move her from poverty to self-sufficiency. Self-sufficiency—that is one of the first points she highlights when discussing that part of her life. "Don't just hand people boxes of food and send them off," Donna implored. "You have to give them the boxes of food, of course, but think about what else is out there to help them."

In the beginning, Donna didn't think much of the suggested program, but she inquired anyway. The social worker started talking about college. That was "crazy stuff" for someone like Donna, who dropped out of school at 15. She was about to leave the agency when she heard the magic words. If she participated in the program, which connects single mothers with college, she would get a Section 8 housing voucher, which would help her pay her rent. Now you're talking, she thought.

She wanted to be a good mother, but people in poverty often cannot think long-term. As Donna explained, "It's what you're going to eat tonight, where you're going to sleep."

That short-term reward of a housing voucher made the difference. Donna was eager to get that voucher for the sake of her kids, and would even do something as crazy as go to college. She would "jump through all the hoops," she decided, but not anything extra. They were not going to change her, she thought. She would get the housing voucher, and then she was out of there.

One of the first "hoops" was picking a career interest. She was asked to pick a job, any job, that she would do if all obstacles were removed and money were no object. Donna was sarcastic, but felt cool and in control—or so she thought. She picked the name of a famous television journalist. "You get me that job," she told them. "That's the job I want." She paused to ask the seminar participants, "Now what am I doing? If you can't get me that job, then who has failed here? That's right, it's not me." Her admittedly rude response was a defense mechanism. It was a way to keep a tiny little bit of control for herself.

The social workers were seemingly not fazed by her attitude. They took it all in stride and responded, "Oh, Donna's interested in journalism!" That was an important difference from many other programs Donna had seen. The social workers did not say she was being unrealistic, or react negatively to her sarcasm. They treated her as if her potential were unknown, and therefore, all things were possible.

They encouraged Donna to go to the financial aid office at a nearby post-secondary school—but they didn't stop there. "They said, 'Come on, Donna, let's go.'" They actually took her there, showed her around, and introduced her to people. "What do we usually do?" Donna asked. "We tell them to go over to the college on their own. When they don't go, we think they don't really want help." She pointed out that those living in generational poverty often believe college is beyond their reach. They would feel too defeated to even try. From Donna's perspective at that time, college was just too overwhelming, too outside the realm of possibilities she could envision for herself. Education wasn't for people like her. She would only venture into this strange new territory if someone guided her.

The social workers brought her to the most important office at the college, the financial aid office. But they did not just introduce the woman who worked there as a financial aid counselor. Instead, they personalized her by telling Donna the woman's name and that she, too, was a mother. That helped Donna connect on a more personal level. She could talk to another mother. They had something in common.

Donna still had not lost all of her sarcasm however. Informed that the woman helps people get money for college, Donna suggested the woman would soon be showing her the door. "You won't want me," Donna assured her. "Just look me up on that computer of yours. I don't have a good credit rating at all." The woman explained that the college did not need to know her credit rating to offer financial assistance. "I said, 'What are you talking about?' I just couldn't believe it. They were offering me money and I didn't even have to have a good credit rating?" There weren't any deals like that in Donna's world. She had not imagined such an opportunity existed for her, nor had anyone in her family or circle of friends.

Despite her initial attitude that the social workers were not going to "change" her, the program opened Donna's eyes to new possibilities, a new way of seeing the world, and a career in journalism. She excelled, completed a bachelor's degree, then a master's degree, and finally, a doctoral degree. She now studies poverty issues. Her research focuses on students from generational poverty who have successfully completed a bachelor's degree, and how they did it. Her consulting firm, Communication Across Barriers, helps agencies identify weak points in their service delivery (Jean 2005).

Donna's story reveals that although the subculture is said to be at odds with the dominant middle-class culture because it downplays the importance of hard work, self-discipline, and deferring gratification, it is not impenetrable. The culture of poverty is an adaptation to poverty, but with the right type of intervention, the subculture is not necessarily reproduced.

Oscar Lewis first introduced the idea of a culture or subculture of poverty as he studied poor barrios in Latin American communities. The idea of a poverty-based subcultural phenomenon caught the media by storm. He wrote:

> The culture of poverty is both an adaptation and a reaction of the poor to their marginal position in a class-stratified, highly individuated, capitalistic society. It represents an effort to cope with feelings of hopelessness and despair which develop from the realization of the improbability of achieving success in terms of the values and goals of the larger society. Indeed, many of the traits of the culture of poverty can be viewed as attempts at local solutions for problems not met by existing institutions and agencies because the people are not eligible for them, cannot afford them, or are ignorant or suspicious of them. The culture of poverty, however, is not only an adaptation to a set of objective conditions about the larger society. Once it comes into existence it tends to perpetuate itself from generation to generation because of its effect on the children. By the time slum children are age six or seven they have usually absorbed the basic values and attitudes of their subculture and are not psychologically geared to take full advantage of changing conditions or increased opportunities which may occur in their lifetime. (*Lewis 1966:xliii–xlv*)

Unfortunately Lewis' work has sometimes been misinterpreted as a victim-blaming approach in which deviant values are seen as the causes of poverty itself. This is not a correct interpretation of his work. Harvey and Reed (1996) suggest that Lewis' ideas are firmly grounded in a Marxist critique of capitalism. A subculture was constructed to ease the pain associated with being a part of the reserve and discarded labor force that is an inherent byproduct of capitalism. They suggest that the culture of poverty is "a positive social construction—the result of a process by which the poor pragmatically winnow what works from what does not, and pass it on to their children" (Harvey and Reed 1996:482).

Wilson attributed poverty among the Black "underclass" in inner cities to their social, economic, and geographic isolation (Wilson 1987; Wilson 1996). He argued that social class, not race, is the primary factor in explaining their poverty. Wilson suggests that the move of well-paying manufacturing jobs from urban inner city areas out to the suburbs has had disastrous effects upon those persons living in the inner city core. Male unemployment and subsequent poverty increased dramatically after the jobs moved, and consequently reduced the pool of men eligible for marriage while at the same time increasing the number of children born out of wedlock and raised in single-parent families. Moreover, the middle class migrated out of urban areas, leading to the development of ghettos. Their migration out to the suburbs means that those persons who remain in the urban core have few role models of mainstream success.

Wilson's work is notable on several fronts. First, he contends that, although social class is more important than race as a cause of intergenerational inequality, his model applies primarily to minorities because few poor whites reside in highly poor inner–city neighborhoods. Second, his model focuses on the interaction of structure and culture. He blames labor markets and demographic changes for isolating the inner-city minority poor, and it is these structural constraints that thereby affect the organization of family and community life. His concept of social isolation does not imply a self-perpetuating or permanent phenomenon. When job opportunities and appropriate social services for inner-city residents are provided, the subcultural adaptation will eventually disappear.

Other scholars have extended Wilson's ideas to include other minority groups. For example, Aponte (1998) notes that Puerto Ricans are also criticized for their relatively high rate of single-parent families. The traditional explanation often used is that these families are being formed primarily to take advantage of welfare benefits. However, a deeper analysis reveals the interplay of structure and culture. He suggests that the fundamental cause of poverty is the economy's inability to generate enough jobs at sufficient wages after manufacturing and other blue-collar employment moved away from large northern cities. Kasarda (1990) reveals that from 1953 to 1986, 1.35 million jobs in the manufacturing and wholesale/retail trades were lost in New York, Boston, Baltimore, and Philadelphia, alone. Because Puerto Ricans are heavily concentrated in these northern cities, their employment prospects declined dramatically, thus leading to a decrease in their rates of marriage and a decline in marriage stability (Aponte 1998).

Fatalism

Finally, Fatalism attributes the causes of wealth and poverty to quirks of birth, chance, luck, human nature, illness, or other forces over which people have no control. Fate here does not necessarily imply destiny, but rather a form of victimization that is rooted in complex events beyond one's immediate control. Poverty is not anyone's immediate fault *per se*, but rather is a potential consequence of unplanned, random, or natural human events or chain of events. Because this perspective claims that poverty is caused by forces outside our control, it can be used to deny the ways that poverty and social inequality are rooted in our social structure. Herrnstein and Murray, for example, suggest that low intelligence is a primary cause of poverty and welfare dependency (Herrnstein and Murray 1994). Arguing that intelligence is largely genetic, they argue that poor people with low IQs give birth to another cohort with low IQs and thus the children remain in poverty.

However, not all fatalistic explanations are quite so victim-blaming. Poverty could be caused by, or related to, factors such as poor health, domestic violence, the ending of a relationship, or other types of "bad luck." For example, in interviews with welfare recipients, I found that many discussed their "bad luck" at getting pregnant (Seccombe 2007). Several who were unmarried teenage girls when they had their first child told me that they were surprised at becoming pregnant—they were unaware that sexual activity caused pregnancy, or they didn't know that they could get pregnant the first time they had sexual intercourse. They were confused and unknowledgeable about sex. Many disclosed that they had intercourse as a way to please a boyfriend, or because of peer pressure from their girlfriends at school or in their neighborhoods. They rarely used birth control. Either they did not know it was necessary, or their partner complained about wearing a condom and they acquiesced to his wishes. When they discovered they were pregnant, they were surprised. How did this happen? Abortion was rarely a consideration among the women interviewed. Instead, these young girls accepted that they somehow got "caught," and they had their babies.

Terri Lynn, a mother of a 6-year-old boy, did well in high school and never suspected that it would "happen" to her.

> Sure, I don't want to be on welfare, but I don't have a choice. You know, I didn't plan to get pregnant with him, but it just happened. You know? I don't want to be on it. I'm going to get off it as soon as I put him in school. (*Seccombe 2007:98*)

Peer pressure among teens to have sex is powerful and challenging to avoid. One recent study involving 1,000 girls in Atlanta found that 82 percent said the subject they wanted to learn most about in their sex education class was "How to say no without hurting the other person's feelings" (Besharov and Gardiner 1997). The average age for first intercourse is 16.9 years for men and 17.4 years for women. By their late teenage years, at least three-quarters of all men and women have had intercourse, and more than two-thirds of all sexually experienced teens have had two or more partners (Alan Guttmacher Institute 2002).

As noted in Chapter 3, there is some good news: there has been a substantial decline in teenage birth rates over the past 15 years and they are now at a record low. The teenage birthrate, at 41.2 per 1,000 women aged 15–19 has plummeted since the 1991 peak of 61.8. The declines are widespread, occurring among both younger and older teens. Even among teenagers 14 and younger, a group that has always had relatively low rates of pregnancy compared to older teens, the declines are substantial. The birthrate for girls aged 10–14 has declined by one-third since 2000 (Hamilton et al. 2005).

Declines also have occurred across racial and ethnic groups, but the decline in birthrates among Black teenagers has been especially striking: their overall rate has dropped 45 percent since 1991, whereas the rate for young Black females aged 15–17 has plunged by more than half. What accounts for these trends? Obviously, declines in birthrates reflect changes in (1) the level of teenage pregnancies and (2) how these pregnancies are resolved. Because we know that the abortion rate among teens also declined during this period, it appears that the decline in teenage birthrates is attributable to reductions in their pregnancy rate. The important question then remains: Why did the pregnancy rate decline? According to a report by the Alan Guttmacher Institute, *Why Is Teenage Pregnancy Declining? The Roles of Abstinence, Sexual Activity, and Contraceptive Use* (2000), there are several reasons, including an increase in abstinence, less frequent sexual activity among those who report being sexually active, and the use of more effective contraceptives.

Despite this good news, there is more work to be done. Although the teenage birthrate is declining, studies find that 21 percent of teenage women fail to use contraceptives at first intercourse, and 20 percent fail to use them at their most recent sexual intercourse (Alan Guttmacher Institute 2006). Adolescent childbearing is far more common in the United States than in other industrialized countries. Our teenage birthrate remains nearly twice that of Canada, three times that of France, and four times that of Sweden (Darroch et al. 2001).

To what degree does the general public attribute poverty to circumstances beyond one's control, or to bad luck? Feagin, in his 1969 survey, found that people shied away from attributing poverty simply to bad luck (Feagin 1975). In his survey of 1,017 adults, only 8 percent of respondents emphasized that "bad luck" was a very important reason for poverty. Smith and Stone, in their study of 200 randomly selected respondents in southeast Texas, also found that fatalistic perspectives were unpopular compared to individualistic explanations (Smith and Stone 1989). For example, only 10 percent of respondents agreed that bad luck or being born inferior is a very important explanation. Moreover, only 14 percent believed that low intelligence is a very important explanation for poverty. More recently, the NPR survey discussed previously found that respondents who are doing well financially do not attribute their success to luck (3 percent), but rather, they attribute their success to their own efforts and abilities (86 percent) (NPR Online 2001). In contrast, among those respondents who claim that they are not doing well financially, 22 percent attribute their financial problems to bad luck, increasing to 29 percent among those living in poverty. Thus, it appears the public is wary of attributing success or failure to luck *per se,* unless they themselves are not doing particularly well. Then, suddenly, luck (or the lack of it) seems relevant after all.

These four perspectives—Individualism, Social Structuralism, Culture of Poverty, and Fatalism—offer competing, yet also complementary, explanations for poverty and social inequality. They reflect historical and persisting dilemmas about human nature, the importance of hard work, and the role of the government and economic systems in perpetuating economic disparities and in ameliorating them. They are competing explanations in the sense that, at first glance, they seem incompatible with one another. Yet, a deeper analysis shows that reasons for poverty are many, and they are multifaceted, complex, and interrelated. Janie, Sheri, Jo Lynn, Donna, and Terri Lynn, the women introduced in this chapter, reveal that structural characteristics have profound implications for our lives, and can ultimately shape the subculture, our attitudes, and the unfortunate circumstances in which we can find ourselves.

Critical Thinking Questions:

1. How do today's views of poverty and the poor reflect historical views? How are they different or similar?
2. The author claims that "Individualism" is a popular explanation in the United States for poverty and welfare use. Can you provide any examples of this explanation from your own experiences?
3. Which explanation(s) for poverty makes the most sense to you, and why? Which explanation is the most controversial, and why? Which explanation may be the most popular among the poor, and why?

5

WELFARE AND ITS REFORM: TEMPORARY ASSISTANCE TO NEEDY FAMILIES (TANF)

WE MAY NOT HEAR A LOT about poverty, but we do hear a lot about welfare and welfare reform these days. The press often reports how "successful" the monumental 1996 changes in the welfare system have been: far fewer families receive cash assistance and more single mothers are working today. In fact, welfare caseloads have declined by more than 60 percent since welfare was changed (U.S. Department of Health and Human Services 2006). Is this good news?

Yes and no. As is often the case, things may be more complex than they first seem. There are both good news and significant challenges that must be addressed. This chapter will trace the history of cash welfare programs, discuss how and why welfare was reformed, and examine the consequences of these changes for poor families.

History of Cash Assistance Programs

Cash welfare programs are not new. They have been around for many years in one form or another, and they reflect societal attitudes toward poverty and toward the worthy and unworthy poor. It is no accident that cash welfare programs are primarily targeted to women and children to protect them from the most serious effects of poverty. They are seen as more vulnerable than men to conditions of poverty, and thus they are seen as potentially deserving of assistance. Nineteenth- and early twentieth-century social reformers were concerned that many children were living in orphanages because their mothers could not support them or could not care for them while they were employed. Moreover, delinquency rates were high and rising among children who were unsupervised at home. However, more implicitly, cash welfare programs also were designed to help single mothers stay out of the labor force. Reformers expressed concern that more than 5 million women working for wages outside the home were taking jobs away from men, and they argued that the future of our nation depended on the proper upbringing of children by their mothers at home (Gordon 1994; Mink 1995; Abramovitz 1996a; Abramovitz 1996b).

Mothers' Pensions

Mothers' Pensions were created during the Progressive Era (1896–1914) to respond to these concerns, and they are generally identified as the first cash welfare program. They are significant because they began the trend of increasing government responsibility for the well-being of poor women and children—particularly those who were white and who were widows. Mothers' pensions were designed as payment for the services of motherhood, thus giving the pensions legitimacy and attempting to remove the stigma that was associated with other types of public aid. However, benefits were low, and the emphasis was placed on moral reform. In exchange for aid, poor mothers were forced to conform to rules and policies designed to weed out suspected fraud and to ensure that women followed strict gender norms. Caseworkers monitored the women for signs of drinking, poor housekeeping, improper child-rearing techniques, and relationships with men, and foreign-born women were urged to quickly assimilate to American culture (Abramovitz 1996b).

Modern-day welfare emerged from these values of moral reform. **Aid to Dependent Children (ADC)**, or "Welfare" as we have come to call it, was created in 1935 as Title IV of the Social Security Act, a critical piece of legislation produced during the New Deal, when millions of families were suffering financial hardship. Approximately one-quarter of the workforce lost their jobs during the Great Depression. Homelessness, hunger, malnutrition, and begging were widespread. Private charities and churches stepped up their efforts to help the needy, but the problem had become so rampant that their efforts could not keep pace with the need. Under President Franklin D. Roosevelt, a wide variety of safety net programs were created to assist vulnerable populations. The Social Security Act established several key social security and unemployment programs, and responsibility for social welfare was transferred from individual states to the federal government.

Aid to Dependent Children (ADC)

The focus of Aid to Dependent Children (ADC) was to keep single mothers from being dependent on their children for labor and income, and to keep both mothers and children out of the workforce. It was considered a pro-family program: it kept mothers in the home so that they could care for, nurture, and protect their children because mothers were not expected to work and raise their children at the same time. The goal was to make welfare synonymous with well-being, prosperity, good health, and good spirits, and the program, therefore, faced relatively little opposition in Congress (Abramovitz 1996a).

ADC was a fundamental departure from the inequitably distributed Mothers' Pensions, which served almost exclusively white widows. ADC recipients included mothers who were abandoned, divorced or never married, or mothers whose husbands were unable to work. ADC was supposed to provide help to minorities as well as to white women; however, only 14 percent of all children who received ADC in the 1937–1938 fiscal year were Black, a figure far below true need (Sterner 1943). To keep Blacks from receiving benefits, many states, particularly in the south, tightened their eligibility requirements so as to exclude them (Quadagno 1994).

Although ADC's goals were admirable, the program fell short of significantly reducing poverty in many respects. For example, although it was a federally created program, ADC gave individual states great authority over eligibility and benefit levels. Southern congressmen fought to limit federal control and would only support ADC if the states were allowed to establish their own eligibility requirements and benefit levels (Quadagno 1988; Quadagno 1994). This resulted in dramatic statewide differences in the level of benefits. For example, in 1939 ADC benefits ranged from an average of $2.46 per child per month in Arkansas to $24.53 in New York (U.S. Social Security Board 1940). In addition to sexism, racism influenced policies. Southern states rationalized their lower-than-average benefit levels by declaring that Black families needed less money than did white families (Abramovitz 1996b).

The program had an aura of social stigma. Keeping with the ideology of the worthy versus unworthy poor, ADC benefits were considerably less than the benefits of other, less stigmatized programs under Social Security, such as Old Age Assistance (OAA) and Aid to the Blind (AB), even though recipients of these two programs were less likely to have children in the home. Furthermore, the program continued the practices, commonly employed with Mothers' Pensions, of using aid to enforce moralistic behavioral standards. Home visits and periodic eligibility checks were routine measures to scrutinize women's parenting, domestic, and sexual behaviors. Most state programs distinguished between deserving and undeserving mothers, closely perpetuating the old model associated with Mothers' Pensions. These provisions were not a part of OAA or AB.

Congress amended ADC in 1939 and moved the assistance given to widows into a new Social Security program, leaving ADC caseloads largely consisting of unmarried, separated, or divorced women and their children. The movement of widows out of ADC resulted in its further stigmatization. Marital status became a defining characteristic of ADC recipients; it was increasingly viewed as a program for children born to "unworthy" women. However, many widows from minority groups were unable to receive widow benefits under the newly restructured program because their husbands had not qualified for Social Security benefits. Thus, these widows had no choice but to turn to ADC. These policy changes contributed to the enduring racialized hostility surrounding welfare: it is seen as a program for unmarried minority women (i.e., Black) and their children.

Growing Caseloads and Growing Concerns

ADC continued to be amended over the years, but the animosity toward the program never subsided. Other social programs that developed over the years managed to avoid the stigma of being labeled as "welfare," such as the GI bill or VA housing loans created after World War II. Veterans were seen as worthy poor, while unmarried women with children were increasingly criticized. These veteran benefits enabled many GIs to get a college education, buy a home, and secure their financial status.

During the 1950s, the composition of various social welfare programs began to change radically. Given the demographics of the era, ADC began to overshadow other programs in size and expense, such as those serving the elderly. As a reaction to this growth, the public focused on rising costs of the program and the moral fitness of welfare mothers. Punitive state policies were enacted to remove people from caseloads. State residency requirements were enforced, names of welfare recipients were publicized, and entire caseloads were closed with recipients required to reapply with new application investigations.

Feminist welfare state theorists suggest that several forces heightened the hostility toward welfare and its recipients (Miller 1992; Gordon 1994; Abramovitz 1996a; Abramovitz 1996b). One force was the competing demand for women's unpaid work in the home and cheap labor in the market. After World War II, the occupations that relied heavily on women's labor and low wages were expanding, while at the same time, the number of women employed outside the home was shrinking. As Betty Friedan notes in her book *The Feminine Mystique* (1963), during the 1950s many women dreamed of husbands, children, station wagons, and houses in the suburbs rather than employment. Women's average age at first marriage dropped to under 20 years, the lowest in more than 100 years. The number of married women in the labor market plummeted (Saluter 1989). In the early 1950s, The Women's Bureau was reporting severe shortages of typists, stenographers, nurses, social workers, teachers, and medical aides, jobs generally held by women (Kessler-Harris 1982).

Not surprisingly, welfare benefits also became restricted and further stigmatized to encourage more women into the labor pool. These changes were particularly seen in the south, where, for example, Louisiana refused ADC to "employable" mothers with young children during the harvest season, as did Georgia when extra pickers were needed in the tobacco and cotton fields (Abramovitz 1996b). Forcing women on welfare to work, or discouraging them from getting the aid to which they were entitled, helped fill jobs at the bottom rungs of the employment sector—jobs that men did not want, and would then be left unfilled.

Feminist welfare theorists also suggest that welfare critics targeted poor women's marriage, sexuality, and childbearing patterns. After World War II, the divorce rate skyrocketed to unprecedented levels. Hasty "shotgun" marriages were short-lived, and the divorce rate climbed to 16 divorces per 1,000 married women aged 15 and older, double the rate before the war. Nonmarital births also increased, almost tripling for white women, and increasing somewhat less, for Blacks. These changes in family structure have been blamed for the breakdown in "family values"—an emotionally charged term heavy with moral overtones about a woman's proper role.

Marital status discrimination was readily apparent. Only women who lived under the safe confines of a husband-as-breadwinner escaped scrutiny. Unmarried working mothers were criticized for neglecting their children's needs and contributing to juvenile delinquency, truancy, and child abuse. Yet, women who did not work and who received ADC also were harshly criticized and blamed for a wide variety of social ills. Policies designed to enforce behavioral, sexual, and gendered norms flourished. Recipients were subject to "midnight raids" and other intrusions into their lives so that authorities could try to catch men staying over at recipients' homes. Some states penalized a woman for having a relationship with a man who was not the father of her children. Arkansas, for example, denied aid to mothers in a "non-stable, non-legal union." Alabama eliminated 25 percent of their welfare clients by cutting off women who were "going with a man." Michigan cut aid to families with "male boarders" (Abramovitz 1996b).

The 1960s and the War on Poverty

The 1960s contained both some gains and some setbacks for the ADC program. Several events occurred during the 1960s that are credited with developing an increased concern for the poor, compassion, and a "rediscovering" of poverty. First, a series of recessions and periods of high unemployment occurred in the late 1950s and early 1960s. The economy bounced back after each of these periods, but with less energy each time. Second, the extent of poverty was exposed during the 1960s, due in part to books and essays such as Michael Harrington's

The Other America (1963). In this popular book, Harrington vividly reported the poverty experienced by millions of America's forgotten people in geographically isolated pockets of our country. Third, the Social Security Administration developed an official poverty index, and thus, the number of poor people and groups in the United States could be systematically counted and compared from year to year. Fourth, the civil rights movement brought increasing attention to the racism and poverty experienced by Black Americans and other minority groups. And finally, the shift in the composition of public assistance rolls that began in the 1950s continued and showed no signs of abatement in the 1960s. Welfare was increasingly becoming synonymous with impoverished divorced and never-married women and their "illegitimate" children.

When running for the presidency, John Kennedy stressed the issues of poverty, unemployment, and rehabilitation of the poor, and after he was elected he began a major effort to address these concerns. He was a firm believer in a human capital approach; he believed that people were poor because they lacked adequate education, job skills, and experience in the labor market, and that they needed further education, job training, and social services to help them succeed. Kennedy argued for greater resources, such as education and job training programs, so that the poor could eventually pull themselves out of poverty. Additionally, he was a believer in the Culture of Poverty perspective and was concerned with the anti-work subcultural values and norms that he believed develop among the poor. President Kennedy sought to create programs that would focus on instilling positive attitudes among poor children that would eventually allow them to become more economically mobile and join the ranks of the middle class. Given the expanded family focus, the name of the ADC program changed to **Aid to *Families* with Dependent Children (AFDC)** (emphasis added). The 1962 amendments to the Social Security Act, referred to as the Social Service Amendments, increased federal funding for social services, "services in addition to support, rehabilitation instead of relief, and training for useful work instead of prolonged dependency . . . to maintain family life where it is adequate and to restore it where it is deficient," claimed President Kennedy (Bandler 1975:380).

This thrust continued after Kennedy's assassination, as President Johnson shared Kennedy's vision of reducing poverty. President Johnson had at his disposal the annual government reports that counted the numbers of poor persons and identified vulnerable sociodemographic groups, such as children, the elderly, large families, single-mother families, rural families, and minority group members. Like Kennedy before him, he believed the government had a critical role in reducing the incidence of poverty and the suffering experienced by millions. In his State of the Union Address in 1964, Johnson announced that "this administration today, here and now, declares unconditional war on poverty in America. . . ." The underlying assumption of the War on Poverty in the 1960s was that poverty is largely the result of inadequate education, job training, and marketable skills, and Johnson posited that the numbers of poor could be significantly reduced with adequate training programs to increase the level of human capital that could be exchanged for wages in the job market. If we could train everyone for a job, and then find them one, poverty will be ameliorated or significantly reduced, human capitalists argued.

During President Johnson's administration, programs were created that focused on job training, education, improving health, and providing jobs. Some of these programs were the Economic Opportunity Act, Head Start, Medicare, and Medicaid. Volunteers in Service to America (VISTA) was designed to help rehabilitate slums and other impoverished areas. Not all programs were created at the federal level; Johnson's War on Poverty also shared a concern that programs should be structured and carried out, at least in part, on the local level. Federal dollars were often targeted to these local efforts. These programs received extensive media attention, leading the public to believe that these efforts would eventually move women off of welfare and out of the ranks of the impoverished.

During this national War on Poverty, the United States' war in Vietnam was escalating, and attention and dollars were diverted from needs at home. Additionally, demographic changes, the growth of the civil rights movement and its white backlash, and the expansion of welfare benefits contributed to what became known as a "welfare crisis." Because of changing eligibility rules, such as allowing women on AFDC to work, allowing some two-parent families to be eligible for aid, and extending benefits to children between the ages of 18 and 21 who were still in school, the number of families receiving welfare continued to rise. The number of welfare recipients soared from 3.5 million in 1961 to almost 5 million in 1967. Costs jumped to $2.2 billion (Abramovitz 1996a). By the late 1960s and early 1970s, many Americans had grown tired of the clamor for social change and had grown resentful of the concerns voiced by the poor, ethnic minorities, and other disadvantaged groups. AFDC came under swift attack. Politicians and the media referred to AFDC and other programs as bloated, claiming that they had become too large and needed to be reformed.

Precursor to Welfare Reform

The late 1960s and early 1970s was a period of many social changes. One change—the increasing number of women in the paid labor market—led many people to question whether poor mothers really constituted a category of the worthy poor any longer. By 1975, 52 percent of married women with children between the ages of 6 and 17, and 37 percent of married women with children under age 6 were employed outside the home (U.S. Department of Labor 1994). Consequently, some politicians voiced serious doubts about the appropriateness of paying poor mothers to stay home and take care of their children. They suggested that welfare benefits had become too attractive to women, that benefits had increased faster than wages, and thus more women were opting to receive AFDC rather than to work in the paid labor market. They worried that the value of the full range of benefits exceeded the amount the recipient could earn in an entry-level job, and thereby women were inclined to choose welfare over work (Tanner, Moore, and Hartman 1995).

Since then, U.S. presidents have generally mirrored these views, and they continued efforts to revamp welfare. For example, President Nixon initiated the Family Assistance Plan, or FAP, which guaranteed that every unemployed family of four would receive at least $1,600 a year from the federal government. The working poor would be allowed to keep benefits until their earnings reached approximately $4,000. Only then would their benefits be discontinued. The FAP contained several other critical features or clauses; most notable, perhaps, is that women with children over the age of 3 would be required to work or would be placed in a job training program.

Nixon's FAP immediately sparked controversy. Quadagno (1994) suggests that it contained an internal contradiction about women's roles because it encouraged single mothers to work, while it encouraged married mothers to stay home. Women's "proper" roles were class-based. Further, FAP contained few programs to really help poor women improve their job skills, or to assist them in finding jobs. Nor did it provide much support for childcare. Nonetheless, in 1970, it passed the House by a vote of 243 to 155. However, because of the controversy surrounding FAP, it remained bogged down in a Senate committee until it expired. Instead of FAP, a multitude of relatively poorly funded work programs were created during the 1960s, 1970s, and 1980s: the Work Incentive Program (WIN), which was later replaced by WIN II; the Job Training Partnership Act (JTPA); and the more recent 1988 Family Support Act, and the Job Opportunities and Basic Skills Training Program (JOBS). Each program received tremendous popular press and blaring headlines, such as "The Most Sweeping Revision of the Nation's Principal Welfare Program" (Szanton 1991). Yet most programs helped only a small fraction of the millions of poor families. For example, funding under the JOBS program covered only 13 percent of recipients (U.S. General Accounting Office 1995 May). Yet, once again, welfare recipients were criticized as being lazy, unmotivated, and not trying hard enough (Berrick 1995).

One of the most dramatic responses to these frustrations with welfare and its recipients occurred during the administration of Ronald Reagan during the 1980s, when several hundred thousand families were eliminated from AFDC eligibility. Spending for all social welfare programs decreased substantially between 1980 and 1986. AFDC was not the only program that was reduced; so were food stamps, Medicaid, school lunch and other nutritional programs, family planning programs, subsidized housing, legal aid, and drug abuse counseling. Welfare expenditures were cut dramatically, down almost 30 percent per person, on average (Ellwood 1988:41).

With the election of George Bush (Senior) as president, the philosophy toward the welfare system remained relatively consistent with that of Ronald Reagan. Bush argued that the best way to overcome poverty is through individual hard work and initiative, rather than through government-sponsored programs. He stressed volunteer charity, school vouchers, and enterprise zones, and he complained that the federal government should back away from welfare. Instead, states and local communities should establish standards and programs. Yet, despite Bush's rhetoric, the number of AFDC recipients rose.

Individual states also experimented with ways to reduce the number of people on welfare. For example, in 1992 lawmakers in New Jersey and Wisconsin passed welfare reform packages commonly referred to as "Bridefare." These reforms were designed to reduce welfare use among women by encouraging them to marry. Arguably fueled by conservative ideologies that are concerned with the presumed breakdown of family values, "Bridefare" extends AFDC eligibility to married women, while restricting benefits to those who are single. The intent was to reverse what politicians have defined as a transfer of power and authority away from men in traditional family settings to the welfare state (Thomas 1995).

New Jersey in 1993 and Arkansas in 1995 enacted further attempts at state-level welfare reform, referred to as "Family Caps." These two states denied higher cash payments to women who have additional children while on welfare. Proponents suggested that a cap would remove financial incentives for AFDC recipients to have more children outside of marriage. Opponents, in contrast, argue that it is a misperception that women who receive AFDC have additional children to get more money. They point out that additional births do not dramatically increase the size of the welfare check; checks increase only $24 to $147 per child depending on the state. This amount is not enough to cover increased expenses of another child.

By 1996, under President Clinton's administration, approximately 14 million persons or nearly 5 million families with children, received AFDC (Committee on Ways and Means 1996: Table 8-27, p. 471). The public, along with a Republican-led Congress, clamored for a reduction in social programs. The human capital approach to helping the poor was becoming out of favor, and instead, the focus was on reducing welfare "dependency" quickly (Bernstein 1993). The primary concern in the 1990s was simply reducing the number of people who received cash welfare assistance. Reforms were not necessarily designed to reduce the number of people impoverished or to reduce the effect that poverty has on individuals and families.

Temporary Assistance to Needy Families (TANF): "Ending Welfare As We Know It"

President Clinton advocated reforming the welfare system, believing that the federal government should institute a comprehensive series of reforms to prevent long-term dependence on the system. He stressed that the focus of welfare should be in getting people back to work, because employment "gives hope and structure and meaning to our lives" (Clinton 1997a). Rather than creating programs to increase the human capital of welfare recipients, he argued that an assortment of services, including health insurance and childcare, should be made available to support lower-wage workers. He acknowledged that, without these services, welfare recipients are unable to leave welfare for work.

> . . . There are things that keep people on welfare. One is the tax burden of low wage work; another is the cost of childcare; another is the cost of medical care . . . today you have this bizarre situation where people on welfare, if they take a job in a place which doesn't offer health insurance, are asked to give up their children's healthcare, and go to work . . . That doesn't make any sense. (*Clinton 1997a*)

The Republican-led Congress came to President Clinton twice with welfare reforms that he considered too punitive and inadequate to support families. However, at the time of their third attempt, Clinton was up for re-election, and early on it looked like it could be a close race. Clinton's Republican opponent would make the most of the fact that Clinton had twice vetoed Republican-initiated welfare reforms that came to his desk. But this time, when the revised legislation came to his desk, the election-year pressure was insurmountable.

Clinton signed the welfare reform legislation into law, promising to make the needed changes to the legislation later. He claimed that the legislation met his general criteria for moving people from welfare to work, offered benefits—such as childcare and healthcare (although, only temporarily)—and would further enforce child support payments on the part of absent parents. Although he felt that this third Republican-led attempt would produce legislation more toward his liking, he also acknowledged, "Some parts of the bill still go too far, and I am determined to see that those areas are corrected" (Clinton 1997b). In particular, Clinton voiced concern over the deep cuts in nutritional assistance for working families with children and the exclusion of benefits for legal immigrants (Haskins 2001a).

On August 22, 1996 President Clinton signed a bill to eliminate AFDC and to revamp welfare "as we know it." From the Personal Responsibility and Work Opportunity Reconciliation Act (PRWORA, P.L. 104–193), **Temporary Assistance to Needy Families (TANF)** was created and went into effect as federal law on July 1, 1997 (Coven 2005). In a nutshell, PRWORA was designed to move families from welfare to work. Proponents hailed the legislation as a powerful way to decrease welfare dependency. Critics, including Clinton himself, felt many of the changes were highly punitive.

Quickly, the Balanced Budget Act (BBA) of 1997 made a number of changes to the TANF program, by partially restoring funding for several of the most extreme cuts enacted in the 1996 welfare law (Haskins 2001b). As a result, changes included such provisions as (1) an increase of $3 billion over a two-year period to help states pay for a variety of employment-related activities aimed toward persons with significant work barriers; (2) possible exemptions for victims of family violence from TANF work and time-limit provisions; (3) restoration of Supplemental Security Income (SSI) benefits to many disabled elderly legal immigrants; (4) waiver of several of the restrictions on food stamp eligibility for adults aged 18–50 who are not caring for minor children; and (5) designation of a $20 billion child health block grant to provide health insurance to many of the 10 million uninsured children in the United States (Center for Law and Social Policy 1997).

It also was recognized that requiring mothers to work full- or part-time meant that someone needed to care for their children. Childcare assistance is an essential part of any strategy to help families avoid or leave welfare. A study of TANF recipients in Michigan found that recipients who had subsidized childcare increased their months employed by 50 percent, and increased their earnings by 100 percent (Danziger, Ananat, and Browning 2004). The final bill included an additional $4.5 billion in childcare to states to be used over the next six years to offset the costs for families who leave welfare for work.

In late June 2006, the Bush administration reauthorized TANF, and issued sweeping changes that diminished some of the state authority for program rules by requiring states to move much larger numbers of people from welfare to work (Pear 2006). The definitions for permissible work activities have become more stringent, and states must now more thoroughly verify and document the number of hours worked by welfare recipients. Under the new rules, 50 percent of adult welfare recipients must be engaged in work or training by fiscal year 2006 (October 1), up from about 32 percent prior to the Bush administration's ruling, or states will face financial penalties. Work participantion rates now increase to 55 percent by 2007, and increase in 5 percent increments until they reach 70 percent by 2010. Moreover, although the basic federal block grant will remain at $16.6 billion despite inflation, the federal government will spend about $150 million on programs to help couples form "healthy marriages." Meanwhile spending to enforce child support payments will be reduced.

How TANF Works

Under the TANF rules, the federal government provides $16.6 million in block grants to states per year. The states can then use these funds to operate their own programs. States can use these dollars in specific ways that meet any or all of the four purposes set out in federal law, which are to (1) provide assistance to needy families so that children may be cared for in their own homes or in the homes of relatives; (2) end the dependence of needy parents on government benefits by promoting job preparation, work, and marriage; (3) prevent and reduce the incidence of out-of-wedlock pregnancies and establish annual numerical goals for preventing and reducing these pregnancies; and (4) encourage the formation and maintenance of two-parent families (Coven 2005). States have chosen to spend TANF funds in a variety of ways, including cash assistance and wage supplements, childcare subsidies, education and job training, transportation assistance, and other services. To receive TANF funds, states must also spend some of their own dollars on programs for needy families, known as the "maintenance of effort," or the MOE requirement. Figure 5.1 illustrates how TANF and MOE funds were spent in fiscal year 2004, at a total of $28.5 billion.

Although the TANF block grants were only authorized until the end of fiscal year 2002, Congress temporarily extended TANF funding several times while working on legislation to reauthorize the block grants and make some modifications to the rules and funding levels. President George W. Bush and his appointees are strong believers in the merits of PRWORA. U.S. Department of Health and Human Services secretary Mike Leavitt announced with pride that TANF rolls continued to decline in 2004: "Throughout the first four years of the Bush administration, we have seen caseloads decline continuously. Now it is important to work with Congress to reauthorize welfare reform so more families can be strengthened by work instead of weakened by welfare dependency" (U.S. Department of Health and Human Services 2005b:1). Likewise, Dr. Wade F. Horn, HHS assistant secretary for children and families, reports, "More Americans are leaving welfare and entering the economic mainstream. The Bush administration is dedicated to welfare reform because it replaces dependency with self-sufficiency" (U.S. Department of Health and Human Services 2005:1). In early 2006, the Bush Administration reauthorized TANF until 2010, with its stricter work requirements.

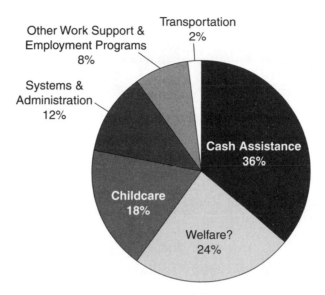

Figure 5.1 How TANF dollars are spent (reflects FY 2004 expenditures of TANF and MOE funds totalling $28.5 billion. *Source:* Coven 2005.)

Federal law now mandates that lifetime welfare payments can total no more than five years, and able-bodied recipients must work after two years, with few exceptions granted. In most cases, there is a two-year limit for TANF out of any 60 consecutive months. Other changes under this reform include some childcare assistance, one year of transitional Medicaid benefits, the required identification of a child's biological father so that child support can more easily be pursued, and the requirement that unmarried minors live at home and stay in school to receive benefits. Cash assistance is no longer an entitlement program available to parents who otherwise meet the financial criteria—today TANF programs provide cash assistance to less than half of the families who meet income eligibility requirements (Coven 2005).

Furthermore, more power was granted to individual states, and under these general federal parameters, states are able to amend the policies to best meet their individual needs. Some hail this as a boon to local control, others fear that poor states have little to offer their poorest residents and consequently either eliminate some families who were previously deemed eligible, or else siphon off money from other state-funded programs such as education or job training programs. The state-run programs operate under different names, as shown in Table 5.1, but are designed to meet any (or all) of the four purposes set out in federal law. Note that many of the names imply that cash assistance represents "dependency" while a job will promote "independence" and empowerment.

Table 5.1 Titles of State TANF Programs

Alabama	FA (Family Assistance Program)
Alaska	ATAP (Alaska Temporary Assistance Program)
Arizona	EMPOWER (Employing and Moving People Off Welfare and Encouraging Responsibility)
Arkansas	TEA (Transitional Employment Assistance)
California	CALWORKS (California Work Opportunity and Responsibility to Kids)
Colorado	Colorado Works
Connecticut	JOBS FIRST
Delaware	ABC (A Better Chance)
Florida	WTP (Welfare Transition Program)
Georgia	TANF
Guam	TANF
Hawaii	TANF
Idaho	Temporary Assistance for Families in Idaho
Illinois	TANF
Indiana	TANF—cash assistance; IMPACT (Indiana Manpower Placement and Comprehensive Training)—TANF work program
Iowa	FIP (Family Investment Program)
Kansas	Kansas Works
Kentucky	K-TAP (Kentucky Transitional Assistance Program)
Louisiana	FITAP (Family Independence Temporary Assistance Program)—cash assistance; FIND WORK (Family Independence Work Program)—TANF work program
Maine	TANF—cash assistance; ASPIRE (Additional Support for People in Retraining and Employment)—TANF work program
Maryland	FIP (Family Investment Program)
Massachusetts	TAFDC (Transitional Aid to Families with Dependent Children)—cash assistance; ESP (Employment Services Program)—TANF work program
Michigan	FIP (Family Independence Program)

Table 5.1 *Continued*

Minnesota	MFIP (Minnesota Family Investment Program)
Mississippi	TANF
Missouri	Beyond Welfare
Montana	FAIM (Families Achieving Independence in Montana)
Nebraska	Employment First
Nevada	TANF
New Hampshire	FAP (Family Assistance Program)—financial aid for work-exempt families; NHEP (New Hampshire Employment Program)—financial aid for work-mandated families
New Jersey	WFNJ (Work First New Jersey)
New Mexico	NM Works
New York	FA (Family Assistance Program)
North Carolina	Work First
North Dakota	TEEM (Training, Employment, Education Management)
Ohio	OWF (Ohio Works First)
Oklahoma	TANF
Oregon	JOBS (Job Opportunities and Basic Skills Program)
Pennsylvania	Pennsylvania TANF
Puerto Rico	TANF
Rhode Island	FIP (Family Independence Program)
South Carolina	Family Independence
South Dakota	TANF
Tennessee	Families First
Texas	Texas Works—cash assistance; Choices—TANF work program
Utah	FEP (Family Employment Program)
Vermont	ANFC (Aid to Needy Families with Children)—cash assistance; Reach Up—TANF work program
Virgin Islands	FIP (Family Improvement Program)
Virginia	VIEW (Virginia Initiative for Employment, Not Welfare)
Washington	WorkFirst

Table 5.1 *Continued*

Washington, D.C.	TANF
West Virginia	West Virginia Works
Wisconsin	W-2 (Wisconsin Works)
Wyoming	POWER (Personal Opportunities with Employment Responsibility)

Source: Coven 2005.

State Policies and State Variation

Since the passage of PRWORA, states have enacted **time limits,** which limit the number of months a family may receive TANF benefits (Rowe and Russell 2004). Many states have enacted welfare reform policies that are more stringent than those imposed by the federal government. There are two types of limits that states can impose on recipients. The first is a *lifetime* time limit, which states when benefits can be permanently eliminated. Although the federal government established a limit of five years, nine states have opted for shorter limits. For example, the limit in Arkansas is 24 months, the limit in Florida is 48 months, and the limit in Utah is 36 months. Some exemptions may be granted in cases of hardship (the definition of which varies by state), usually up to 20 percent of the caseload. For example, 17 states will provide an exemption to verifiable victims of domestic violence, and seven states will provide an exemption if caring for an infant under a few months of age (Rowe and Russell 2004).

Thirteen states impose an additional type of time limit that limits benefits *temporarily* for a specific period of time. For example, in Nevada, families who receive TANF for 24 months are then ineligible to receive benefits for the next 12 months, even though ultimately they could receive five years of lifetime benefits.

The federal government imposed **work requirements** that require recipients to work as soon as the state determines they are able, or after 24 months of benefit receipt, whichever is earlier. Most states require recipients to begin work or finish their high school education immediately, and to work a minimum of 30 hours per week. Post-secondary education while on TANF is generally not allowed in most states, despite the fact that a college degree would significantly improve job prospects, pay, and job benefits like health insurance coverage. Some exemptions are allowed, and these vary by state. For example, 37 states provide an exemption to care for an ill or incapacitated person, and 45 states allow exemptions to care for a young infant, usually defined as less than 12 months of age, but 11 states require work after the child is over three months of age. Six states offer no exemptions for young children at all (Rowe and Russell 2004). Noncompliance with the work requirements may reduce the adult portion of the benefits, or terminate benefits for the entire family for six months or longer.

The pressure exerted on TANF recipients to "just get a job" is keenly felt. TANF recipients feel that they must take any job that becomes available to them, regardless of pay or benefits. This mentality can deflect attention from gathering needed information for planning to find a "good job"—one with a livable wage and benefits such as health insurance. In the interviews conducted with families leaving TANF for work in Oregon, most respondents reported having experienced pressure from their caseworkers to take any job to get off TANF, even one without insurance. They received little information from caseworkers regarding the qualifications for Medicaid eligibility after the transitional year of coverage expired (Seccombe et al. 2005:100–01). Ellen and Rita discussed these pressures to get a job:

> They didn't care what it [the job] was and yeah, there was the constant pressure of that . . . It was pretty clear to me what I was looking for wasn't going to be handed to me through working at Burger King or any of those type jobs, and I didn't have the training or the skills to do anything but that. So really it was a big quandary there. (Ellen)

> They just pretty much wanted you to get a job and get off of TANF, was my experience. It would be mentioned, "Oh, look, this one has benefits." That's really great if it did have benefits. However, they wanted me to be a bell-ringer [laughs], which is a very temporary position that is not going to offer benefits. So benefits didn't seem to be a big concern. (Rita)

Likewise, when Dinesha left welfare for work, she was advised not to worry about securing health insurance, because of the one-year transitional coverage. In essence, she was advised to think "short term" about health insurance options. Dinesha said:

> [T]he line of work, the jobs I can do, I would still qualify for medical, and my caseworker helped me figure that out, that getting a job is more important than worrying about healthcare right now because you are still going to be covered under the state.

Another woman, Jocelyn, made a similar point, as she explained:

> Their big push was just finding a job, any job. Don't care if it pays minimum wage, don't care what it does, just get a job. I tried to talk to her because I had been with

the state before . . . saying I really would like to go where I can get the benefits and stuff I need for the family, and it was like, well you can try, but in the meantime, you're going to have to take anything you can get.

The emphasis on getting a job—without considering pay or health insurance benefits—presents a barrier to sound planning; TANF leavers who hope to find a job with insurance—or make other plans for insurance—could benefit from caseworker support on this matter. Chelsea's remarks indicate how frustrating this lack of support can be:

They don't really explain nothing to you. Not really. Like, if you get into it and ask, they will say something little to push you off but if you keep bugging them about it, they will sit there and make time to explain it for you, but other than that no. . . . They don't really tell you what you are going to have, what you're not going to have, what's gonna be covered, what's not going to be covered. I mean, you just find out on your own.

In addition to time limits and work requirements, 21 states imposed **family cap** policies that limit or deny additional benefits to families who have a child while on TANF, even though this policy was not part of the federal mandate. For example, in California, if a child is born within 10 months after a family begins TANF, there will be no increase in the cash benefit for that child (Rowe and Russell 2004).

Other TANF Policies and Regulations

Under the old AFDC program, all families that met federal income eligibility criteria were entitled to receive cash assistance. Under TANF, eligibility is primarily determined by state rules, and families are no longer automatically entitled to assistance even if they meet financial criteria. States now decide who can receive assistance, under what circumstances, and for how long. Yet, these decisions are complex because of federal mandates, fiscal constraints at the state level, conflicting goals of TANF, and the myriad of exemptions to work requirements or time limits that may be granted because of extenuating circumstances.

For example, the new law retains a federal requirement that those receiving assistance must assign their **child support rights** over to the state. As in the past, to receive assistance, recipients must cooperate with the state in establishing paternity (if this is in question), obtaining a support order, and enforcing that order. In the past, a mother was required to appear at all relevant court/administrative agency hearings, and turn over to the state any child support payments received directly from the father. However, with "good cause" (e.g., the child was conceived as the result of a forcible rape or incest; pursuing support could result in physical or emotional harm; adoption was under consideration or was pending) she could be exempt from these requirements. PRWORA established stricter child support enforcement policies (U.S. Department of Health and Human Services 2004). Respondents must assign rights to child support and cooperate with paternity establishment efforts. States have the option to either deny cash assistance or reduce assistance by at least 25 percent to those individuals who fail to cooperate. These policies have the potential to either help or to harm women and their children, depending on the situation surrounding paternity. Yet under the 2006 reauthorization bill, money for child support enforcement has been cut.

Policies toward **assets** also vary among states. Families are allowed to have a vehicle while receiving TANF funds, although most states allow only one per family (including two-parent families). Twenty-three states limit the value of the vehicle, often to under $5,000. For example, in New York, the fair market value of an allowable vehicle is capped at $4,650. Other allowable assets are even more meager. In 33 states, a family can have no more than $2,000 in assets, above and beyond their vehicle (Rowe and Russell 2004). These policies severely restrict the mobility and transportation needs of families.

What Do Welfare Recipients Think of Welfare Reform?

Many people are surprised to discover that welfare recipients do not like welfare. I asked women to describe, in one word, what life is like on welfare. "Hell," "difficult," "miserable," "challenging," "degrading—very degrading" were just a few of their responses. They described life on welfare as "a strain," "depressing," "rough," "a struggle," "aggravating," "a trap," and "scary." Comments such as these contradict ideas that women on welfare enjoy being "on the system," are purposefully lazy, and enjoy the "free ride" that they receive at taxpayers' expense. Instead, I found that welfare recipients do not like welfare and I had to push them to say anything positive about it (Seccombe 2007).

If welfare recipients do not like welfare, how do they feel about welfare reforms? I conducted interviews in Florida in 1996, on the eve of welfare reform, and found that women generally were eager for substantial reforms of the welfare system. When specifically asked about the policies of time limits, work requirements, and family caps, many women somewhat less enthusiastically endorsed these policy changes, noting that there could be exceptional circumstances that should override the policies. For example, although the majority of women— regardless of age, race, level of education, or number of children—embraced work requirements in particular, they also felt that children should be over the age of 3 or should be in school before their parents are required to work; that recipients should be allowed to finish school if they were already enrolled; that the job should pay above minimum wage; and that benefits should not be automatically and immediately eliminated, "or else it just wouldn't work." Jo Lynn expressed the sentiment held by many that she supports work requirements, but only if these other conditions are met. Otherwise, she suggests, working becomes prohibitive. She told me of her dilemma, of wanting to work, but wondering if work will enhance or detract from her meager standard of living. When asked if she supported work requirements, she replied,

> Yes, depending on the situation. Depending on your youngest child's age. Maybe on how long a person has been on welfare, and depending on how much money that person gets from a job, or what benefits are going to be cut. I think a lot of people would be willing to go to work, even want to work. It's a scary thing, where, like me, okay, I have $241 a month and I want to get a part-time job. And they say, "Okay, you can take the job, but we're going to start cutting everything off." You know, it takes a little while to establish yourself. I think if they would help establish people, like give them six months to keep their check and their work check, where they could put some money aside maybe or build up for their own apartment, or whatever they need to build up. With health insurance, if you get a job and make over a certain amount of money you lose your Medicaid completely and everything. And I think that's a really serious situation for a lot of people. (*Seccombe 2007:178*)

Women I interviewed worried about their children. First and foremost, these women wanted to ensure that work would be compatible with motherhood and would better their families' lives. If it did not, either financially or psychologically, then work was less enticing.

Alexandra is one of the many women who support welfare reform, along with a high degree of caution. She is divorced, has one child, and has been on welfare for several years, although she anticipates being off welfare shortly. She has an associate's degree from a community college and would like to transfer to a four-year university for a bachelor's degree in art. The walls in her home are decorated with her own artwork, revealing keen talent. Echoing the sentiments of many, Alexandra suggested it is unrealistic to simply expect women to go to work without some assistance from the government. She questioned the benefits of putting infants and toddlers in daycare for nine or ten hours a day. She also brought up the cost of childcare and questioned whether a job would even cover these costs. Although she supports work requirements in theory, she does not believe it is desirable to work full-time when her child is young, nor is it even possible to work unless her childcare needs are taken care of.

> Work or go to school is good. I wouldn't mind having a part-time job or something. But how much money can I make at a part-time job? And how much does a

sitter charge? A lot, you know? Is your entire paycheck even going to be able to pay for a week or a month's babysitter? So, I don't know. It's a good idea, but they would have to pay childcare. You see what I mean? Otherwise, it just wouldn't work. (*Seccombe 2007:179*)

When I discussed time limits and family caps with women, they voiced similar concerns. Most believed that allowances must be made for specific circumstances and needs, such as allowing additional time for women whose lives are especially difficult or disorganized; giving women additional time for schooling or training; or ensuring that women are guaranteed a job above minimum wage. Time limits make many women nervous: how can they ensure that their lives would smoothly progress through the stages necessary to be off welfare in two to three years, when their lives are so disorganized and a constant struggle today?

Doreen is a 31-year-old woman living in Florida who received $241 a month for herself and her 15-year-old daughter Latasha in 1996, an amount that would remain the same 10 years later in 2006 as this book goes to press. Latasha is seven months pregnant with her first child and requires complete bed rest after going into early labor. She is being home schooled so that she can continue high school. Doreen said that she would like to get a job, and she has earnestly looked for work in the past, but usually can only turn up part-time pay in the fast-food industry. So, instead, she babysits occasionally for extra money, but does not report this income to her case-worker. And now, without a car, with Latasha needing full-time care, and with a new grandbaby on the way to help care for, finding a job seems a near impossibility. She summarized the concerns of many regarding time limits when she said:

If they can get a job within that time, then yeah. But if they can't get a job within that time period, then allow another three or four years until they can. Because if you go out and put out applications, that doesn't mean that person is going to hire you. You know, you can get out there and do it, but there's no guarantee that the person is going to hire you. They might hire the next person, or the next person . . . You know, actually it would be really good if they guaranteed that you would get a job. It's my opinion that if they can go and guarantee you a job, then get off welfare. But if they can't guarantee that they're going to get you a job, then leave them alone because it's going to hurt the kids in the long run. (Seccombe 2007:176).

With respect to family caps, many women I interviewed opposed them in principle. They believed that family caps unfairly penalize innocent children "from something that they need." Yet there is significant disagreement as to whether women on welfare deliberately have children to increase the size of their benefit level. Some women argue that other recipients will be influenced to have more children if their welfare benefit is increased. However, even some women who believe that others do have additional children to augment their welfare check still opposed family caps, arguing that children should not be punished for the decisions of their parents. Jessie, a 42-year-old mother, spoke for most women when she said, "You shouldn't jeopardize a woman for having a baby or make children suffer because of their parents." (Seccombe 2007:180).

Reference was often made to the additional costs associated with having a child, and that the current benefit probably could not realistically be stretched to cover these costs. Again, the child would ultimately suffer as a result. Marissa spoke of inflation, and that a child's needs cannot be squeezed out of an already low welfare grant.

> There's inflation, you know, and prices go up. I think it should be increased. You know, the basics of buying clothes and stuff. That's another family member, and you can't live off the amount it is. Well, you can live, but as far as buying Pampers and stuff like that, you couldn't do it without an increase. (Seccombe 2007:180)

Despite opposing them in principle, many women conceded that caps might be necessary if women continue to have many children while on welfare. My respondents had varied opinions about the threshold at which caps should be implemented. Some claimed that if a woman had one or two more children while on welfare she should still receive additional benefits for that child or children, but caps should be imposed for subsequent births. Others were more tolerant and would allow three or more additional births. Not surprisingly, their tolerance closely mirrored their own experience with nonmarital births. For example, one woman, who had one child while receiving welfare, maintained that caps should be applied to the second pregnancy.

> I feel that if they do it this one time, okay. I don't see to give them more money if they have more than one child on welfare. Because one time, it could have been an accident, or whatever the case may be. But if they have more than one child when you're on welfare—if you see a pattern there—you shouldn't get any more. (*Seccombe 2007:181*)

How Is TANF Working? Research Findings

One year after signing reform legislation, President Clinton hailed welfare reform a resounding success by citing statistics indicating a 1.4 million drop in the number of welfare recipients. "I think it's fair to say that the debate is over. We know that welfare reform works," he said in a speech in St. Louis (Broder 1997). By

June 2005, there were 3 million fewer families on welfare, down to only 1,895,756 families (U.S. Department of Health and Human Services 2006). However, these statistics only indicate that the number of people on welfare fell. It tells us nothing about whether welfare reform "works," in the sense of whether poverty has declined. "You can't tell whether welfare reform is working simply from caseload numbers," said Wendell Primus, a welfare expert who quit the Clinton administration in protest over Clinton's signing of the welfare legislation. "Those figures do not tell how many former recipients moved from welfare to work, or simply from dependency to despondency. You have to look at where these people went," he suggested (Broder 1997).

What has happened to families on welfare? Initially, many feared that welfare reform would erode the social safety net for vulnerable individuals and families. They wondered what would happen to the many poor people who may not be able to find work for one reason or another when they reach the government's time limit. They questioned whether jobs were available for all the people now on assistance, without a massive job creation effort. They lamented that even the lucky people who did find employment would most likely be paid wages that fail to bring their incomes above the poverty line. They were concerned that the job training would be superficial and would not really be effective in increasing recipients' employment prospects. They wanted to know why welfare recipients were no longer allowed to go to college to further their education. They asked who would care for the children when childcare reimbursements are inadequate to pay for quality childcare. And, they wondered how the healthcare needs of the influx of low-income workers and their children would be met after their transitional Medicaid expired.

These are critical questions because, despite a multitude of welfare reforms over this century, they have never been adequately addressed. Two-parent welfare families were targeted as the first to be cut off of welfare assistance. By October 1, 1997, a little more than one year after welfare reform became law, 75 percent of two-parent welfare families were mandated by the federal government to either have jobs or be in job training programs. In the first real test of welfare reform, approximately half the states fell short of these employment goals—goals that, in retrospect, many people suggest were unrealistic (DeParle 1997). This first failure to meet employment goals is held up for its symbolism. Work requirements among two-parent families, at first glance at least, should be relatively easy to fulfill. The requirements stipulate a total of 35 hours per week between two adults, and while one is working, the other should seemingly be able to provide childcare. If the difficulties of employing two-parent households have been so seriously underestimated, then what does that suggest about the other, more challenging cases involving single parents? Despite the severity of federal guidelines, states are free to impose stricter time limits and work requirements, which many have elected to do.

Today, ten years after TANF was created, there is a burgeoning amount of research that shows us what has happened to families in the aftermath of welfare reform. I will attempt to summarize some of the key findings here.

Poverty Rates Among Families That Leave TANF Are Very High

Many studies report that between 50 and 75 percent of families remain poor even two to three years after leaving welfare (Blank 2002). Moreover, even those families with incomes above the poverty threshold have very low incomes. One state study found that about 90 percent of TANF leavers lived below 185 percent of poverty—many are therefore not counted in official statistics, but they continue to live on the margins of society (Acs and Loprest 2004). Although the chances of living in poverty declines over time, it is at a very modest rate. For example, a California study sponsored by the U.S. Department of Health and Human Services (HHS) that looked at leavers at two points in time—first 5–10 months after leaving welfare, and again 11–16 months after leaving welfare—found that income gains averaged only $60 to $70 per month (Macurdy, Marruto, and O'Brien-Strain 2003). Another HHS-sponsored study of welfare reform, this time in Wisconsin, reported that the net income of welfare leavers in the year after they left welfare was actually lower than their income prior to leaving welfare. Although their earned income was significantly higher, their benefits declined by more than their earned income (Cancian et al. 2003). A study of Michigan women who received TANF in 1997 when the program was newly formed, found that by the fall of 2001, only one-quarter were working in "good jobs," defined as full-time jobs paying at least $7 per hour and offering health insurance, or full-time jobs that do not offer health insurance but pay at least $8.50 an hour (Pavetti and Acs 2001).

Families That Left Welfare Recently Are More At Risk Than Early TANF-Leavers

Recent TANF-leavers are less likely to be employed, and are less likely to have another stable source of support. For example, a report by the Urban Institute shows that the proportion of families that leave welfare and are not employed rose from 50 percent in 2000 to 58 percent in 2002. This study found a marked increase in the number of families that are "disconnected"—they are not working, do not have a working spouse, and are not receiving TANF or SSI—rising from 9.8

percent in 1999 to 13.8 percent in 2002 (Loprest 2003). These families face significant health, education, language, or other barriers to employment and suffer from hunger. They report that they are "barely making it from day to day" (Wood and Rangarajan 2003; Zedlewski 2003).

Susan and her teenage son illustrate how families may be disconnected (Seccombe et al. 2005:62–63). They had recently moved to Oregon from Montana after her son was diagnosed with cancer, and participated in my study of 552 Oregonians who left TANF for work. Because of her son's illness, Susan lost her full-time job that provided health benefits for both of them. At the time she was first interviewed, Susan had Medicaid insurance, known as the Oregon Health Plan (OHP). She also was being treated for fibromyalgia, acid reflux, and Type II diabetes. During the first interview, she noted that her own health had suffered as a result of the stress of having a child with a life-threatening disease. However, it was difficult to get her to talk about her own health given the magnitude of her son's illness and her involvement in his daily care. Mental and emotional stresses are especially troublesome for Type II diabetics, because they have a negative impact on blood glucose levels. Thus, medical management becomes even more imperative for these individuals.

In addition, Susan's marriage ended in divorce during her child's illness, and she moved to a new state where the only person she knew was her grown daughter. She relied on this daughter for financial support because she had none and had exhausted her TANF benefits. She tried to find work that would help support herself and her child while leaving her flexible enough to make frequent visits to the hospital for cancer treatments. She also needed to make sure she did not go over the allowable earnings limit that might disqualify her from OHP/Medicaid eligibility. During her initial interview, Susan was well aware of the cutoff date for her one year of transitional OHP/Medicaid benefits. She stated that if she were to lose her benefits, she would be unable to afford her doctor visits or medications due to the prohibitive cost of each. Susan's discussion of her medications and their cost is representative of the vast majority of respondents in the study.

> They give you one year of medical. So I have until January. I have to take Prevacid, which is $139 approximately. I take Avandia, which is for my diabetes, and it's a hundred-and-something dollars. I take Zocor to help bring down my cholesterol because of my history. My mother died of heart condition related to diabetes. The Zocor is to help keep me healthy. And that is a hundred-and-something dollars. And believe me, if I have no insurance, Zocor is going to go. I'm going to suffer because Prevacid I can't afford it, and I will do Avandia because of the diabetes. Trazodone. That's for the fibromyalgia. So we're talking $300–$400 [of] medicine a month.

Susan understood the system well and had maximized her benefits for as long as possible to attend to the needs of her ill child. When asked at the first interview about her future plans for meeting her healthcare needs if she should lose her OHP/Medicaid, she replied: "There's just no system to help you with that. You fall through the cracks. You either are on the system or you have nothing."

Susan finally found a job—one without insurance coverage—and did lose her OHP/Medicaid benefits after her transitional year ended. At the time of her second interview one year later, she had not been seen by a doctor or taken any of her medications in eight months. Prior to losing her OHP/Medicaid benefits, an endocrinologist followed Susan closely, but that has now changed. She explained:

> I was seeing the doctor on average every other month, at least two to three months for sure, that I was on [OHP]. That's what the doctor felt I needed to be monitored.... Anyway, I have not taken any medication for diabetes since January. I don't know how it is. I have no idea how I'm doing, but I try to be careful and I know the signs of when I don't feel good because of it. I'm in a danger zone ... I have always controlled it. I was taking medicine for all of this time; I was taking Avandia when I had insurance.

People like Susan with uncontrolled Type II diabetes are at higher risk for developing the same complications of Type I diabetes including neuropathy, retinopathy, heart failure and stroke, and renal disease. It was clear from Susan's interview that she was aware of these threats to her health, but that she had no other options due to her uninsured status. In addition to forgoing medication and regular monitoring by her physician, Susan is unable to afford the diabetic supplies she needs to measure her blood sugar.

> I can't tell you right now where my diabetes is and that bothers me, because it's much better when it's being watched. Before, every three months I would have lab work and stuff done to see where I was at, and as long as I knew I was okay, I was okay. Now, I have this lingering concern, now I don't know. I could be higher than I think I am. I can't buy testers and stuff, I can't afford that.

Families Leaving Welfare Are More Likely to Have Significant Health Problems

TANF-leavers and their children have high rates of illness that interferes with their ability to obtain and maintain steady employment. In my statewide study in Oregon, I found that 24 percent of adults who had recently left TANF for work rated their health as only fair or poor, compared to 9 percent of adults nationally (and 22 percent of poor adults) (Schiller, Adams, and Coriaty Nelson 2005). Likewise, I found that 15 percent of parents who had recently left TANF reported having at least one child in fair or poor health. Nationally, 2 percent of children overall and 5 percent of poor children are in fair or poor health (Dey and Bloom 2005; Seccombe et al. 2005).

There is a strong relationship between health (of adult or child) and employment (Zedlewski 2003; Powers 2003). A Michigan study found that physical and mental health problems, as well as child health problems, are each related to lower employment durations over a five-year period, even after controlling for important factors that affect employability, such as job skills, prior work experience, or availability of transportation (Corcoran, Danziger, and Tolman 2003).

Guiliana is a 28-year-old Hispanic woman living with her husband and two children in rural eastern Oregon. Both of her children have frequent bouts of illness. Her story illustrates how children's health problems are exacerbated by poverty, and how a child's illness affects a parent's ability to rise out of poverty through employment (Seccombe et al. 2005:53–54).

> . . . At that time it was snowing, and freezing, and I had just started to work, barely . . . So . . . I worked in the afternoon, Ernesto stayed with the boy, I took the girl to someone else to watch because she was smaller and it was difficult for him. So I took her out in the afternoon when it was raining, and then I went to pick her up at night. My car didn't have heat, she got the flu and then bronchitis and she got like asthma. But also the problem was that she didn't get better, or it didn't get under control very quickly because in my apartment, it was humid . . . there was a leak in the room where we slept, and the bedroom is close to the bathroom, so there was also a leak in the bathroom from the apartment upstairs. And the person who lived upstairs went to the bathroom to get high . . . and all of the smoke came down through this hole. Well, the manager made a hole to check the water, to see where the leak was, and all the smoke came down. So all this smoke got stuck in my room, so my son also, that's why he had problems with asthma, because every night they inhaled this smoke, and the humidity of the room which had a lot of leaks, so, that is why it lasted so long, like a month and a half.

Guiliana's children were experiencing so much respiratory difficulty that their pediatrician offered to write a letter to the apartment manager. The physician believed that it was medically necessary to make the household repairs. "The doctor even told me that she would write a letter to the manager to tell him it was because of the way we lived the kids didn't get well quickly." But Guiliana was fearful of angering her apartment manager, because her earlier reporting of the leaks had upset him. She ended up quitting her job to stay home with her sick children.

> And so I told the doctor that it was okay, that we were probably going to move, that that would be better, and then time passed and then . . . the weather started changing, and then I quit. I stopped going to work. I stayed home to take care of the kids. I was just taking them in for a check-up every two weeks, or later every month when they started to get better. And that's all, and now they are, since summer started, they are doing well.

A Large Share of Very Poor and Needy Families Do Not Receive TANF

Not only do poor families not receive TANF, but their numbers are increasing. Data indicate that about 45–50 percent of families who would be eligible for TANF do not receive assistance, up from only about 20 percent in 1996 (Fremstad 2003; Fremstad 2004). Many families are diverted from TANF when they go to apply for aid, and the few studies on those persons diverted show some interesting trends. London found that TANF applicants who were diverted from the program were more likely to have significantly lower or higher educational levels than TANF recipients (London 2003). Although it may be argued that applicants with more education may have greater alternatives to them, it is perplexing why those with very low education levels also are diverted, because they may be most vulnerable and in need of aid. Likewise, other studies have found that persons diverted from TANF were more likely to be Black, were more likely to speak Spanish as their primary language, and were more likely to be disabled or have other health problems (Fremstad 2004).

Childcare Assistance Is Crucial to Helping Families Move from Welfare to Work

Concern over the lack of safe and affordable childcare is a common reason why women turned to, or remain on, welfare. Childcare is often patched together in a fashion that leaves mothers anxious (Seccombe 2007). Although extended families are the preferred childcare provider, relatives cannot always be counted on. Living in high-density and high crime areas, poor families worry about the safety of their children in daycare centers or with other babysitters that they did not know well. As one woman I interviewed told me, "I'm not going to leave him with someone I don't know until he's old enough to tell me what happened." They also worry about the psychological effects of inadequate care—crowded, dirty, or impersonal conditions—upon their children. These concerns have largely been overlooked in quantitative studies that simply focus on the availability of daycare—are there enough daycare slots for the children who need them? My in-depth interviews revealed that the availability of childcare slots is not the primary consideration; rather, it is the quality of care that is most imperative. Mothers also worry about the cost of childcare. Costs vary dramatically across the country, but they are beyond the reach of most poor and low-income families.

Providing subsidized, high-quality childcare increases the likelihood that current and former welfare recipients will leave welfare and work full-time (Danziger, Ananat, and Browning 2004; Fuller et al. 2002; Scott, London, and Hurst 2005). Childcare subsidies are associated with higher rates of employment, an increase in full-time employment, and a decreased likelihood of returning to welfare. However, subsidies are generally low, often less than $2.00 an hour, and therefore they limit what type of childcare a family can realistically use. Yet, research indicates that higher subsidies are further associated with increased employment (Fremstad 2004).

Consequently, funds to increase the number (and in some states the amount) of childcare subsidies were an important component of TANF, and the initial funding seemed promising. However, since 2002, funding has been stagnant, while the need is increasing. Consequently, there is tremendous unmet need. Only one in seven children eligible for childcare assistance actually receives it (Children's Defense Fund 2005a). Moreover, with caseloads inching up again, and with the inflationary erosion of TANF block grants to states, at least 23 states have reduced childcare funding for low-income families since 2003. For example, Nebraska cut 1,600 children off subsidies when it reduced the income cutoff from 185 percent to 120 percent of poverty (Friedlin 2004). At least one-third of states place eligible families who apply for assistance on waiting lists or turn them away without even taking their names because there are not enough funds to provide services (Schulman and Blank 2004).

This chapter has revealed that many of our recent concerns about poverty and cash assistance programs are rooted in longstanding tensions about the worthy and unworthy poor, women's roles in society, and the goal of public aid. These tensions are not new. A review of recent welfare reform legislation shows that we still see poverty as largely a personal problem rather than a structural one. Reforms in the 1990s were predicated on this belief. So where are we today? Far fewer families receive cash assistance and more single mothers are working. In fact, welfare caseloads have declined by 60 percent since welfare was changed. I leave you with the original question: Is this good news?

Critical Thinking Questions:

1. Would early welfare programs have been stigmatized to the same degree if assistance to widows were included, rather than separated in another program? Do you think the separation was deliberate? Why or why not?
2. Which aspects of TANF policies do you support, and which aspects do you oppose? Defend your answers.
3. Do you think that welfare recipients would say that TANF policies are working? Why or why not?

6

BUILDING RESILIENCY:
PROGRAMS AND POLICIES
FOR FAMILIES

MANY PROGRAMS AND POLICIES have been created, particularly over the past 40 years, to ameliorate the effects of poverty. This chapter will discuss several of the more prominent programs, including food stamps; health insurance programs such as Medicaid, Medicare, and the State Children's Health Insurance Program (SCHIP); and economic programs such as the Earned Income Tax Credit (EITC) and Social Security. However, before we turn to specific policies and programs, let us begin this chapter with a general question: What do poor families need to become stronger and flourish?

Family Resiliency

We know that many people, both adults and children, do not have picture-perfect family lives. Many people grow up in impoverished environments or face significant other problems. Yet, despite the toll that these events can take, some adults and children overcome this adversity and lead successful, well-adjusted, and competent lives. They have overcome most or all of life's many obstacles. These individuals are **resilient**. Resilience is a multi-faceted phenomenon that produces the ability to thrive despite adversity. The term is derived from Latin roots, meaning to jump (or bounce) back (Silliman 1994; Walsh 1998). It can be defined as the capacity to rebound from adversity, misfortune, trauma, or other transitional crises strengthened and more resourceful (McCubbin et al. 1997; Walsh 1998; Walsh 2002).

Although most social scientists seem to focus on problems rather than resiliency *per se*, the *Kauai Longitudinal Study* is a notable exception (Werner 1994; Werner 1995; Werner and Smith 1989; Werner and Smith 1992). This study, based on 698 children born in 1955 on the Hawaiian island of Kauai, examines the long-term effects of growing up in high-risk environments. This unusual study followed the children for nearly 40 years. Most of the children were born to unskilled sugar plantation workers of Japanese, Filipino, Hawaiian, Portuguese, Polynesian, and mixed racial descent. Fifty-four percent of the children lived in poverty. Approximately one-third were considered "high risk" because of exposure to a combination of at least four individual, parental, or household risk factors, such as having a serious health problem, poverty, familial alcoholism, violence, divorce, or mental illness in the family. The children were assessed from the perinatal period to ages 1, 2, 10, 18, and 32 years.

The research team found that two-thirds of high-risk 2-year-olds who experienced four or more risk factors by age 2 developed learning or behavior problems by age 18. However, this finding also meant that one-third did not. These children developed into stable, competent, confident, and productive adults, as rated on a variety of measures. In a later follow-up, at age 40, all but two of these individuals were still successful. In fact, many of them had outperformed the children from low-risk families.

Perhaps a key finding was that resiliency can be developed at any point in the life course. Among the two-thirds of high-risk children who had learning or behavioral problems at age 18, one-half of them did not exhibit these problems at age 30. Instead, they had satisfying jobs, stable marriages, and in other measures were deemed successful by the research team. The researchers noted that teenage delinquency is not automatically a precursor to a life of crime. Meanwhile, a few individuals identified as resilient at age 18 had developed significant problems by age 30.

The evidence shows us that many adults and children reared in poverty (and other disadvantaged statuses) do overcome their adversities. How can we explain this finding?

Individual, Family, and Community Factors

Most research on resilience has focused on three types of factors that improve resiliency in the face of adverse conditions: (1) individual traits and disposition, (2) family protective and recovery factors, and (3) community strengths. **Individual-level protective factors** include such traits as a positive self-concept, sociability, intelligence and scholastic competence, autonomy, self-esteem, androgyny, good communication and problem-solving skills, humor, and good mental and physical health (Garmezy 1991; Werner 1994; Rouse 1998; Walsh 1998). Wolin and Wolin (1993), in their review of research and clinic experience, identified seven traits of adults who survived a troubled childhood: insight (awareness of dysfunction); independence (distancing self from troubles), supportive relationships; initiative; creativity; humor (reframing the situation in a less threatening way); and morality (justice and compassion rather than revenge). For example, the resilient high-risk adolescents in the longitudinal Kauai study had developed a sense that obstacles were not insurmountable, and they believed that they had control over their fate. They had a high degree of self-esteem and self-efficacy, and many developed a special skill or hobby that was a source of pride.

Family protective and recovery factors are central features of the resiliency literature. **Family protective factors (FPF)** are those characteristics or dynamics that shape the family's ability to endure in the face of risk factors. **Family recovery factors (FRF)** assist families in "bouncing back" from a crisis situation (McCubbin et al. 1997). Key characteristics of resilient families include warmth, affection, cohesion, commitment, and emotional support for one another. However, if parents are not able to provide this environment, other kin (e.g., siblings, grandparents) may step in to provide it. Resilient families generally have reasonable and clear-cut expectations for their children. They participate in family celebrations, share spiritual connections, and have specific traditions and predictable routines. Moreover, resilient families generally share core values around financial management and the use of leisure time, even when money and time are in short supply (Stinnett and DeFrain 1985; McCubbin and McCubbin 1988; Abbott and Meredith 1998; Silliman 1998; Walsh 1998).

There are also factors in the **community** (e.g., geographic space, social networks, religious and faith-based fellowships) that affect resilience (Silliman 1998; Miller 2000). Community institutions are important aspects of developing resilient youth and fostering resiliency among adults. Blyth and Roelkepartian (1993) indicate several key community strengths. First, a strong community provides opportunities for participation in community life. Among youth, extracurricular activities in school, religious youth groups, Scouting, or other activities help to bond youth to their schools, churches, or communities. In these settings, they can learn important skills such as teamwork, group pride, or leadership. Adults also have a frequent need for opportunities to hone these skills. Second, Blyth and Roelkepartian suggest that a strong community should provide avenues to enable its members to contribute to the welfare of others. This involvement can foster a sense of inner strength and self-esteem. Third, a strong community provides opportunities to connect with peers and other adults. Resiliency is more likely when there is access to a role model, a friend, or a confidant. For youth, teachers may play a critical role in providing this type of social support. Finally, Blyth and Roelkepartian propose that healthy communities have adequate access to community facilities and events for youth. There should be a funding priority for education and youth activities, with a functioning committee focusing on youth issues.

What Is Missing? Structural Conditions

There is a growing appreciation for a broader, systemic view of resiliency—the recognition that strengthening families requires the interaction of individual, familial, and community contingencies (Walsh 1998; Walsh 2002). Although this broader view pays homage to ecological and developmental nuances, it still places the focus on individual versus *structural-level* conditions. It virtually ignores the position that national and statewide policies and programs must play in strengthening families. Can we really expect families to be resilient without this assistance? For example, how do we best help a child who is chronically hungry? In addition to strong individual attributes, an involved family, and a supportive community, developing sound economic and social policies and programs designed to strengthen *all* families (healthy as well as vulnerable) can go a long way toward giving families and youth the necessary tools to master resiliency (Seccombe 2002).

What are some of the programs and policies in the United States that have been effective in fighting poverty and helping increase family resilience? While no means an exhaustive list, the rest of the chapter describes several critical programs and social policies that have made a clear difference in the lives of millions of poor or low-income families.

Food Stamp Program

The **Food Stamp program (FSP)** is the primary mechanism in U.S. policy to reduce hunger and poverty. It was created in the 1960s and was extended nationwide in 1974 to increase the food purchasing power of low-income households so that they are better able to afford a nutritionally adequate low-cost diet (Castner and Schirm 2005; USDA 2005 December). It has been amended considerably since then, to both extend the program to the neediest and to cut back program growth. Today, the FSP is the largest of the 15 domestic food and nutrition assistance programs administered by the U.S. Department of Agriculture's (USDA) Food and Nutrition Service and cost more than $31 billion in 2005 (USDA 2006). Food stamps are no longer "stamps" as originally designed; they are electronic benefits similar to a debit card that can be used like cash to buy food at any of the 150,000 eligible stores across the United States.

Food stamp allotments are based on the Thrifty food plan developed by the USDA, the least expensive of the four food plans they created. It is a lean budget, and it provides little more than half the amount of money the USDA affords its Liberal food plan that is more in line with spending habits of middle-class America. A mythical family of four containing 2 adults between the ages of 20 and 50, one child between the ages of 6 and 8, and another child aged 9 to 11, would have only $516 per month in 2006 to spend in the Thrifty plan versus $997 per month in the Liberal food plan. More specifically, the Thrifty food plan allows this family of four only $119 per week, or $17 per day for food (USDA June 2006).

Trends in food stamp use closely follow trends in poverty, as shown in Figure 6.1 (USDA 2005). During the middle and late 1980s, there were 18 to 20 million FSP participants. Participation increased by 37 percent between 1990 and 1994 to a peak of 28 million as the number of people in poverty rose dramatically during this period. FSP participation then declined to a low of 17 million during the economic boom of the late 1990s. However, the number of participants increased by nearly 40 percent between 2000 and 2005, as poverty rates and unemployment rose.

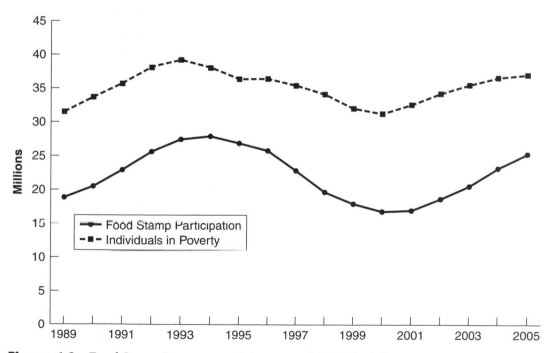

Figure 6.1 Food Stamp Program participants, and individuals in poverty
Source: FY 1989 to 2005 Food Stamp Program Quality Control samples (Food Research and Action Center (FRAC) 2006; DeNavas-Walt, Proctor, and Lee 2006).

By 2005, nearly 26 million people living in 10.5 million households received food stamps each month, with an average benefit of $93 per person or $213 per household (USDA 2006). However, one little known fact is that only about 56 percent of eligible people actually receive food stamp benefits. The USDA's budget request for fiscal year 2006 includes a performance target to reach at least 68 percent of the eligible population by 2010 (Castner and Schirm 2005). Participation rates vary widely from state to state, according to federal data, ranging from around 84 percent of people eligible in Oregon, to only about 43 percent of those eligible in Massachusetts. Why would an eligible person fail to receive food stamps? Reasons vary: they may not know about the program; they may have logistical barriers such as language differences, transportation, or childcare that prevent them from applying for benefits; they may be a dependent child and unable to apply for benefits for themselves; or they may proudly not want to receive government aid.

Eligibility

How would a person qualify for food stamps? Certain households are categorically eligible and therefore not subject to income or asset limits, such as a household that receives Temporary Assistance to Needy Families (TANF). However, the majority of households that apply for food stamps must meet two income eligibility standards: a gross income standard and a net income standard. They also must have assets that are below a certain threshold.

With respect to income, to be eligible for the FSP, a household must have a gross monthly income at or below 130 percent of poverty *guidelines*, which is $2,167 for a family of four in the contiguous United States in fiscal year 2006 and net monthly income at or below 100 percent of the poverty *guidelines*, which is $1,667 for a family of four. Remember that the "guidelines" are used for administrative and program purposes, and are somewhat higher than the poverty "thresholds" or "lines" that are used to count the number of persons in poverty. Net income is determined by subtracting permitted deductions, such as a standard deduction, earned income deduction, dependent care deduction, medical deduction, child support payment deduction, and excess shelter expense deduction (USDA 2005).

With respect to assets, households are permitted up to $2,000 in countable assets, or $3,000 in countable assets if at least one member is at least 60 years of age or disabled. Countable assets include cash and other assets that can easily be converted into cash, such as checking or saving accounts, stocks, or bonds. Vehicles beyond a single one per household, or vehicles exceeding $4,650 were formerly included under countable assets. However, by January 2004, 25 states had adopted policies that excluded the value of all vehicles from the asset test, and most other states increased the allowable value of one or more vehicles (USDA 2005).

In addition to these financial criteria, there are some nonfinancial eligibility requirements that place restrictions on the participation of students, strikers, people who are living in institutions, unauthorized immigrants, and nonimmigrant visitors. Moreover, adults aged 18–49 who are not disabled and who live in households without children, can only receive three months of food stamp benefits in any 36-month period (USDA 2005).

Characteristics of Food Stamp Households

Who then receives food stamps? The FSP serves a broad spectrum of people.

- **Most food stamp recipients are poor.** Eighty-eight percent of food stamp households have gross incomes less than or equal to 100 percent of the federal poverty guideline, 62 percent of all food stamp households have gross incomes less than or equal to only 75 percent of poverty, and 40 percent of all food stamp households are extremely poor and have gross incomes only 50 percent or less than the federal guidelines. Moreover, this poorest group received 57 percent of all benefits; thus, the FSP effectively targets benefits to the neediest households. Overall, the typical food stamp household had gross income of $643 per month (USDA 2005). The average food stamp household possessed only about $143 in countable resources, including the nonexcluded portion of vehicles and the entire value of checking and savings accounts.

- **Most food stamp households contain children, elderly, or the disabled.** In fiscal year 2004, 84 percent of all food stamp households contained a child (54 percent), an elderly person (17 percent), or a disabled nonelderly person (23 percent). Collectively, these households received 89 percent of food stamp benefits. Compared with other Food Stamp households, those that contained children received a higher than average benefit of $280 per month, reflecting their larger than average household size of 3.3 people (USDA 2005).

- **Many food stamp households have a working adult, and most do not receive cash welfare benefits.** Nearly 30 percent of food stamp households have earnings, up from 19 percent in 1990. For these households, earnings are the primary source of income. Working women represent 28 percent of the food stamp households, and working-age men represent 13 percent. The vast majority of households without a wage earner are those containing elderly or disabled persons. Only 16 percent of food stamp households receive TANF cash welfare benefits, a decrease from 42 percent in 1990, when the cash program was called Aid to Families with Dependent Children (AFDC).

Instead of cash welfare, 27 percent of food stamp households receive Supplemental Security Income (SSI), and 23 percent receive Social Security benefits (USDA 2005).

Inadequacy of Food Stamps

The Thrifty food plan is the basis for food stamps, and this plan can be criticized on several grounds. First, it was designed to be a temporary budget, "for temporary or emergency use when funds are low" (Peterkin 1964), not a threshold at which families are to survive indefinitely. The USDA has stressed, "The cost of this plan is not a reasonable measure of basic money needs for a good diet," and they suggested it be increased by approximately 25 percent (Peterkin and Kerr 1982).

Second, the Thrifty food plan is based on the poor's spending patterns 40 years ago adjusted for inflation (Ruggles 1990), but it does not provide for changing spending habits. For example, it still assumes that families will bake daily and cook foods from scratch, and that they will not buy prepared convenience foods. The plan fails to take into account important changes in cooking styles, family tastes, and women's lifestyles since its creation four decades ago.

Despite its claim of enabling poor households to buy nutritionally adequate diets, many recipients argue that this plan does not allow sufficient funds to buy nutritious foods. Therefore, it comes as no surprise that the lowest-income households consume about 25 percent less fresh fruit than the national average, while the highest income level consumes about 40 percent more than the national average (Lutz, Blaylock, and Smallwood 1993).

Because the Thrifty food plan, which is the basis for food stamps, is generally inadequate to meet the food needs of most households, many people must dip into their small cash reserves to make ends meet after their food stamps are exhausted. How do people try to make their food stamp allotment last to keep from having to use too much of their own money? I interviewed Alexandra, a 29-year-old divorced woman who received $212 for herself and one child, and she revealed a common strategy (Seccombe 2007:121):

Alexandra: They never last. I get $212. But when you go to the store, you spend at least $50 easily on food, a week. So usually, the last week of every month I have no more food stamps. It gets pretty bad.

Interviewer: So, then what do you do?

Alexandra: Rent money. I spend money from the rent that's coming up. I'll buy something like peanut butter and jelly. She'll eat peanut butter and jelly for a week. Breakfast, lunch, and dinner. But it's food. It works. If she complains, I say, "Hey you can have grape or strawberry jelly. It's a choice today."

Interviewer: Would some people say that you should just figure out how to budget better?

Alexandra: I basically buy things that last a long time. Lots of spaghetti. You can make massive amounts for 63 cents. Lots of spaghetti, peanut butter and jelly. I like those frozen pot pies. At least there's a whole day's nutrition in just that. Five for a dollar.

Another woman, Stephanie, revealed that eating healthy foods can be more costly than filling up on junk food. When I asked her if she received enough food stamps every month, she answered emphatically:

No! I eat out very rarely, so I find that food stamps rarely last the month for me. I eat very little meat. But I try to eat a lot of fresh fruits and vegetables. I try to be very healthful in my diet. I eat a low fat diet. And unfortunately, those foods are expensive. When it comes to the end of the month, I sometimes have to pay $20 or $30 until the next time I can get food stamps. Some months are four weeks, and some are five. Like, right now, it's tight. I only have one gallon of milk in the fridge, a half a loaf of bread, and some orange juice. I have to be real creative about what I make to eat. There haven't been any fruits or veggies this past week. (*Seccombe 2007:120*)

My interviews with poor women revealed important strategies for making food stamps last the entire month. One common method was to go grocery shopping only once a month. Food stamp recipients purchased foods designed to last the entire month—particularly pastas and canned goods. They bragged to me that they "shopped the sale" and shied away from name-brand goods. As the weeks progressed, if they were running low on food, they cooked creatively and sparsely, they spent portions of their cash grant, they visited food banks or charities, or they ate meals with friends or relatives.

Some women, particularly those without reliable transportation, shopped for many of their food items in convenience stores near their homes. These small neighborhood stores generally carry significantly higher prices for food than do the large chain grocery stores, but they are used nonetheless because they are conveniently located. It is ironic that those who have the least money often pay the most for their food because of where they shop (Rank 1994).

Some food stamp households experience food insecurity—defined by the USDA as uncertainty of having, or inability to acquire, enough food for all household members because of insufficient money or other resources. Others experience food insecurity with hunger—defined as households that were food insecure to the extent that one or more household members were hungry. The number of households experiencing food insecurities are on the rise (Nord et al. 2005). In my study of Oregon families who had recently left welfare for work, I found that 30 percent of respondents were food insecure, and another 22 percent could be classified as food insecure with hunger (Seccombe et al. 2005). Nearly 30 percent reported that they sometimes, often, or always worry about where their next meal is coming from. Thirty-eight percent reported cutting the size of their own meals almost every month and 37 percent reported that they have cut their meal size or skipped meals for their children because of lack of money (or food stamps) (Seccombe et al. 2005).

Worry over inadequate food supplies can lead to depression and anxiety (Hamelin, Habicht, and Beaudry 1999; Siefert et al. 2004). For example, in a qualitative study of 98 low-income households, researchers found that respondents suffered many detrimental effects from food insecurity, including a preoccupation with access to enough food, lack of control over their situation and the need to hide it, and disrupted eating patterns. Researchers also found that respondents felt an acute sense of alienation, frustration, powerlessness, guilt, shame, and inequality.

This preoccupation with food also can lead to obesity. It is ironic that food insecure individuals have some of the highest rates of obesity (Townsend et al. 2001; Vozoris and Tarasuk 2003). For example, using data from the national 1994–1996 Continuing Survey of Food Intakes by Individuals (CSFII), Townsend, Peerson, Love, Achterberg, and Murphy found that the prevalence of overweight women increased as food insecurity increased (with the exception of 11 severely food insecure women) (Townsend et al. 2001). Forty-one percent of mildly food insecure women and 52 percent of moderately food insecure women were overweight, compared to 34 percent of women considered food secure. The researchers were unable to provide any causal explanations, but suggested that it may be due to the "food stamp cycle" in which relatively abundant food supplies are available for the first three weeks of the month, followed by one week without food stamps when food supply is severely limited. When food stamps are restored the next month, overeating may occur.

Health Insurance

The lack of health insurance is a serious and disturbing social problem in the United States because health insurance is one of the primary mechanisms of accessing healthcare services. The ability to obtain healthcare is fundamental to the security, stability, and well-being of families. Uninsured families, or even one uninsured member of a family, risk not only their health but also the families' entire economic viability. Not surprisingly, the Institute of Medicine refers to health insurance as a "family matter" (Committee on the Consequences of Uninsurance 2002:1392). Paying for health insurance can cause families to spiral down into poverty, and it now is a leading cause of worker strikes. Families know that without health insurance, they may not be able to get the healthcare that they need.

Forty-seven million Americans, or 16 percent of the population, had no health insurance in 2005 (DeNavas-Walt, Proctor, and Lee 2006). This represents a significant increase from 39 million in 2000 (U.S. Census Bureau Public Information Office 2001a). Millions more are "underinsured"—their high deductibles or copayments render their insurance virtually useless except in the most catastrophic conditions.

Having health insurance can make a tremendous difference in the amount and type of healthcare that families receive. Without insurance, both adults and children use the healthcare system less often, are less likely to have a regular source of healthcare, rely on emergency rooms for their treatment, and often experience unnecessary pain, suffering, and even death. The uninsured are twice as likely to postpone seeking medical care, four times as likely to forgo needed medical care, and more than twice as likely to have a needed prescription go unfilled (Kaiser Commission on Medicaid and the Uninsured 2003). Uninsured adults and children are more likely to suffer a wide variety of chronic and acute ailments compared to those with insurance, and they have higher death rates (Baker et al. 2002; Feinberg et al. 2002; Hadley 2003).

In the United States, about 60 percent of Americans receive their health insurance from an employer, either as a worker or as a dependent of a worker. We assume that the ideal way to get health insurance is from an employer—this is "playing by the rules" (Seccombe and Amey 1995:168). Health insurance is considered a fringe benefit of employment and a supplement to a worker's wages. However, employers are not required to offer health insurance to their workers, and an increasing number are choosing not to do so (DeNavas-Walt, Proctor, and Lee 2006). This mechanism of employer-sponsored insurance is virtually unheard of in other industrialized nations, as well as in many nonindustrialized ones. Instead, they have national health insurance. This means that access to healthcare is considered a public right of all citizens. It is viewed as a public good, like education, police protection, and parks, and, therefore, is funded out of taxes and general revenues. Consequently, healthcare coverage is universal in these countries.

Poor and low-income families, especially those families that have an employed member, are particularly hard-hit with respect to being uninsured. Only 41 percent of workers earning less than $10 an hour have access to employer-sponsored insurance (Collins et al. 2004). Moreover, the working poor generally do not qualify for public health insurance programs even when their employers fail to insure them. Although Medicaid and SCHIP were designed to fill in the gaps, the safety net appears to be woefully inadequate, as millions remain uninsured. Therefore, the working poor are twice as likely to be uninsured as are poor persons without jobs (Berk and Wilensky 1987).

Yet, poor and low-income persons have poorer health than others; and therefore, health insurance is of critical concern (Wood et al. 2002; Corcoran, Danziger, and Tolman 2003; Levin-Epstein 2003; Centers for Disease Control 2004). For example, nearly one-third of women in the four counties that were part of the Manpower Demonstration Research Corporation's Urban Change Project had low physical well-being scores, compared to one-tenth of adults nationally (London, Martinez, and Polit 2001). Another study using data from the National Health Interview Survey (NHIS) reports that about one in four children enrolled in TANF during the study year had some form of chronic illness (Wise et al. 2002).

The Stress of Being Uninsured

Being without insurance is extremely stressful to families. They know that without insurance, they may not be able to get needed care. In in-depth interviews with families who were on welfare and who had recently left welfare for work, I found that people rated Medicaid as their most important benefit (Seccombe et al. 2005; Seccombe 2007). It was evaluated as more important than food stamps, subsidized housing, or even the welfare check itself.

Bob was one of the many people who were interviewed in Oregon as part of a study looking at what happens to families' health insurance after leaving TANF for work. He was part of a married-couple household that received TANF in the past for the care of their young children and foster children. Bob had diabetes, was disabled, and received Supplemental Security Income (SSI) for his disability.

He and his wife lived in a small town community in eastern Oregon, that is known for its harsh winters and blistering summers. Driving through the small town, there were many streets littered with abandoned cars, piles of garbage, and remnants of old appliances. Bob's house was typical of those in his community— small, dilapidated, weather-beaten. The region had been experiencing a typical winter, which means lows in the teens and wind chills much lower than that. Although the sun was shining brightly, the air was chilling and recent storms had left large snow banks along the sides of the streets. As we approached Bob's front door, anxious to get in out of the cold, nothing could have prepared us for the severe chill *inside* the house; the air inside even *smelled* cold.

Though in many ways Bob looked like a typical thirty-something with brown eyes, dark blonde hair, and a pockmarked face, the lack of color in his face and hands provided a window into the physical suffering he was enduring, despite his warm smile. Bob walked us through the sparsely furnished living room with threadbare blue carpet. We sat together at his dining room table about ten feet away from what seemed to be the only heat source in the house: a cross between a small wood stove and an old "trash burner."

Bob and his wife typify families who fall between the gaps in a complicated maze of insurance programs. At the time of our interview, both Bob and his wife were working, and technically both had insurance from their jobs. One plan served as the primary insurer, the other as the secondary insurer.

Yet, despite this seemingly good news, the insurance plans were woefully inadequate. One carried a $3,000 deductible and paid a maximum of $3,500 per year. It was difficult to meet his deductible given his family's low income; however, the real problem is that, given his wide array of serious and costly health conditions, his medical costs far exceeded the maximum benefit. Therefore, Bob had been relying on the second insurance plan from his wife's job, but that plan was suspended because she was on unpaid maternity leave after the recent birth of their child. She now had to pay her own premium in full, and the family could not pay its cost. Now all medical expenses had to be paid for out of pocket.

> She's been on maternity leave for nine weeks now. We've had no income. So what happened is that she hasn't been at work, the $48 a month hasn't been deducted, so we've been cut off. We've got really bad insurance problems right now . . . My newborn is covered for a year, but my 2-year-old and our 3-year-old are not covered.

The family struggled monthly to make ends meet while also securing the healthcare they need. The financial costs to this family had taken their toll, and Bob and his wife have had to make some very difficult choices.

> The State paid for this month, but we weren't at work and we didn't use the money for what we were supposed to use it for . . . we used it for daycare. We've sort of had to rob Peter to pay Paul because we've both been out of work for so long.

What are the consequences of being poor and having inadequate insurance? Bob and his family had to forgo needed medical care. Making choices between basic necessities had been especially heartbreaking for him when his children were the ones affected. Bob described his dilemmas and explained how these decisions had affected his ability to provide for his family's health needs.

> I have always had insurance problems, and it's at the pharmacy where it's at. It's so frustrating to go somewhere to get your meds and they're saying no, you have to pay $100, $200, or $300 for what you used to get for $3. You're going, "Sorry, I can't take it," and you walk away. It's frustrating, especially when it is for your

kids. Just last week they prescribed some steroids for their lungs, but we couldn't get the medication.

When we interviewed him the second time, Bob's own health was particularly precarious. Forced to steal, and then ration what remained of his medications, Bob explained how he was maintaining his physical health as best as he possibly could.

I haven't been able to meet those expenses, so I'm suffering. I've had to go on a fourth of the medications I usually take to make sure they last until her insurance picks back up. The medications I'm on are expensive. Thank God I have been able to get samples. I've been able to continue that, but I haven't been able to get my samples of the Neurontin, so I'm down to, instead of four pills, I'm down to one pill. . . . I only have one more day's worth of medication. But the most important is my insulin pump. I'm getting infections from the sites because I'm keeping them on five times longer than I'm supposed to. I haven't received an order since April, and I refuse to go back on the injections of the long acting insulin because that's what puts me in the hospital with seizures. I've been taking 15–20 shots a day to try to mimic this pump. Nothing has gone through with this company insurance-wise. My blood sugars are suffering a lot. I just had a hemoglobin test, and it's four times higher than it should be. . . . It's supposed to be 3 and it's at 10.7, which is killing my heart, my liver, my kidneys, my eyes, my circulation. I've had two surgeries on my feet since last year too. High blood sugars affect your circulation. There's a loss of sensation, tingling, pain, lots of pain.

Bob acknowledged that by forgoing timely needed care, his health problems end up costing even more in the long run. He was especially concerned about how his own shortened life expectancy might affect his family.

I have no control. Say I don't eat at the right time, boom, I go into low blood sugar reaction and I end up in the hospital. It happened to me three or four times a month before I went on the pump. That's why OHP paid the $6,000 for this pump because it was cheaper to keep me out of the hospital. Diabetes is terminal if it's untreated when insurance, policies, budget cuts, every little thing affects it. They need to say, "He's here, he doesn't have cancer, but it is terminal if it's not treated."

How has Bob coped? He acknowledged that he would have been better off if he had been able to stay on the Oregon Health Plan (OHP), Oregon's version of Medicaid. But the family was no longer eligible because of his wife's employment. He felt guilty that he was not self-sufficient and that his family had needed public assistance. Nonetheless, he also noted that he and his wife had been hardworking taxpayers.

If I would have known the problems I would have had getting on that primary, I would have never done it, never. I would have remained on OHP and I would probably be healthy right now. I'd probably have a whole box full of equipment to use. But I'm a taxpayer too. My wife is a taxpayer. I felt this guilt, I'm not quite self-sufficient. Our will is to get off public assistance altogether, because our will is to be self-sufficient as much as we can. . . . I know I could be if we did this or tried this . . . I have a lot of faith in the Lord and He has been a big issue in our lives. He has been giving me the strength to make it through this.

Bob and his family reveal the ways that poor health can impoverish families. Although they have always lived somewhat on the financial margins, their situation reminds us that even many middle-class families are only one health crisis away from losing their jobs, their income, and their assets. Insurance coverage is increasingly inadequate to meet a family's true needs. Moreover, a pre-existing condition or disability may make it impossible to obtain insurance from an employer. Given that our healthcare system is structured as a for-profit enterprise with for-profit insurance companies as a first line of defense, and that medical costs are rising well beyond the rate of inflation, should we be surprised that families like Bob's fall through the cracks?

Medicaid

The **Medicaid** program provides medical benefits to specific groups of poor people who have no insurance or inadequate insurance. It is not available to all poor persons; Medicaid is available only to certain low-income individuals and families who fit into an eligibility group that is recognized by federal and state law. There are about 25 different eligibility categories that are classified into five broad coverage groups: pregnant women, children and teenagers, the aged, the blind, and the disabled. Even within these groups, though, certain requirements must be met, including income and resources (like bank accounts, real property, or other items that can be sold for cash); and whether you are a U.S. citizen or a lawfully admitted immigrant. Most poor persons without insurance do not qualify for Medicaid. For example, in Texas, only 23 percent of poor adults are eligible for Medicaid, compared to a national average of 48 percent. Among low-income adults (defined as up to 200 percent of the poverty line), only one-third qualify nationally, and 14 percent in Texas (Davidoff, Yemane, and Adams 2005).

Nonetheless, about 42 million Americans were enrolled in Medicaid in 2005, with about 20 million being children. The elderly comprise another large group of Medicaid beneficiaries (13 million) and receive substantial benefits to augment their Medicare (Kaiser Commission on Medicaid and the Uninsured 2005). For example, Medicaid pays for nearly 60 percent of all nursing home residents (Wikipedia 2005).

Medicaid is a federally created program that is largely state administered. Each state sets its own guidelines regarding eligibility and service (Centers for Medicare and Medicaid Services 2005b). This arrangement results in complex policies for eligibility, services, and payments that vary considerably. A person who is eligible for Medicaid in one state may not be eligible in a neighboring state, and the services available may differ in amount, duration, and scope (Davidoff, Yemane, and Adams 2005).

Some states have created programs to extend health insurance coverage to low-income or medically needy persons through Medicaid or through a special health-care financing program. One of the most well known of these programs is found in Oregon.

State Plans: The Oregon Health Plan

Beginning in the 1990s, several unique pieces of legislation were passed in the Oregon state legislature collectively known as the **Oregon Health Plan (OHP),** and they are of interest to policymakers throughout the country. OHP contains three primary components:

1. Extending Medicaid eligibility to all state residents with incomes below the federal poverty level. For those who would not otherwise be covered by Medicaid if not for the expansion of the OHP, small monthly premiums have been instituted on a sliding scale. Persons who are at up to 170 percent of the poverty line can qualify for OHP if they fall in a particular category (e.g., low-income pregnant women or children meeting certain criteria).
2. Establishing a high risk insurance pool for people refused health coverage because of pre-existing medical conditions.
3. Providing small businesses with a broader range of insurance options and incentives, and their employees with an improved chance to retain their insurance when changing jobs.

Oregon has made substantial progress with the implementation of OHP in protecting the health of poor and low-income persons. Thousands of Oregonians are insured through OHP who would otherwise likely be without health insurance. In 1992, approximately 18 percent of the statewide population was uninsured; by 2000, it had been reduced to 12 percent overall, and 8 percent of children (Office of Oregon Health Policy and Research Fall 2002).

Nonetheless, despite the widespread gains made by the implementation of OHP in its early years, by 2004, 17 percent of Oregonians and 12 percent of Oregon's children remained uninsured. Data from the 2004 Oregon Population Survey indicate that race, ethnicity, and income are highly associated with insurance status. Almost 16 percent of Hispanic children were uninsured, compared to 9.5 percent of non-Hispanic children. Families with incomes under the federal poverty line were six times more likely to be uninsured than those with incomes over 500 percent of the federal poverty line (Office of Oregon Health Policy and Research Fall 2006).

SCHIP

Because children are especially vulnerable and in need of preventive care, the **State Children's Health Insurance Program (SCHIP)** was enacted to help children in working families with incomes too high to qualify for Medicaid, but too low to afford private family coverage (Children's Defense Fund 2004). As part of the Balanced Budget Act of 1997, Congress created SCHIP as a federal/state partnership, similar to Medicaid, with the goal of expanding health insurance to children. It is the single largest expansion of health insurance coverage for children since the initiation of Medicaid in the mid-1960s. Although eligibility criteria differ somewhat by state, the federal target is one who resides in a family with income below 200 percent of the federal poverty level or whose family has an income 50 percent higher than the state's Medicaid eligibility threshold (Centers for Medicare and Medicaid Services 2005a). Generally, most uninsured children in families of four who earned up to $36,200 a year in 2005 would qualify, with relatively modest copayments and deductibles (Centers for Medicare and Medicaid Services 2005). For little or no cost, SCHIP pays for children's doctor visits, immunizations, hospitalizations, and emergency room visits.

Yet, despite this program, millions of needy families remain ineligible, do not know about SCHIP, or otherwise do not enroll. As revealed in Chapter 3, 16 percent of poor children under age 19 remain uninsured, compared to only 5 percent of non-poor children (Cohen and Bloom 2005). Recent changes to SCHIP have rendered more children ineligible for assistance due to an increase in premiums, and the implementation of a 90–day waiting period in some states.

Maria is a single mother of three whose employer does not provide health coverage. In August of 2001, when her 3-year-old son Billy developed an ear infection, she took him to the emergency room of Texas Children's Hospital in Houston, where he was diagnosed not only with an ear infection but also a life-threatening heart condition. The hospital helped her apply for the Children's Health Insurance Program. She completed the application on September 2001 and was approved for coverage before her son had heart surgery on October 31, 2001. Mary is so grateful to the

SCHIP coverage that saved her son's life with the operation she never could have afforded. If new SCHIP requirements that make families wait 90 days before receiving coverage had been in effect, Billy's life-saving operation would not have been possible. (*Children's Defense Fund 2005b*)

Medicare

Healthcare is a rapidly growing segment of the U.S. economy, and the elderly use a sizable portion of healthcare services. Because most elderly persons no longer work, how do they get their health insurance? **Medicare** is a federal health insurance program for people aged 65 and older (and some people with disabilities under 65, including people with permanent kidney failure requiring dialysis or a transplant). It was created in 1965 and today is virtually universal among the elderly.

Medicare really is made up of several distinct programs, the two largest of which have the interesting names of Part A and Part B. **Part A** is sometimes called hospital insurance. Most people receive Part A automatically when they turn 65, and they do not have to pay any monthly premiums for it. It covers overnight stays in hospitals, 100 days in a skilled nursing facility, hospice care, and some home healthcare. The yearly **deductible** (the amount that the recipient must pay before Medicare chips in) was $952 in 2006 (Centers for Medicare and Medicaid Services 2005b).

Part B is sometimes called supplemental insurance. It is optional and required an $88.50 monthly premium in 2006. Part B covers 80 percent of the costs of such things as physicians' fees, outpatient hospital treatment, and lab services (after a deductible of $124 per year). The other 20 percent, which is referred to as a **copayment,** is the part that the elderly pay themselves out of pocket (Centers for Medicare and Medicaid Services 2005b).

Medicare has made health insurance far more affordable and available to elders. It has recently expanded services, offering prescription coverage in 2006. Because it is a universal program rather than means-tested, Medicare has virtually no stigma attached to it.

Yet, Medicare is not without its critics. Given high deductibles, co-payments, and payments for things not covered under Medicare, most elderly persons spend thousands of additional dollars each year on medical care, averaging 21 percent of their medical costs (Committee on Ways and Means 1997). Elders' healthcare is far from free. In fact, even with Medicare, rising costs and gaps in coverage result in elders paying more out of their own pockets today than they did before Medicare existed (Morgan and Kunkel 1998). Consequently, nearly 70 percent of elders have some form of additional insurance, a "medigap" policy. The poorest elderly may qualify for Medicaid, the healthcare program that is designed to serve poor persons, regardless of age.

In any case, our healthcare system is not designed to serve the elderly well. This situation is certainly not the fault of Medicare, but it does dampen the efficiency of the program. Elders commonly suffer from chronic conditions, such as arthritis or heart disease. In contrast to these needs, our healthcare system is more geared toward acute care, such as surgical or high–tech treatments to fix short-term problems. Many health problems the elderly experience cannot be cured. A system that focused more on the social dimensions of health and well-being, rather than simply on the absence of disease, would be more responsive to their needs.

Our rapidly increasing elderly population has some potentially distressing repercussions for the Medicare program. Medicare is primarily funded through taxes—working people pay taxes today for programs used by the elderly today. In the future, as our population ages, there will be fewer working adults paying taxes relative to the number of elderly persons needing Medicare services. There were approximately five workers for each beneficiary in 1960 and three in 2000, but there will be only 1.9 by 2040 (De Lew, Greenbery, and Kinchen 1992). Couple this with our rising healthcare costs, and we have the prescription for a major financing disaster. To deal with this problem, Congress will continue to increase the amount that elders pay out of their own pockets by raising deductibles and copayments, and possibly covering fewer services. The goal is to keep Medicare solvent well into the future. Americans recognize that the health of our seniors is, at least in part, a social concern, not merely an individual problem. Securing their access to adequate healthcare is seen as a social responsibility falling to all Americans. Compare this approach with our policies toward children.

Head Start

Head Start is an educational program for poor children that began in 1965 as part of the War on Poverty program launched by the administration of President Lyndon B. Johnson (Gale Encyclopedia of Childhood and Adolescence 1998; Head Start Bureau 2005). At that time, nearly half of the nation's poor people were children under age 12, and Head Start was developed to respond to the needs of poor children as early as possible. A few privately funded preschool programs for poor children in inner cities and rural areas had shown marked success in raising children's cognitive skills. Research showed that early intervention through high-quality programs enhances children's physical, social, emotional, and cognitive development; enables parents to be better caregivers and teachers to their children; and helps parents meet their own goals, including economic independence. Moreover, many low-income children also had unrecognized health problems and had not been immunized. Head Start was envisioned as a comprehensive program that would provide health and nutritional services to poor children, while also developing their school readiness. The program aimed to involve parents as well. Many parents of children in the program were employed as teacher's aides so that they would understand what their children were learning and help carry on that learning at home.

The program was political from its inception. The first lady, Lady Bird Johnson, launched Head Start with much fanfare, and presidents from Lyndon Johnson to Bill Clinton have praised the program and taken credit for its successes. Measuring the program's actual success is not a simple matter, however. Head Start programs have an average cost of $7,222 per child, but proponents argue that Head Start saves taxpayers' money, because children who attend Head Start are more likely to graduate high school and get a job than their peers who do not attend. However, the precise long-term benefits of Head Start are difficult to gauge, and researchers disagree even about the short-term benefits. Nevertheless, it has been estimated that, in the long term, $6 are saved for every $1 invested in the Head Start program. Other studies merely suggest that Head Start graduates are more likely than their peers to stay in the proper grade level for their age in elementary school.

Most programs are half-day and include lunch. The curriculum is not the same in every program, but in most cases, school readiness is stressed. Children may be taught the alphabet and numbers, and to recognize colors and shapes. Healthcare is an important aspect of the program, and children in Head Start are monitored to keep them up to date on their immunizations; testing is also available for hearing and vision. Many programs are integrated to include children with special needs, such as a physical or mental handicap. Class size is limited to between 17 and 20 children, with two teachers. Parents are encouraged to volunteer their time in the classroom or to work as teacher aides.

Head Start began by primarily serving 4-year-olds, who attend for one year before starting kindergarten. However, with the reauthorization of the Head Start program in 1994, Congress established a new program for low-income families with infants, toddlers, and pregnant women called Early Head Start. The Early Head Start program provides resources to community programs to address the needs of younger children and their families. Its goals are similar to Head Start— to demonstrate the impact that can be gained when early, continuous, intensive, and comprehensive services are provided to pregnant women and very young children and their families.

Head Start served approximately 905,000 children across the nation in fiscal year 2004, but the demand for services is far greater than the actual numbers served. Head Start remains skewed toward older children, although the numbers of younger children are increasing: in 2004, 57 percent of the children were 4 years or older, 32 percent were age 3, and 9 percent were under 3. Minorities are overrepresented given their size in the population, reflecting their higher than average rates of poverty. Three percent of children enrolled in Head Start in 2004 were Native American, 31 percent were Hispanic, 31 percent were Black, 27 percent were white, and 3 percent were Asian, Hawaiian, or Pacific Islander (Gale Encyclopedia of Childhood and Adolescence 1998; Head Start Bureau 2005).

Economic policies also play a crucial role in fighting poverty. Two of the largest ones with the most far-reaching impact, the Earned Income Tax Credit (EITC) and Social Security, are discussed in the following sections.

The Earned Income Tax Credit

The **Earned Income Tax Credit (EITC)** is a refundable federal tax credit for low-income working families. The credit can reduce the amount of taxes owed and result in a tax refund to those who claim and qualify for the credit. To qualify for the credit, the adjusted gross income for 2005 must have been less than $37,263 for a married-couple family with more than one child, $33,030 for a married couple with one child, and $13,750 for a married-couple family without children. The thresholds for single-parent families (and single adults) are somewhat lower (Center on Budget and Policy Priorities 2005; Internal Revenue Service 2005).

The EITC is applauded for lifting millions of families out of poverty each year. In the United States, where family allowances, health insurance, and worker benefits are largely excluded from national policy, the EITC is considered one of the country's largest sources of assistance for poor and low-income families (Hotz, Mullin, and Scholz 2001; Schiller 2001). It is a cash subsidy that applies to low-income workers. Enacted in 1975, and expanded in the 1990s, almost 21 million taxpayers received more than $36 billion in EITC payments in 2004. These EITC dollars had a significant impact on the lives and communities of the nation's lowest paid working people, lifting more than 5 million of these families above the federal poverty line.

Not surprisingly, the EITC has had a positive effect on employment because it offers a real supplement to wages for those low-income workers who qualify. The EITC has been credited with making it easier for families to transition from welfare into work in the late 1990s (Ellwood 1999; Hotz, Mullin, and Scholz 2001). Ellwood's research on single-mother employment suggests that welfare reform accounted for only one-half of the changing employment of female-headed households. The EITC, and other work supports, accounted for roughly 30 percent of the change, and the relatively robust economy of the 1990s accounted for the remainder (Ellwood 1999).

More than one-half of all payments go to families who live below the poverty line. For a family with an income of approximately $10,000 per year, the EITC reflects nearly a 40 percent increase in income, or approximately $2.00 an hour (Hotz, Mullin, and Scholz 2001). This increase provides a critical element of security for poor families. It can contribute to basic necessities, it can enable families to make special needed purchases, or it can be used as a savings cushion to offset a future job loss, illness, or other situation that could leave a family at risk.

Economists suggest that every increased dollar received by low and moderate-income families has a multiplier effect of between 1.5 to 2 times the original amount, in terms of its impact on the local economy and how much money is spent in and around the communities where these families live. Using the conservative estimate that for every $1 in EITC funds received, $1.50 ends up being spent locally, would mean that low-income neighborhoods are effectively gaining as much as $18.4 billion.

Nonetheless, the EITC does have its critics. Not all low-income eligible working families receive the credit. Applying for it requires some sophistication with tax laws and forms, and not surprisingly, some low-income persons do not know how to apply for it. In particular, persons who do their own taxes may have little information or understanding of the EITC. Moreover, the EITC provides financial relief only once a year. As will be shown in Chapter 7, other countries tend to offer relief to low-income working families on a monthly basis.

Social Security

Another important program is **Social Security**, the cash program targeted toward people aged 65 and older. Nearly 10 percent of elders lived in poverty in 2004. On first look, the elderly seem to be doing quite well compared to others, especially children, whose poverty rate was 17.8 percent. Indeed, the elderly (along with Asian Americans) are one of the few groups who have not experienced a rise in poverty in recent years.

Yet, to truly understand the economic well-being of the elderly, we must examine more than just the likelihood of living below the poverty threshold. This would be highly misleading because many elderly live only slightly above poverty. They are not represented in the statistics, but they are fragile nonetheless.

Ideally, in the United States, elders' income comes from three primary sources: (1) retirement benefits from Social Security, (2) payments from private pensions, and (3) income from assets and personal savings. The imagery used by the Social Security Administration is that of a "three-legged stool"—all three legs are needed in balance for the stool to provide support.

The United States is one of at least 155 countries that have some sort of financial program for elders, known here as Social Security. It was created to decrease the numbers of elderly living in poverty. In the late nineteenth and early twentieth century, few companies had private pensions for seniors, and the government did not provide public pensions. Consequently, elderly persons who could still physically work usually did so. Many other industrialized nations had created publicly funded programs that provided pensions for the elderly. Germany implemented such a program in 1889, Great Britain in 1908, Sweden in 1913, Canada in 1927 and France in 1930 (Cockerham 1997).

In the United States, bills for public pensions were introduced many times between 1900 and 1935 with no success. But during the Great Depression it became obvious that the elderly could not rely on jobs, private pensions, savings, or their families for financial support. While people of all ages faced hard times during this period, the elderly were particularly hard hit. By 1935 unemployment rates among those 65 and older were well above 50 percent (Hardy and Shuey 2000). Moreover, pension plans were still relatively rare. A federal commission determined that nearly half of all seniors in the U.S. could not realistically support themselves (Achenbaum 1978). The Social Security Act was born in 1935 as a response to the austere poverty that enveloped many of our nations' elders. The Act, referred to today as Social Security, is actually many programs under one umbrella, including Medicare, Medicaid, cash welfare assistance, and cash assistance for survivors and for seniors. But Social Security has become synonymous with a cash assistance entitlement program for seniors. It is seen as an earned right for seniors, not a form of welfare (Trattner 1999).

Payments from Social Security have successfully reduced the percentage of seniors who are impoverished. Today, the poverty rate among the elderly is slightly below that for the rest of the population. However, generalizations mask large differences in income and assets among elderly subgroups. Chances are, an 80-year-old Black female who lives alone is significantly worse off than a 66-year-old married white male. Sex, race, and age interact to significantly influence median income and likelihood of living in poverty. Sociologists refer to the notions of **cumulative advantage and cumulative disadvantage** to describe how early life chances influence one's status in later life. Individuals who have greater opportunities for financial success (i.e., white males) can build upon their successes to perpetuate their advantages into older age, while those who have faced disadvantage carry these over, often resulting in poverty. The "three-legged stool" of Social

Security, pensions, and assets may be adequate for white married couples, but something is clearly amiss for widowed, divorced, or never-married women, especially minorities, who have high rates of poverty. Their cumulative disadvantage results in lower pay, fewer savings and assets, and reduced Social Security benefits.

These are but a sample of programs and policies that are designed to remedy some of the effects of poverty. Most are available only to families that meet specific income thresholds, and they require a degree of sophistication on the part of potential recipients to understand and apply to the system. The income thresholds are deliberately kept low so as to keep too many people from qualifying, and the poor have described their frustration with trying to access the social and health service "maze" (Seccombe et al. 2005; Seccombe 2007). For example, Alexandra, a mother of one young daughter, describes the frustration she encountered when she lost her job and turned to welfare for help:

> I mean, when you start on welfare, you have to start depending on people that are already on welfare to get you into the system because nobody is there to help you and there are no guidelines to go by to tell you how. I just needed some assistance at the time and I wanted to go back to school and stuff, but I couldn't get assistance because I couldn't figure out how. I kept going down for appointments, and I couldn't get in there. It's just like you have to know somebody to be able to get on it and get through it. It's like a maze; it's like a puzzle, and you have to fit the pieces together and you have to start learning how to work the system, basically. It's like a job learning how to do it, and I was real naïve. I never saw a food stamp in my life. I didn't even know what a check looked like. I had never known a person who used them. (*Seccombe 2007:172*)

Likewise, Amera, who had recently left welfare for work, described the difficulties associated with trying to continue her medical coverage after the one year of transitional Medicaid—completing paperwork, making visits to state offices, or receiving mailed notices. Amera was unable to renew her Medicaid coverage because of the constraints of her work schedule, so it was cancelled. She explains that she was literally unable to contact the OHP office via phone or go to the welfare office to pick up needed materials, for what amounts to a relatively minor technicality: incompatible schedules (Seccombe et al. 2005):

> I haven't had any [OHP coverage] for about a year, because they're 8 to 5 . . . I work an 8 to 5 shift, so it's been really hard to get hold of them. I call at noon from work; I get a busy signal. By the time I get home at night, they're not there. They need to extend their hours from 7 to 6 or 7 to 7, because there's a lot of other people out there that can't get hold of them for the same reason. I don't have time to

run out to the local welfare office for the same reason. They're 8 to 5. It just drives me up a wall.

This chapter examined several critical social programs and policies to ameliorate poverty and strengthen families. However, instead of truly focusing on ways to make families more resilient, policies are created within a framework fearing that generous programs will make people "dependent" on the system. Our programs and policies tend to have an implicit goal of preventing people from getting too comfortable with assistance, and serve as a powerful reminder that needing assistance is an undesirable state and comes at an emotionally expensive price. How do other countries deal with these concerns? This will be the focus of Chapter 7.

Critical Thinking Questions:

1. What do you think poor families need to thrive? How do the needs of poor families differ from the needs of families that are not poor?
2. How does Bob's situation reflect structural conditions rather than just his own personal problems?
3. Why are healthcare and cash grants available for all elders regardless of income, but not for all children, or all adults? What attitudes and values do these policies reflect?

7

CAN POVERTY BE ELIMINATED? LESSONS WE COULD LEARN

HOW DOES POVERTY IN THE UNITED STATES compare to other developed countries? Precise comparisons have been challenging because measures of poverty vary from one country to another. However, the Luxembourg Income Study, begun in the 1980s, has standardized variables across 70 data sets to allow for some comparisons of poverty across a limited number of countries (Smeeding 1997; Smeeding, Rainwater, and Burtless 2000). Using several different measures of poverty across 18 comparable nations, researchers are now able to make relatively valid cross-national comparisons within these countries. Comparing poverty rates, and exploring how others deal with poverty, lead us to several critical questions. Is poverty inevitable? Can it be eliminated, or at least reduced significantly? What lessons can be learned from the experiences of other countries?

This chapter examines the range of possibilities made available by proactive and comprehensive family policies that recognize the structural causes and consequences of poverty and social inequality. My goal is to impart a sense of optimism—all is not hopeless because there are many things that the United States could do to lift millions of families out of the depths of poverty and enhance their lives. As President Franklin D. Roosevelt said:

> I see a great nation upon a great continent, blessed with a great wealth of natural resources. . . . I see a United States which can demonstrate that, under democratic methods of government, national wealth can be translated into a spreading volume of human comforts hitherto unknown, and the lowest standard of living can be raised far above the level of mere subsistence. But here is the challenge to our

democracy: In this nation I see tens of millions of its citizens—a substantial part of its whole population—who at this very moment are denied the greater part of what the very lowest standards of today call the necessities of life. I see millions of families trying to live on incomes so meager that the pall of family disaster hangs over them day by day. I see millions whose daily lives in city and on farm continue under conditions labeled indecent by a so-called polite society half a century ago. I see millions more denied education, recreation, and the opportunity to better their lot and the lot of their children. (*Children's Defense Fund Action Council 2005*)

To better understand the extent of poverty in the United States, let us compare it to other developed countries. The Luxembourg Income Study reveals a startling conclusion: regardless of the measure used, the United States poverty rate exceeds those of the other 17 developed countries. For example, using one method that defines poverty as the percentage of persons living with incomes at or below 50 percent of the median income, Smeeding, Rainwater, and Burtless (2000) found that 17.8 percent of Americans were in poverty in the 1990s, far exceeding the 8.6 percent average for the other 17 countries. The percentage of American children who live below 50 percent of the median income also is greater than in any of the other countries, at 22.3 percent for the United States, compared to an average of 9.9 percent. Among the aged, only Australia has a higher proportion of seniors living in poverty than does the United States.

Likewise, 2000 data from UNICEF, which compare the rate of child poverty in all families and in single-parent families across developed and developing nations, found similar trends (UNICEF Innocenti Research Centre June 2000). The results, shown in Table 7.1, reveal that the United States poverty rate among children, particularly children in single-parent families, is considerably higher than in other developed nations and is higher than in many developing nations as well. For example, the poverty rate for children in single-parent families in the United States hovered around 55 percent in 2000, although the comparable figure in Mexico was only 28 percent. Comparative data such as these indicate that high rates of poverty in a wealthy, developed nation such as the United States are not inevitable.

Reason for High Poverty in the United States

Why does the United States have greater poverty, despite its vast wealth and resources? The reasons can be traced to early attitudes and resulting social policies. The United States has a long history of "rugged individualism" and a distrust of government and governmental programs as revealed in Chapter 4. Policies in the United States reflect and promote the concept of self-sufficiency. Americans

Table 7.1 Child Poverty* in Single-Parent Families Relative to Other
Family Types: 2000

	Poverty rate of children in:	
	Single-parent families (%)	Other families (%)
Australia	36	9
Belgium	14	4
Canada	52	10
Czech Republic	31	4
Denmark	14	4
Finland	7	4
France	26	6
Germany	51	6
Greece	25	12
Hungary	10	10
Ireland	46	14
Italy	22	20
Luxembourg	30	3
Mexico	28	26
Netherlands	24	7
Norway	13	2
Poland	20	15
Spain	32	12
Sweden	7	2
Turkey	29	20
United Kingdom	46	13
United States	**55**	**16**

*Poverty defined as 50% of median national income.
Source: UNICEF Innocenti Research Centre, June 2000.

expect people to be in charge of their own destinies, and they display little tolerance for those who seem to be unwilling or unable to pull themselves up "by their bootstraps" (Quadagno 1982; Trattner 1999). Borrowing from early English "Poor Laws," our policies evolved over the seventeenth and eighteenth centuries and make clear distinctions between "worthy" needy people (i.e., people who cannot support themselves through no fault of their own) and the "unworthy."

Not surprisingly then, the United States has embraced a laissez-faire approach in which families are largely left to fend for themselves. This approach includes the arena of work, where employers have near-complete discretion on matters of pay and benefits. With the inflationary erosion of the minimum wage, the rise in service-sector jobs, and no requirement that employers offer benefits such as health insurance, retirement, or sick leave, low-income workers are becoming increasingly unprotected.

The laissez-faire approach also is apparent in the lack of a cohesive national family policy and safety net for poor families. Many of the programs we do have tend to be **means-tested,** meaning that persons generally need to meet some income eligibility requirement—often excruciating low—to qualify for benefits. For example, people have to be well below the poverty line—and meet other criteria—to qualify for Medicaid. Income thresholds vary across states, and they are kept relatively low to limit the number of users of the program and control costs. Yet, not all programs in the United States are means-tested. Police and fire protection, as well as public schools, are available to all persons, regardless of income. These services are considered a right of citizenship. It is not always clear why some programs are available to everyone and others are not. Why is education a "right," but health insurance a "privilege" only available to those with generous employers or to those who are poor enough (and meet additional criteria) to qualify for Medicaid?

When we compare the philosophy of the United States to the philosophies of most of Europe, Canada, Australia, and many other locales, we see vastly different approaches. Most developed nations have an interrelated, coordinated set of proactive and **universal** economic and social programs to help strengthen all families. Universal programs are not means-tested; rather, they are available to everyone regardless of their income. They are a right of citizenship, and no one is denied services. For example, as shown in Table 7.2, in a recent review of 23 developed nations, the United States was the only country that had no universal health insurance coverage, paid maternal/parental leave at childbirth, or a family allowance/child dependency grant (Social Security Online 2004). The United States sees these family issues in individualistic terms and expects parents to figure

Table 7.2 Child Safety Net Policies in 23 Industrialized Countries Compared with the United States

Country	Universal Health Insurance/ Health Care	Paid Maternal/ Parental Leave at Childbirth	Family Allowance/ Child Dependency Grant
Australia	Y	Y	Y
Austria	Y	Y	Y
Belgium	Y	Y	Y
Canada	Y	Y	Y
Czech Republic	Y	Y	Y
Denmark	Y	Y	Y
Finland	Y	Y	Y
France	Y	Y	Y
Germany	Y	Y	Y
Hungary	Y	Y	Y
Iceland	Y	Y	Y
Italy	Y	Y	Y
Japan	Y	Y	Y
Luxembourg	Y	Y	Y
Netherlands	Y	Y	Y
New Zealand	Y	Y	Y
Norway	Y	Y	Y
Poland	Y	Y	Y
Portugal	Y	Y	Y
Spain	Y	Y	Y
Sweden	Y	Y	Y
Switzerland	Y	Y	Y
United Kingdom	Y	Y	Y
United States	N	N	N

Source: Social Security Online 2004.

it out on their own; other countries have specific policies to ensure that all people can receive these benefits. Yet, many American parents are not able to "figure it out themselves." How does one go about figuring out how to get health insurance when an employer does not offer it and the costs of purchasing it yourself far exceed your budget? How do you arrange for a paid maternity leave after the birth of your child when an employer tells you that you will be fired if you don't quickly come back to work? How do you go about finding a family allowance, when most people in the United States have never even heard of such a program?

Likewise, in many other countries, childcare is often subsidized so that it is free or available at a very low cost. Most developed nations have an interrelated set of proactive and universal programs that keep families from slipping into poverty, or that help the poor improve their financial circumstances. These programs are financed by **progressive** forms of taxation—those who earn more, pay more in taxes. Countries offer these programs because residents favor structural explanations for inequality over individual explanations by a wide margin. For example, when asked, "Why are there people in this country who live in need?" 35 percent of Swedes claimed it was due to societal injustice and only 16 percent claimed it was because of personal laziness. The results in France were even more telling: 42 percent of those surveyed blamed societal injustice, compared to only 15 percent who believed it was due to personal laziness. In the United States, the explanations are reversed: 33 percent invoked structural explanations, while 39 percent blamed personal laziness (World Values Survey 1994). These differences in values add up to vastly different approaches in dealing with poverty.

Comparative Family Policies

Family policy is a term to describe what government does to and for families. It includes those explicit and implicit policies that are designed to improve the lives of families with children. Programs may be designed to assist families with the costs of raising children, or encourage and enable families to have more children (Kamerman 2003). Policies could include such things as family law (e.g., laws regarding marriage, divorce, child custody); family allowances (i.e., a cash benefit provided on the basis of the presence, number, and age of children); tax benefits (e.g., credits or allowances); paid job-protected leaves following childbirth or adoption (i.e., maternity or paternity leaves); early childhood education benefits and services; child support or advanced maintenance policies providing child support by the noncustodial parent; child protection services (e.g., foster care, adoption); subsidized goods or services (e.g., housing allowance); maternal and child healthcare; and other critical benefits. Some of these policies are explicitly designed to compensate families for the costs of children (e.g., family allowances); other policies are universal in nature, but have an implicit goal of helping children and families (e.g., national health insurance).

The United States has a weak and relatively unsystematic family policy. Unlike other developed nations, it seems to have little comprehensive, collective vision for families (Kamerman and Kahn 1978; Bergmann 1996; Elrod 1999; Bogenschneider 2000; Warner 2005).

In the following sections, I describe three particular examples of the ways in which other countries commonly assist families—family allowances, childcare, and maternity and family leaves. These policies keep many families from falling into poverty, and they help many struggling families improve their lives. This discussion is certainly not an exhaustive list of relevant social policies. The goal here is to give Americans some idea of what *could* be done to drastically reduce the rate of poverty and the deleterious effects of poverty on families.

Family Allowance

A **family allowance**, or child allowance, is a cash benefit provided by the government to families with children as a universal right of citizenship (Kamerman and Gatenio 2002; Centre des Liaisons Europeennes et Internationales de Securite Sociale 2006). Currently, 88 countries provide family allowances to parents, yet surprisingly, few Americans have even heard of them. In some countries, family allowances may be supplemented by birth grants, school grants, childrearing or childcare allowances, adoption benefits, special supplements for single parents, guaranteed minimum child support benefits, and allowances for adult dependents and disabled children. By providing these cash benefits, governments are directly helping families with the costs associated with raising children and indirectly helping to lower the rate of child poverty.

Typically, family allowances have one or more of the following objectives: (1) redistributing income from childless households to families with children, in recognition of the heavier financial burden incurred by childrearing; (2) supplementing the incomes of poor and modest-income families with children as a means of reducing or preventing poverty; (3) strengthening labor force attachment, because in some countries benefits are only available to families with children who have at least one parent in the workforce (or higher benefit levels are offered to families attached to the labor force); and (4) increasing feelings of social cohesion and progress among people—this last objective is particularly of interest to the European Union as they move toward greater unity among member states.

For the most part, family allowances are modest benefits, for each child worth a little less than 10 percent of average wages, but they can contribute a significant component of family income to large or low-income families. Family allowance benefit levels vary in different ways. Several countries provide a uniform rate per child, regardless of the number of children in the family (Australia, Spain, Norway, and Sweden), while in other countries, benefits increase with each additional child or are larger for later children, such as the third, fourth, or fifth child (Italy, Belgium, France, Germany, and Luxembourg). In still others, such as the United Kingdom, the benefit is higher for the first child, while in France a family is only eligible for the allowance after the second child is born. Notice that benefits generally *increase* as family size grows; this policy is contrary to the philosophy of family caps in the United States that curtail or eliminate further cash welfare benefits if families have additional children. In other words, explicit policy in other countries encourages births, while in the United States, we encourage families to limit them.

Many countries provide higher benefits for older children (Austria, Belgium, France, Luxembourg, and the Netherlands). Some countries provide a higher or special benefit for families with very young children (Austria, France, Germany, and Portugal) to make it possible for a parent to remain at home during a child's early years (usually until the child is age 3; age 1 in Portugal). In Finland and Norway, parents have the option of subsidized childcare or a cash benefit of equivalent value, making it possible for a parent of a very young child (under 3) to stop working and stay home. Benefit levels may be reduced as income rises or by including the benefit in taxable income, as in Spain and Greece. In some countries, benefit levels vary by geographic regions. Austria, Germany, and Spain offer national benefits that vary by region, due to differences in the cost of living. Likewise Norway supplements the allowances of families in the Arctic region.

Allowances are generally provided to families from the time of a child's birth to the age of majority or completion of formal education. In almost all developed countries, the universal cash allowance is awarded to the mother, or to the person caring for the child. An income-related cash benefit is more likely to go to the wage-earning parent.

In recent years, some countries have begun to deliver family allowances through the tax system, have substituted targeted benefits for family allowances, or have supplemented allowances by adding child or family tax benefits. For example, the family allowance was Canada's first universal welfare program, begun in 1944, because families feared that the Canadian economy would return to a depression after World War II. It was available to all families with children under the age of 16, regardless of income. However, the program had its critics who argued that the benefits should only go to needy families. Beginning in 1978, a series of reforms was initiated in Canada to more closely target the benefit to lower-income families. In 1993, the family allowance was replaced by a new income-tested child tax benefit that provided monthly benefits based on the number of children and the level of family income. Thus, although the benefit is now means-tested, Canada continues to provide a monthly benefit to lower-income families (Government of Canada 2005).

Ultimately, regardless of the method, the issue is how much money reaches families with children. Given the high child and family poverty rates in the United States, we might want to consider enriching our package so that more families are covered, and the compensation is adequate to lift them out of poverty (Kamerman and Gatenio 2002).

Childcare Policies

About two-thirds of mothers with children under age 6, and more than three-quarters of mothers with children ages 6 to 13 years are employed in the labor force (U.S. Department of Labor 2005b). As we have learned, childcare is expensive. Given that most families have more than one child and they are spaced only a few years apart, it is possible that many families have daycare bills that approach $10,000–$20,000 per year (Children's Defense Fund 2005a; Johnson 2005). These costs are comparable to, or even exceed, costs for college, and they are out of the reach of many families (Schulman 2000). Yet, where is the "financial aid" to help these parents? There are no federal loans, scholarships, or work-study programs for childcare. Families themselves pay most of the cost. Looking at childcare expenditures, approximately 60–80 percent of the costs are borne by families, with the public and private sector paying the remaining share. In contrast, families on average pay only one-quarter to one-third of the costs of their child's college tuition.

In the United States, there are two ways the public sector assists with the costs of childcare. One mechanism is a childcare tax credit on the family's income tax form. Under current law, the **Child and Dependent Care tax credit** can cover 20–30 percent of expenses to care for children younger than 13 years of age. There is a dollar limit on the expenses toward which you can apply the credit: in 2005, a family could deduct up to $3,000 for the care of one child, $6,000 for two or more (Internal Revenue Service 2006).

As a second option, available only if an employer offers this benefit, a family can set aside up to $5,000 **pretax dollars** for childcare (regardless of the number of children). They do not pay taxes on this amount, so if a family is in the 25 percent tax bracket, it is as though they were getting an extra 25 percent bonus on this money ($1,250). This tax credit is a real boon to many families. However, there are two problems with this program. First, given that most childcare costs far exceed $5,000, these savings, while helpful, are inadequate to meet the needs of most families. For example, if the real cost of childcare is $10,000, and by law the 25 percent tax benefit can only be taken on half of that amount—$5,000—it thereby reduces real savings by half, to 12.5 percent. Second, wealthier families, who are in higher tax brackets, save more money than do lower-income persons in lower income tax brackets. Therefore, a program like this is highly regressive: the wealthier end up getting a higher benefit than do those families who need it the most.

Childcare is a necessity for most families, but it remains largely a private matter. Families are left on their own to find the highest-quality care that they can afford. However, quality controls are limited and vary by state. For example, CPR and first aid requirements for childcare workers vary dramatically and are nonexistent in some states. Pay for childcare workers is low (the median was $8.90 an hour in 2005). Many childcare workers live in poverty; few workers receive fringe benefits such as health insurance, sick pay, or vacation time; and turnover is high (U.S. Department of Labor May 24, 2006). The story of Marie and her family illustrates the consequences of the poor wages and benefits we pay to valuable childcare workers.

> It is suppertime and Marie, the mother of two young children and one handicapped adult daughter who contracted spinal meningitis as a toddler, surveys the nearly bare shelves in the kitchen—some beans, vegetables, and canned potato soup. The week's meat, which she buys when it is on sale, has been rationed and stretched as far as possible, and is gone by now. Marie always makes sure the children eat dinner first, although it might be just canned soup, and sometimes she goes hungry for the night. "As long as they get something," she says. Marie has been working for more than a decade and a half. She is not on welfare. When she tried to apply for food stamps last year, she was told that she earned one dollar above the income requirement to be eligible. She is a childcare provider. She works hard every day to make sure the toddlers in her care are safe and well fed, comforted when they cry, and given as much love and stimulation as possible. For her crucial work, she brings home so little money she can barely feed and house her own children. The average childcare worker makes $16,000 and is usually without health benefits. (*Children's Defense Fund* 2002)

Unlike the United States, many developed countries do not think of childcare as a private matter. They see quality childcare as a public concern, as a social good that can ultimately benefit everyone. They recognize that our lives will be better for having well-cared-for and well-educated children because these children are more likely to stay in school, are less likely to become delinquent, and more likely to become productive adults contributing to the economy. We all will depend upon children to grow up and to take care of us, whether as vascular surgeons or as garbage collectors. All tasks are beneficial for society, and all children should be well cared for so that they can make their contributions, whatever they may be.

What can other countries teach us about how to structure quality childcare and early education for the benefit of everyone? Sheila B. Kamerman, director of the Columbia University Institute for Child and Family Policy, states:

> If school readiness is a key goal, if meeting the needs of working mothers is an essential response, and if maximizing the health and well-being of children is a desirable outcome, Americans should take a look at what is occurring in other developed countries. The contrast is dramatic. (*The Clearinghouse on International Developments in Child, Youth, and Family Policies 2001:1*)

Early childhood education and care (ECEC) is a service for young children involving both physical care and education. Begun 100 years ago in many countries, programs were expanded considerably in the 1970s because of the dramatic rise in labor force participation of mothers, the push for single mothers to work rather than receive public aid, and a growing interest in ensuring that all children begin elementary school with basic skills and ready to learn (The Clearinghouse on International Developments in Child, Youth, and Family Policies 2005). These ECEC programs enhance and support children's cognitive, social, and emotional development.

The Project on Global Working Families examined the ECEC policies of 168 countries and found that the United States is tied with Ecuador and Suriname for 39th in enrollment in early childhood education for 3–5 year olds, at 57 percent. Nearly all European countries perform better. In terms of the percentage of gross domestic product (GDP) spent on early childhood education, the United States is in a seven-way tie for 13th place out of 30 studied countries at 0.4 percent. The United States tied for 91st place out of 151 countries in the area of student-staff ratios. Among developed nations, only the United Kingdom and Japan do worse (Heymann et al. 2004).

The Organization for Economic Cooperation and Development sponsored a three-year study of 12 developed nations to compare the availability and structure of ECEC programs. How do the programs differ? In several countries, access to ECEC is a statutory right. Although compulsory school begins at age 6 or 7, ECEC availability begins at age 1 in Denmark, Finland, and Sweden (after generous maternity and family leave benefits are exhausted); at age 2½ in Belgium; at age 3 in Italy and Germany; and at age 4 in Britain. Most countries have full coverage for 3–6 year olds. In contrast, in the United States there is no statutory entitlement until children are 5–7 years old, depending on the state. Access to publicly funded

ECEC programs is generally restricted to at-risk children, usually defined as poor or near-poor (e.g., the Head Start Program). The demand for these programs far outstrips their availability. Only New York and Georgia have developed universal prekindergarten programs for all 4-year-olds regardless of family income (The Clearinghouse on International Developments in Child, Youth, and Family Policies 2001).

In most of the 12 countries reviewed, governments pay the largest share of the costs, with parents covering only 25–30 percent. Countries also may make arrangements for sliding scale payments for low-income families to help make programs affordable. Most countries require staff to complete at least three years of training at universities or other institutes of higher education. Their earnings are in accordance. In contrast, American parents pay an average of 60–80 percent of ECEC costs. Some of these costs can be recouped through tax benefits, but many low-income families find the tax system confusing and therefore end up using informal or unregulated childcare. There is also no agreed-upon set of qualifications for staff; their status and pay are low and turnover is high, unlike in the other countries (The Clearinghouse on International Developments in Child, Youth, and Family Policies 2001).

The result is that American families tend to scramble to find private care, while families in other countries rely on publicly funded programs. Table 7.3 illustrates the percentage of children in publicly funded childcare from age 0 to 2, and age 3 to school age. Of the 14 countries listed, the United States ranks last in the percentage of children in publicly funded programs, with only 1 percent of children age 2 and under, and 14 percent of children age 3 to school age in publicly funded programs. Compare these data with Denmark, where 48 percent of children up to age 2, and 85 percent of children age 3 to school age are in publicly funded daycare. Or, compare the United States with France and Belgium, where 20 percent of children to age 2 and 95 percent of children age 3 and older are in publicly funded daycare. In the United States, the costs of childcare are largely borne by the parents themselves. Quality care is seen as a private good rather than a public one, even though we all benefit from having well-cared-for and educated children.

Ironically, although the United States is a national leader in research on child development, it has not developed the programs that research suggests are needed and that are increasingly available in other developed nations. Dr. Kamerman says:

> Most countries are giving major attention to ECEC. [There is] progress at an accelerated rate almost everywhere. But the United States has not yet made the critical political commitment. The U.S. leads in child development research; I think it is time for us to catch up in practice. (*The Clearinghouse on International Developments in Child, Youth, and Family Policies 2001:1*)

Table 7.3   Publicly Funded Childcare, Index of Policies Supporting Employment for Mothers, and Government Payment in Child Support Arrangements

	% Children in Publicly Funded Childcare	
	Age 0 to 2	Age 3 to School
Australia	2	26
Belgium	20	95
Canada	5	35
Denmark	48	85
Finland	32	59
France	20	95
Germany	2	78
Italy	5	88
Luxembourg	2	58
Netherlands	2	53
Norway	12	40
Sweden	32	79
United Kingdom	2	38
United States	**1**	**14**

Source: Cited in "When Mom Must Work: Family Day Care as a Welfare-to-Work Option," Ontario Coalition for Better Child Care. April 2000.

Maternity and Parental Leaves

Another critically important way to invest in families is by providing paid maternity leaves after the birth of a child and parental leaves for other serious family events. As Canada's former prime minister Jean Chretien has said:

> There is now overwhelming scientific evidence that success in a child's early years is the key to long-term healthy development. Nothing is more important than for parents to be able to spend the maximum amount of time with newborn children in the critical early months of a child's life. Therefore, I am proud to announce today that the government will introduce legislation in this parliament to extend employment insurance maternity and parental benefits from the current maximum of six months to one full year. (*Center for Families 2001*)

What "scientific" information is the former prime minister referring to? A growing body of research is informing us of the benefit that leaves have for children, their parents, and their parents' employers (Galtry 1997; Ruhm 1998; Glass and Riley 1998; McCaine and Mustard 1999; Center for Families 2001). Long leaves are associated with better maternal health, vitality, and lower rates of infant mortality. Moreover, women are likely to breastfeed for longer periods if they have extended leave benefits. The benefits of longer maternity leaves also extend to employers. Women are more likely to return to work after childbirth in those countries that have more lengthy leaves. It is more cost-effective to develop a well-planned leave policy than it is to rehire and retrain new employees.

Out of 168 countries examined by the Project on Global Working Families, 163 guarantee paid leave to women in connection with childbirth (Heymann et al. 2004). The United States has, by far, the least generous maternity leave policy of any nation, including poor and developing nations. A sample of the benefits in these countries is reported in Table 7.4. The United States provides no paid leave to women as a national policy, and is only one of five countries (and one of only two developed nations) that lack this protection. Australia, the only other developed nation that does not provide paid leave to mothers, does offer one full year (52 weeks) of unpaid leave. The only other countries studied that do not provide paid leave to mothers are Lesotho, Papua New Guinea, and Swaziland (Heymann et al. 2004).

What is the U.S. policy? The Family Medical Leave Act of 1993, signed by former President Clinton, requires employers with more than 50 employees to give 12 weeks of *unpaid* leave to women or men for a family need deemed serious, such as the birth of a baby, or to care for a sick or injured relative. Employers in small firms are not required to offer leaves. Among those who work in larger employee settings, the reality is that few people can really afford to take unpaid leave. Therefore, many come back to work shortly after their short-term disability, vacation, or sick pay has been exhausted. In a survey about the use and impact of family and medical leave, 34 percent of workers said they needed it but did not take leave (Commission on Family and Medical Leave 1996). Data from the Census Bureau indicates that the percentage that did not take maternity leave because they could not afford to was even higher. Minority women and women with less education are least likely to take leave after giving birth (U.S. Census Bureau 2001). By way of contrast:

- Denmark offers 18 weeks of paid maternity leave at 90 percent of a person's salary.
- The Netherlands and Spain each offer 16 weeks of leave at 100 percent of a person's salary.

- Sweden allows for 450 days of leave per child until the child is 8 years old. The time can be configured as the parents choose. Of the 450 days of leave, at least 30 are reserved for the mother and 30 are reserved for the father, with the remaining days being split as they wish. Parents receive 80 percent of their income for the first 390 days, while for the remainder it is a flat rate. Some employers offer a supplement that replaces a parent's full salary for up to four months.
- The United Kingdom allows 26 weeks of maternity pay at 90 percent for six weeks, and a flat rate for the remainder. They also offer 40 weeks of unpaid leave.
- Canada provides up to 17–18 weeks of maternity benefits depending on the province, and 10 weeks of parental benefits for fathers and parents who are caring for an adopted child at 55 percent of average insured earnings, up to a ceiling (Center for Families 2001; United Nations Statistics Division 2005).

Maternity leave also is far more generous in many developing nations than it is in the United States. Even in Bangladesh, one of the poorest nations on earth, women can receive 12 weeks of maternity leave, paid at 100 percent. In Vietnam, women may receive 4–6 months of pay at 100 percent, depending on their occupation. Women in Egypt may be eligible for 90 days of leave, also paid at 100 percent. Realistically, not all women in these countries receive these benefits because many work in the underground economy, or in positions that fail to offer coverage. However, as a matter of law, many women in these poorer countries are indeed entitled to receive benefits that women in the United States can only dream about. These benefits can keep families resilient and prevent them from slipping into poverty.

Maternity and parental leave benefits are most often provided by that country's social security program. Social Security payments in the United States focus primarily on seniors, the disabled, or survivors in the event of parental death. However, why not allow parents to draw Social Security benefits during their prime child-rearing years? Rankin (2002) offers a tantalizing proposal: Allow parents to draw benefits up to three years during their prime child-rearing years. This policy would give mothers and fathers a real choice about how much time to spend working and how much time to spend at home with their children. Research indicates that after factoring in taxes and the various expenses associated with a family's second job (childcare, transportation, additional clothing, lunches out, and miscellaneous other costs), even a $30,000 income translates into only a little over $10,000 net income for the family—the average Social Security payment for current retirees. The real financial gain among poor and low-income workers is even more paltry. Extending Social Security to parents would subsidize family income

Table 7.4 Maternity Leave Benefits, 2004

	Length of Maternity Leave	Percentage of Wages Paid in Covered Period	Source
Developing Nations			
Bangladesh	12 weeks	100	Employer
Bulgaria	135 days	90	Social Security
Bolivia	60 days	100 of min wage + 70 percent of wages	Social Security
China	90 days	100	Employer
Cuba	18 weeks	100	Social Security
Egypt	90 days	100	Employer
India	12 weeks	100	Social Security/ Employer
Iran	90 days	67	Social Security
Iraq	62 days	100	Social Security
Mexico	12 weeks	100	Social Security
Morocco	14 weeks	100	Social Security
Nigeria	12 weeks	50	Employer
Vietnam	4–6 months	100	Social Security
Developed Nations			
Canada	17–18 weeks	55 percent for 15 weeks	Employment Ins
Denmark	18 weeks	90	State
Finland	105 days	70	Social Security
France	16 weeks	100 up to a ceiling	Social Security
Ireland	18 weeks	70	Social Security
Italy	5 months	80	Social Security
Japan	14 weeks	60	Health Ins/Social Security

Table 7.4 *Continued*

	Length of Maternity Leave	Percentage of Wages Paid in Covered Period	Source
Netherlands	16 weeks	100	Unemployment Fund
New Zealand	14 weeks	100 up to a ceiling	State
Spain	16 weeks	100	Social Security
Sweden	14 weeks	390 days @ 80 percent; 90 days @ flat rate	Social Security
Switzerland	98 days	80	Social Security
United Kingdom	26 weeks	6 weeks @ 90 percent; flat rate after	Employer
United States	**12 weeks**(a)	0	—

(a) Applies only to workers in companies with 50 or more workers.
Source: Adapted from: United Nations Statistics Division 2005, Table 5c.

at a crucial time in their lives, and it could offer real relief from the time crunch and financial stress that millions of families with young children face every day. Families could use their payment to allow them to stay home with children, to work part-time, or to help finance the added costs associated with full-time employment.

Rankin further suggests that those parents who draw on their Social Security benefits could repay the system in a number of ways if reimbursement is desired. The employee's share of the payroll tax they pay when they return to work could be increased; the age of retirement could be increased in some pro-rated fashion; or, the monthly retirement benefit could be reduced as it is for those who opt for early retirement now. Possibilities abound. As Rankin suggests, our Social Security system has long been thought of as providing a measure of financial security in return for work. What could be a more vital contribution to the future of our country than attending to the well-being of children?

Case Study: France

France is one of many countries that can provide a rich contrast to the United States. Why look at France? In the book *Saving Our Children From Poverty* (1996), economist Barbara Bergmann notes that there are many demographic and economic similarities between the two nations. The annual rate of growth is comparable, and both countries have similar rates of female labor force participation and births outside of marriage, and both countries have minority populations of comparable proportions. France has a significantly higher unemployment rate, yet its poverty rate is considerably less than that of the United States. The child poverty rate in France is one-third that of the United States. The poverty rate of children in single-parent families in France is half the rate in the United States. Moreover, only about a quarter of single mothers in France received welfare-type benefits, compared to two-thirds of American single mothers.

There are at least two reasons for these differences. First, France has made a successful commitment to enhance low-tier work. They have improved the conditions surrounding these jobs so that they are no longer necessarily associated with low wages, and they do not automatically reduce the array of benefits that are vital to an individual's and a family's well-being. Second, the investment in low-tier work in France is not only monetary, but it is reflected in the entire orientation to caring for their citizens. France provides extensive benefits, mostly universal, that are successful in preventing families living on the margins from slipping into poverty. Author Judith Warner, in her book *Perfect Madness: Motherhood in the Age of Anxiety* (2005), describes the assistance available to her as a new mother living in France, and presents the jolting contrast she found after returning to the United States:

. . . For my first three-and-a-half blessed years of motherhood, I know something was very different. I didn't realize it then, but I was in paradise.

I was living in France, a country that has an astounding array of benefits for families—and for mothers in particular. When my children were born, I stayed in the hospital for five comfortable days. I found a nanny through a free, community-based referral service, then employed her, legally and full-time, for a cost to me of about $10,500 a year, after tax breaks. My elder daughter, from the time she was eighteen months, attended excellent part-time preschools, where she painted and played with modeling clay and ate cookies and napped for about $150 per month—the top end of the fee scale. She could have started public school at age three, and could have opted to stay until 5 p.m. daily. My friends who were covered by the French social security system (which I did not pay into), had even greater benefits: at least four months of paid maternity leave, the right to stop working for up to three years and have jobs held for them, cash grants after their second children were born starting at about $105 per month.

And that was just the beginning. There was more: a culture. An atmosphere. A set of deeply held attitudes toward motherhood—toward adult womanhood—that had the effect of allowing me to have two children, work in an office, work out in a gym, and go out to dinner at night and away for a short vacation with my husband without ever hearing, without ever thinking, the word "guilt."

... [after returning to the United States] I knew what had worked for me in France. It wasn't just that I had access to a slew of government-run or subsidized support services; it was also that I'd had a whole unofficial network of people to help and support me—materially and emotionally—as I navigated the new world of motherhood. There was the midwife who'd appeared as if by magic on day four in the hospital to offer tissues as I succumbed to the tears of the "baby blues," and who'd said matter-of-factly, "Everything is coming out now. Blood, milk, tears. You have to let it flow."

There was my local pharmacist who, unasked, filled my shopping bag with breast pads. The pediatrician who answered his own phone. The network of on-call doctors who made house calls at any time of the day or night. The public elementary school principal who gave us a personal tour of her school and encouraged us to call her if we had any questions. In short, an extended community of people who'd guaranteed that I was never, from the moment I became a mother onward, left to fend for myself alone. . . . I knew that there was a kind of existential safety to be derived from a world in which there were structures in place to help you take care of your children: Day-care centers that had guaranteed standards of quality. Public schools whose early education programs were a source of national pride. Small things, independent of government support; reasonably priced agencies that could be counted on to provide quality babysitters, a community center that made referrals to childcare services. . . . A general message that it was a bad thing to go it alone. (*9–10, 30–31*)

What is the impact of this collectivist orientation? French parents at all income levels get a great deal of government assistance with childcare and healthcare, for example. Infants are usually cared for in the home by one of their parents, a situation made possible by the existence of three kinds of parental leaves: 16 weeks of paid maternity leave; 11 days of paid paternity leave; and up to three years of unpaid leave for either parent with their job guaranteed (provided they have been on the job for at least one year) (Embassy of France 2006). After this leave period, state-subsidized individual or group care provides childcare. Of the more than 4 million children age 6 and under, the vast majority receive some degree of state-subsidized care. Even stay-at-home parents can use this care on a part-time, as needed basis. By the time French children are 3 years old, attendance in preschool is virtually 100 percent. There is also a well-coordinated before and after school care program for a nominal fee. Childcare workers are an educated work force, they are well compensated, and it is considered valued and important work.

Likewise, free health care is available to everyone by right of citizenship, and it is not lost when a person loses a job, develops an illness that is expensive to treat, or leaves welfare, as is often the case in the United States. The French government further supplements the income of families with children by providing family allowances, housing assistance, and cash payments to pregnant women. These programs are not limited to poor families, unemployed families, or single parents. Moreover, because most of these programs are universal and available regardless of income, they have little or no stigma attached to them. They are considered to be normal facets of the social structure, much in the way public education is in our country. These programs are rights of all citizens, not privileges, and therefore, there is no shame in receiving them. In contrast, in the United States, we have families who need assistance but do not know what is available, do not know how to access it, or have been so absorbed by the Individualist perspective that their ego or guilt prevents them from seeking the help that they qualify for and need.

Workers in France with low wages get even more help from these and other programs. For example, a single mother in France who moves from welfare to work retains $6,000 in government cash and housing grants. She continues to receive free health insurance and pays a negligible amount for childcare, as do all French citizens. She does not have to face the hardships associated with low-tier work, as do her sisters in the United States. Thus, despite the fact that the welfare programs in France are more generous than are ours, women are still more likely to leave them to pursue jobs. They can make this move because of the security that the French government provides to all its workers. It is wrong to assume that we must have a punitive approach and keep benefits low so that women will not abuse the welfare system. Here, as in France, women would prefer employment, and they will work, if they continue to have the security that they need to care for their families.

How did these policies and programs come about? The need for a national family policy was first discussed in France in the nineteenth century and led, in 1939, to the drafting of the Family Code. This Code provided the first institutional basis for a genuine policy on families and was incorporated under the Social Security System (Embassy of France 2001). Family policies in France are dynamic and take into account the changing nature of families. For example, there has been a gradual shift away from the model focusing on traditional marriage and children, and increasing attention paid to single-parent households, unmarried-couple households with children, and families in which the mother is employed for pay. Policies and programs are designed to help all families, although there is a particular emphasis on increasing the security of low-income and large families.

CONCLUSION

My goal in this book has been to illustrate that poverty is a structural problem, not merely a personal one. Poverty is a large and important public issue *directly* affecting the lives of millions of persons, young and old, in profound ways. However, *indirectly*, poverty affects us all by contributing to higher health, mental health, education, and welfare costs, which all adults, as taxpayers, must bear. Moreover, poverty also stunts the productivity and well-being of millions of adults and future adults, denying the rest of America the benefits coming from a fully engaged, and physically and emotionally healthy population.

When poverty and its effects touch so many people, it ceases to be simply a personal problem, and therefore, we must look beyond individualist solutions. Yes, some poor people are indeed lazy, lack motivation, or are happy living off government supports. However, some wealthy people also share these same characteristics. Most people—rich, poor, and those in-between—share basic core values that emphasize the importance of hard work, thrift, and self-sufficiency.

Poverty is not simply a personal problem. It is rooted in the social arrangements of society, and therefore, any real hope of ending poverty must also examine our social structure to see how we perpetuate poverty and social inequality. This can then provide the clues as to how to ameliorate those problems.

What lessons about poverty, and responses to poverty, have we learned as we look at other countries? Data reveal that the United States lags dramatically behind others, both developed and developing nations, when it comes to enacting public policies designed to enhance the economic and social well-being of families. Initial inequalities across social classes are exacerbated by weak and fragmented policies that emphasize individualism over social structure. In most other countries, families can rely upon a set of proactive policies and programs that enhance the structure of low-tier work by providing livable wages and important benefits, and that provide a secure safety net for fragile families. These programs minimize disparities across social class, while our programs exacerbate them. We expect families to go it alone, while other countries know that this approach is detrimental to families and does not build resiliency.

Critics may scoff that the costs for these policies and programs are prohibitive. According to data compiled by Bergmann (1996), the United States would need to spend approximately 59 percent more than its current level to increase our spending on programs for child well-being to match those of the French. As the richest country in the world, with one of the lowest tax rates, investing in our families in this fashion is eminently possible. However, our money is being spent in other ways—it is a matter of priority. For example, the United States spends more than twice as much money on defense (in nonwar years) as it does for programs that promote children's well-being (e.g., childcare and development, income supplements, income tax reductions, medical care for low-income children), whereas in France the opposite occurs. Proudly, children are their explicit priority. The United States also spends an inordinate amount of money on the enforcement of means-tested policies. That money would be better spent reinforcing the security of the vulnerable members of our society, which, despite our comfort in thinking to the contrary, could be any one of us. I leave you with this thought from the Children's Defense Fund (2004):

Where America Stands

Among developed countries: the United States ranks:

First in military technology

First in military exports

First in Gross Domestic Product

First in the number of millionaires and billionaires

First in health technology

First in defense expenditures

12th in living standards among our poorest one-fifth

13th in the gap between rich and poor

14th in efforts to lift children out of poverty

23th in infant mortality

Last in protecting our children against gun violence

I believe that we can do better than this.

Critical Thinking Questions:

1. What can one person, (i.e., you) do to help the plight of poor families? Does your solution (or solutions) focus on the individual level or the structural level?

2. If family allowances, maternity and parental leaves, and early education programs have such promising results, why has the United States failed to adopt these programs? Who opposes them, and why?

3. Can you think of any other examples of ways in which other countries try to reduce poverty or help the poor?

REFERENCES

Abbott, Douglas A. and William Meredith. 1998. "Characteristics of Strong Families: Perceptions of Ethnic Parents." *Home Economics Research Journal* 17:140–47.

Abramovitz, Mimi. 1996a. *Regulating the Lives of Women: Social Welfare Policy from Colonial Times to the Present, (Rev. ed)*. Boston: South End Press.

———. 1996b. *Under Attack, Fighting Back: Women and Welfare in the United States*. New York: Monthly Review Press.

Achenbaum, W. Andrew. 1978. *Old Age in the New Land: The American Experience Since 1790*. Baltimore, MD: Johns Hopkins University Press.

Acs, Gregory and Pamela Loprest. 2004. *Leaving Welfare: Employment and Well-Being of Families That Left Welfare in the Post-Entitlement Era*. Kalamazoo, MI: W.E. Upjohn Institute for Employment Research.

Alaimo, Katherine, Christine M. Olson, and Edward A. Frongillo, Jr. 2001. "Food Insufficiency and American School-Aged Children's Cognitive, Academic, and Psychosocial Development." *Pediatrics* 108(1):44–53 (Abstract available at: http://www.pediatrics .org/cgi/content/abstract/108/1/44).

The Alan Guttmacher Institute. 2000. "Why Is Teenage Pregnancy Declining? The Roles of Abstinence, Sexual Activity and Contraceptive Use." Retrieved 14 June 2000 (http:// www.agi-usa.org/pubs/or_teen_preg_decline.html).

———. 2002. *In Their Own Right: Addressing the Sexual and Reproductive Health Needs of American Men*. New York: The Alan Guttmacher Institute.

———. 19 February 2004. *U.S. Teenage Pregnancy Statistics: Overall Trends, Trends by Race and Ethnicity And State-by-State Information*. New York: The Alan Guttmacher Institute.

———. 2006. "Facts in Brief: Contraceptive Use." Retrieved 23 June 2006 (www .guttmacher.org/pubs/fb_contr_use.pdf).

Anderson, Martin. 1978. *Welfare: The Political Economy of Welfare Reform in the United States*. Stanford, CA: Hoover Institution.

The Annie E. Casey Foundation. 2005. *Kids Count* Data Book. Baltimore, MD: The Annie E. Casey Foundation.

Aponte, Robert. 1998. "Hispanic Families in Poverty: Diversity, Context, and Interpretation." Pp. 578–92 in *Shifting the Center: Understanding Contemporary Families*, edited by S.J. Ferguson. Mountain View, CA: Mayfield Publishing Co.

Baker, David W., Joseph J. Sudano, Jeffrey M. Albert, Elaine A. Borawski, and Avi Dor. 2002. "Loss of Health Insurance and the Risk for a Decline in Self-Reported Health and Physical Functioning." *Medical Care* 40(11):1126–31.

Bandler, Jean Taft Douglas. 1975. "Family Issues in Social Policy: An Analysis of Social Security." Ph. D. Diss., School of Social Work, Columbia University.

Bergman, Mike. 28 March 2005. *Educational Attainment in the United States: 2004*. Press Release. Washington, D.C.: U.S. Census Bureau.

Bergmann, Barbara R. 1996. *Saving Our Children from Poverty: What the United States Can Learn from France*. New York: Russell Sage Foundation.

Berk, Marc L. and Gail R. Wilensky. 1987. "Health Insurance Coverage of the Working Poor." *Social Science and Medicine* 25:1183–87.

Bernstein, Jared. 1993. "Rethinking Welfare Reform." *Dissent* Summer:277–79.

Bernstein, Jared and Isaac Shapiro. 1 September 2005. *Unhappy Anniversary: Federal Minimum Wage Remains Unchanged for Eighth Straight Year, Falls to 56-Year Low Relative to the Average Wage*. Washington, D.C.: Economic Policy Institute and Center on Budget and Policy Priorities.

Berrick, Jill Duerr. 1995. *Faces of Poverty*. New York: Oxford University Press.

Besharov, Douglas and Karen M. Gardiner. 1997. "Sex Education and Abstinence: Programs and Evaluation." *Children and Youth Services Review* 19(65/6):327–39.

Betson, David M. and Jennifer L. Warlick. 1998. "Alternative Historical Trends in Poverty." *American Economic Review* 88:348–51.

Billingsley, Andrew. 1968. *Black Families in White America*. Upper Saddle River, NJ: Prentice Hall.

Blank, Rebecca M. 2002. "Evaluating Welfare Reform in the United States." *Journal of Economic Literature* 40(December):1105–66.

Blyth, Dale A. and Eugene C. Roelkepartian. 1993. *Healthy Communities, Healthy Youth*. Minneapolis: Search Institute.

Bogenschneider, Karen. 2000. "Has Family Policy Come of Age? A Decade Review of the State of U.S. Family Policy in the 1990s." *Journal of Marriage and the Family* 62:1136–59.

Bowen, Gary L. and Mimi V. Chapman. 1996. "Poverty, Neighborhood Danger, Social Support, and the Individual Adaptation Among At-Risk Youth." *Journal of Family Issues* 17:641–66.

Brady, David. 2003. "Rethinking the Sociological Measurement of Poverty." *Social Forces* 81:715–52.

Breslau, Naomi, Nigel S. Paneth, and Victoria C. Lucia. 2004. "The Lingering Academic Deficits of Low Birth Weight Children." *Pediatrics* 114(4, October):1035–40.

Broder, John M. 1997. "Big Social Changes Revive the False God of Numbers." *New York Times*, 17 August, Week in Review 4–1.

Brodie, Mollyann, Annie Steffenson, Jaime Valdez, Rebecca Levin and Roberto Suro. December 2002. *2002 National Survey of Latinos: Summary of Findings*. Washington, D.C.: Pew Hispanic Center/Kaiser Family Foundation.

Brooks-Gunn, Jeanne and Greg J. Duncan. 1997. "The Effects of Poverty on Children." *The Future of Children (Children and Poverty)* 7(2, Summer/Fall):55–71.

Burton, C. Emory. 1992. *The Poverty Debate*. Westport, CT: Praeger.

California Department of Health Services. 1998. *Lead Hazards in California's Public Elementary Schools and Child Care Facilities*. Report to the California State Legislature (15 April).

Cancian, Maria, Robert Haveman, Daniel R. Meyer, and Barbara Wolfe. 2003 January. *The Employment, Earnings, and Income of Single Mothers in Wisconsin Who Left Cash Assistance: Comparisons Among Three Cohorts*. Madison, WI: Institute for Research on Poverty.

Capizzano, Jeffrey and Regan Main. 2005. "Many Young Children Spend Long Hours in Child Care." In *No. 22 in "Snapshots of America's Families III."* Retrieved 11 July 2005. Urban Institute (www.urban.org/urlprint.cfm?ID=9232).

Carnevale, Anthony P. and Stephen J. Rose. 2001. "Low Earners: Who Are They? Do They Have a Way Out?" Pp. 45–66 in *Low-Wage Workers in the New Economy*, edited by R. Kazis and M. S. Miller. Washington, D.C.: The Urban Institute Press.

Castner, Laura A. and Allen L. Schirm. 2005. *Reaching Those in Need: State Food Stamp Participation Rates in 2003*. Mathematica Policy Research, Inc. Washington, D.C.: U.S. Department of Agriculture Food and Nutrition Service.

Center for Families, Work, and Well-Being. 2001. "Response to Extension of Parental Leaves." Retrieved 19 October 2001 (http://www.worklifecanada.ca/index.shtml).

Center for Law and Social Policy. 1997. "Welfare Changes Enacted" Retrieved 10 October 2004 (www.igc.apc.org/handsnet2/welfare.reform/Articles/art .876261804.htm).

Center on Budget and Policy Priorities. 2005. *Facts About Tax Credits for Working Families—the Earned Income Credit and Child Tax Credit: Tax Time Can Pay for Working Families*. Washington, D.C.

Center on Hunger and Poverty. 2002 June. *The Consequences of Hunger and Food Insecurity for Children: Evidence from Recent Scientific Studies*. Heller School for Social Policy and Management. Boston: Brandeis University.

Centers for Disease Control and Prevention, National Center for Environmental Health. 2006. "General Lead Information: Questions and Answers." Retrieved 19 March 2006 (www.cdc.gov/nceh/lead/faq/about.htm).

Centers for Disease Control and Prevention. 2004. "Early Release of Selected Estimates Based on Data from the 2003 National Health Interview Survey" Retrieved 14 July 2005 (www.cdc.gov/nchs/data/nhis/earlyrelease/200406_11.pdf).

Centers for Medicare and Medicaid Services. 2005a. *Medicaid At-A-Glance 2005: A Medicaid Information Source*. Washington, D.C.: U.S. Department of Health and Human Services.

———. 2005b. "Medicare Premiums and Coinsurance Rates for 2006: Frequently Asked Questions." Retrieved 2 January 2006. U.S. Department of Health and Human Services (questions.medicare.gov/cgi–bin/medicare.cfg/php/enduser/std_adp.php?p_faqid=1701).

———. 2005. "Insure Kids Now." U.S. Department of Health and Human Services (www.cms.hhs.gov/LowCostHealthInsFamChild/02_InsureKidsNow.asp).

Center des Liaisons Europeennes et Internationales de Securite Sociale. 2006. "The French Social Security System." Retrieved 15 January 2006 (www.cleiss.fr/docs/regimes/regime_france/an_3html).

Child Trends Database. 2005. "Children in Poverty." Retrieved 6 October 2005 (http://www.childtrendsdatabank.org/indicators/4Poverty.cfm).

Children's Defense Fund Action Council. 2005. *Stand Up for Children Now!: State of America's Children Action Guide*. Washington, D.C.: Children's Defense Fund Action Council.

Children's Defense Fund. 1994. *Wasting America's Future: The Children's Defense Fund Report on the Cost of Child Poverty*. Washington, D.C.: Children's Defense Fund.

———. 2 June 2005. *Over 13 Million Children Face Food Insecurity*.

———. 2001. "Child Care Basics." Retrieved 27 July 2003 (http://www.childrensdefense.org/cc_facts.htm).

———. 2002. *The State of Children in America's Union: A 2002 Action Guide to No Child Left Behind*. Technical Report No. Page 8.

———. 2004. "Frequently Asked Questions: CHIP, Medicaid, and Uninsured Children." Retrieved 23 August 2005 (www.childrensdefense.org/childhealth/chip/faqs.aspx).

———. 2005a. "Child Care Basics" (Issue Basics).

———. 2005b. "Defining Poverty and Why It Matters for Children" (www.childrensdefensefund.org).

———. 2005c. "Increasing the Minimum Wage: An Issue of Children's Well-Being." Retrieved 26 November 2005 (www.childrensdefense.org/familyincome/jobs/minimumwagereport2005.pdf).

Chilton, Mariana and Angelo Giardino. 2004. "Who's Looking Out for the Little Ones?" Opinion Editorial. *The Philadelphia Daily News*, 2 November, p. 16.

The Clearinghouse on International Developments in Child, Youth, & Family Policies. 2001. "New 12 Country Study Reveals Substantial Gaps In U.S. Early Childhood Education and Care Policies." Retrieved 28 July 2003. Columbia University (www.childpolicyintl.org/issuebrief/issuebrief1.htm).

———. 2005. "Section 1.2: Early Childhood Education and Care." Retrieved 17 January 2006. New York/Columbia University (www.childpolicyintl.org/ecec.html).

Clinton, Bill. 1997a. "Welfare Should Be Reformed." Pp. 26–27 in *Welfare: Opposing Viewpoints*, edited by C. Cozic. San Diego, CA: Greenhaven Press.

———. 1997b. "Welfare Reform Must Protect Children and Legal Immigrants." Pp. 40–44 in *Welfare Reform*, edited by C. Cozic. San Diego, CA: Greenhaven Press.

Cockerham, William C. 1997. *This Aging Society*. Upper Saddle River, NJ: Prentice Hall.

———. 2001. *Medical Sociology*, 8th ed. Upper Saddle River, NJ: Prentice Hall.

Cohen, Robin A. and Barbara Bloom. 2005. *Trends in Health Insurance and Access to Medical Care for Children Under Age 19 Years: United States, 1998–2003*. Advance Data from Vital and Health Statistics No. 355. Hyattsville, MD: National Center for Health Statistics.

Collins, Sara R., Karen Davis, Michelle Doty, and Alice Ho. 2004. *Wages, Health Benefits, and Workers' Health*. Washington, D.C.: The Commonwealth Fund (www.cmwf.org/USR_doc/Collins_workers_IB_788.pdf).

Commission on Family and Medical Leave. 1996. "A Workable Balance: Report to Congress on Family and Medical Leave Policies." Retrieved February 2000 (http://www.dol.gov/dol/esa/fmla.htm).

Committee on the Consequences of Uninsurance. 2002. "Health Insurance Is a Family Matter." Retrieved 20 May 2005. Institute of Medicine (www.iom.edu/file.asp?id=4161).

Conger, Rand, Katherine Conger, and Glen Elder. 1997. "Family Economic Hardship and Adolescent Adjustment: Mediating and Moderating Processes." Pp. 288–310 in *Consequences of Growing Up Poor*, edited by G. Duncan and J. Brooks-Gunn. New York: Russell Sage Foundation.

Conger, Rand D., Xiao-Jia Ge, and Frederick O. Lorenz. 1994. "Economic Stress and Marital Relations." Pp. 187–203 in *Families in Troubled Times: Adapting to Change in Rural America*, edited by R. D. Conger and G. H. Elder Jr. New York: Aldine de Gruyter.

Conger, Rand D., Martha A. Rueter, and Glen H. Elder Jr. 1999. "Couple Resilience to Economic Pressure." *Journal of Personality and Social Psychology* 76:54–71.

Congressional Budget Office. 2005. "Historical Effective Federal Tax Rates, 1979 to 2002." Retrieved 25 October 2005 (www.cbo.gov/showdoc.cfm?index=6133& sequence=0).

Cook, John T., Deborah A. Frank, Carol Berkowitz, Maureen M. Black, Patrick H. Casey, Diana B. Cutts, Alan F. Meyers, Nieves Zaldivar, Anne Skalicky, Suzanne Levenson, Tim Heeren, and Mark Nord. 2004. "Food Insecurity Is Associated with Adverse Health Outcomes Among Human Infants and Toddlers." *Journal of Nutrition* 134(June):1432–38.

Corcoran, Mary, Sheldon Danziger, and Richard Tolman. 2003. *Long-Term Employment of African-American and White Welfare Recipients and the Role of Persistent Health and Mental Health Problems*. Ann Arbor, MI: University of Michigan National Poverty Center Working Paper Series #03-5.

Coryn, Chris L. 2002. "Antecedents of Attitudes Toward the Poor." Retrieved 20 October 2005 (www.iusb.edu/~journal/2002/coryn/coryn.html).

Coulton, Claudia J., Jill E. Korbin, Marilyn Su, and Julian Chow. 1995. "Community Level Factors and Child Maltreatment Rates." *Child Development* 66:1262–76.

Coven, Martha. 2005. "An Introduction to TANF." Retrieved 3 January 2006. Center on Budget and Policy Priorities (www.centeronbudget.org/1-22-02tanf2.htm).

Cozzarelli, Catherine, Anne V. Wilkinson, and Michael J. Tagler. 2001. "Attitudes Towards the Poor and Attributions for Poverty." *Journal of Social Issues* 57(2):207–27.

Dalaker, Joe. 2005 June. *Alternative Poverty Estimates in the United States: 2003*. Current Population Reports. Washington, D.C.: U.S. Census Bureau.

Danziger, Sandra K., Elizabeth Oltmans Ananat, and Kimberly G. Browning. 2004. "Childcare Subsidies and the Transition from Welfare to Work." *Family Relations* 52(2, March):219–28.

Darroch, Jacqueline E., Susheela Singh, Jennifer J. Frost, and the Study Team. 2001. "Differences in Teenage Pregnancy Rates Among Five Developed Countries: The Role of Sexual Activity and Contraceptive Use." *Family Planning Perspectives* 33:244–50 & 281 (www.agi-usa.org/pubs/journals/3324401.html).

Davidoff, Amy, Alshadye Yemane, and Emerald Adams. 2005. *Health Coverage for Low-Income Adults: Eligibility and Enrollment in Medicaid and State Programs, 2002.* Washington, D.C.: Kaiser Commission on Medicaid and the Uninsured.

Davis, James A. and Tom W. Smith. 1990. *General Social Surveys, 1972–1990: Cumulative Codebook.* Chicago: National Opinion Research Center (NORC).

De Lew, Nancy, George Greenbery, and Kraig Kinchen. 1992. "A Layman's Guide to the U.S. Health Care System." *Health Care Financing Review* 14:151–65.

DeBell, Matthew. 2003. "Rates of Computer and Internet Use by Children in Nursery School and Students in Kindergarten Through Twelfth Grade: 2003." *Education Statistics Quarterly* 7(1–2). National Center for Education Statistics.

DeNavas-Walt, Carmen, Bernadette D. Proctor, and Cheryl Hill Lee. 2006 August. *Income, Poverty, and Health Insurance Coverage in the United States: 2005.* Current Population Reports No. P60-231. Washington, D.C.: U.S. Census Bureau.

DeParle, Jason. 1997. "A Sharp Decrease in Welfare Cases Is Decreasing Speed." *New York Times*, 7 February.

Dey, Achintya N. and Barbara Bloom. 2005. *Summary Health Statistics for U.S. Children: National Health Interview Survey, 2003.* National Center for Health Statistics. Vital Health Stat 10(223). Washington, D.C.: U.S. Government Printing Office.

Dodson, Lisa and Jillian Dickert. 2004. "Girls' Family Labor in Low-Income Households: A Decade of Qualitative Research." *Journal of Marriage and Family* 66:318–32.

"Don't Fence Us Out." 2006. *The Economist*, 1–7 April, pp. 25–26.

Donnelly, Cindy. 2006. Letter to the Editor. *Brain, Child*, p. 4. Gibsonia, PA, Winter.

Doty, Michelle M., Jennifer N. Edwards, and Alyssa L. Holmgren. 2005. "Medical Bills Land Millions in Debt." Retrieved 20 October 2005. The Commonwealth Fund (www.cmwf.org/topics/topics.htm?attrib_id=12001).

Douglas-Hall, Ayana and Heather Koball. 2004. "Parental Employment in Low-Income Families." Retrieved 9 September 2005. New York/National Center for Children in Poverty (www.nccp.org/pub_pe1104b.html).

Downey, Douglas B. 1994. "The School Performance of Children from Single-Mother and Single-Father Families: Economics or Interpersonal Deprivation?" *Journal of Family Issues* 15:129–47.

Drake, Brett and Shanta Pandey. 1995. "Understanding the Relationship Between Neighborhood Poverty and Specific Types of Child Maltreatment." *Child Abuse and Neglect* 20:1003–18.

Dubow, Eric F. and Maria F. Ippolito. 1994. "Effects of Poverty and Quality of the Home Environment on Changes in the Academic and Behavioral Adjustment of Elementary School–Age Children." *Journal of Clinical Child Psychology* 23(4):401–12.

Duncan, Greg J. and Jeanne Brooks-Gunn. 1997. *Consequences of Growing Up Poor.* New York: Russell Sage Foundation.

Duncan, Greg J., Wei-Jun Yeung, Jeanne Brooks-Gunn, and Judith R. Smith. 1998. "How Much Does Childhood Poverty Affect the Life Chances of Children?" *American Sociological Review* 63:406–23.

Economic Policy Institute. 2002. "Living Wage: Frequently Asked Questions." Retrieved 28 December 2005 (www.epinet.org/content.cfm/issueguides_livingwage_livingwage faq).

———. 2005. "Minimum Wage." In *EPI Issue Guide*. Retrieved 19 December 2005 (www.epinet.org/content.cfm/issueguides_minwage_minwage).

Edin, Kathryn and Maria Kefalas. 2005. *Promises I Can Keep: Why Poor Women Put Motherhood Before Marriage*. Chicago: University of Chicago Press.

Edin, Kathryn and Laura Lein. 1997. *Making Ends Meet*. New York: Russell Sage Foundation.

Ehrenreich, Barbara. 2001. *Nickel and Dimed: On (Not) Getting By in America*. New York: Henry Holt and Co.

Ellwood, David T. 1988. *Poor Support: Poverty in the American Family*. New York: Basic Books.

———. 1999. "The Impact of the Earned Income Tax Credit and Social Policy Reforms on Work, Marriage, and Living Arrangements," Cambridge, MA: Kennedy School of Government, Harvard University, Unpublished manuscript.

Elrod, Linda. 1999. "Epilogue: Of Families, Federalism, and a Quest for Policy." *Family Law Quarterly* 33:843–63.

Embassy of France. 2001. "Family Policy in France." Retrieved 15 January 2006 (www.ambafrance-us.org/atoz/fam_pol.asp).

———. 2006. "Childcare." Retrieved 15 January 2006. Embassy of France in the United States (www.ambafrance-us.org/atoz/childcare.asp).

Evans, Gary W., Carrie Gonnella, Lyscha A. Marcynyszyn, Lauren Gentile, and Nicholas Salpekar. 2005. "The Role of Chaos in Poverty and Children's Socioemotional Adjustment." *Psychological Science* 16(7, July):560–65.

Family Economics and Nutrition Review. 1997. "Cost of Food at Home." *Family Economics and Nutrition Review* 10:56.

Farber, Nancy. 1990. "The Significance of Racc and Class in Marital Decisions Among Unmarried Adolescent Mothers." *Social Problems* 37:51–63.

Feagin, Joe R. 1975. *Subordinating the Poor: Welfare and American Beliefs*. Upper Saddle River, NJ: Prentice Hall.

Feinberg, Emily, Katherine Swartz, Alan Zaslavsky, Jane Gardner, and Deborah K. Walker. 2002. "Family Income and the Impact of a Children's Health Insurance Program on Reported Need for Health Services and Unmet Health Need." *Pediatrics* 109(2):E29.

Fergusson, David M. and Lianne J. Woodward. 2000. "Teenage Pregnancy and Female Educational Underachievement: A Prospective Study of a New Zealand Birth Cohort." *Journal of Marriage and the Family* 62:147–61.

Fields, Jason M., Kristin Smith, Loretta E. Bass, and Terry Lugaila. 2001. *A Child's Day: Home, School, and Play (Selected Indicators of Child Well-Being)*. Current Population Reports. Washington, D.C.: Governmental Printing Office.

Fisher, Gordon M. 1997. "The Development and History of the U.S. Poverty Thresholds—A Brief Overview." In *Newsletter of the Government Statistics Section and the Social Statistics Section of the American Statistical Association*. pp. 6–7. Retrieved: 11 October 2005 (aspe.os.dhhs.gov/poverty/papers/hptgssiv.htm).

Food Research and Action Center (FRAC). 2006. "Food Stamp Participation in August 2005 Nearly 1.2 Million Above August 2004 Level" (Current News & Analyses). Retrieved 4 April 2006 (www.frac.org/html/news/fsp/05.08_FSP.html).

Fremstad, Shawn. 2003 September. *Falling TANF Caseloads Amidst Rising Poverty Should Be a Cause of Concern*. Washington, D.C.: Center on Budget and Policy Priorities.

———. 2004. "Recent Welfare Reform Research Findings." Retrieved 3 January 2006. Center on Budget and Policy Priorities (www.centeronbudget.org/1-30-04wel.htm).

Friedan, Betty. 1963. *The Feminine Mystique*. New York: Dell.

Friedlin, Jennifer. 2004. "Welfare Series: Child Care Promises Fall Through." Retrieved 8 January 2006. Women's eNews (www.womensenews.org/article.cfm/dyn/aid/1947).

Fuller, Bruce, Sharon L. Kagan, Gretchen L. Caspary, and Christiane A. Gauthier. 2002 Winter/Spring. *Welfare Reform and Child Care Options for Low-Income Families*. The Future of Children.

Furness, Bruce W., Paul A. Simon, Cheryl M. Wold, and Johanna Asarian-Anderson. 2004. "Prevalence and Predictors of Food Insecurity Among Low Income Households in Los Angeles County." *Public Health Nutrition* 7(6):791–94.

Gale Encyclopedia of Childhood and Adolescence. 1998. "Head Start Programs." Gale Research. Retrieved 10 March 2006 (http://www.findarticles.com/p/articles/mi_q2602/is_0002/ai_/2602000293).

Galtry, Judith. 1997. "Suckling and Silence in the USA: The Costs and Benefits of Breast Feeding." *Feminist Economics* 3(3):1–24 (http://www.lawsocietyalberta.com/legalinfo/parental.htm).

Garfinkel, Irwin, Daniel R. Meyer, and Sara S. McLanahan. 1998. "A Brief History of Child Support Policies in the United States." Pp. 14–30 in *Fathers Under Fire: The Revolution in Child Support Enforcement*, edited by Irwin Garfinkel, Sara S. McLanahan, Daniel R. Meyer and Judith A. Seltzer. New York: Russell Sage Foundation.

Garmezy, Norman. 1991. "Resilience and Vulnerability to Adverse Developmental Outcomes Associated with Poverty." *American Behavioral Scientist* 34:416–30.

Garrett, Patricia, Nicholas Ng'andu, and John Ferron. 1994. "Poverty Experiences of Young Children and the Quality of Their Home Environments." *Child Development* 65(2):331–45.

Geller, Adam. 2005. "CEO Pay Rises Even as Questions Linger About Overcompensation." *The Detroit News, Business*, 16 April. Retrieved 4 April 2006 (www.detnews.com/2005/business/0504/16/biz-152196.htm).

Gelles, Richard J. 1992. "Poverty and Violence Toward Children." *American Behavioral Scientist* 335:258-74.

Gilbert, Dennis and Joseph A. Kahl. 1993. *The American Class Structure: A New Synthesis*, 4th ed. Belmont, CA: Wadsworth.

Gilder, George. 1981. *Wealth and Poverty*. New York, NY: Basic Books.

Gilmer, Todd and Richard Kronick. 2005. "It's the Premium, Stupid: Projection of the Uninsured Through 2013." In *Health Affairs* 10.1377: hlthaff.w5.143.

Glass, Jennifer L. and Lisa Riley. 1998. "Family Responsive Policies and Employee Retention Following Childbirth." *Social Forces* 76(4):1401–35.

Glennerster, Howard. 2000, October. *U.S. Poverty Studies and Poverty Measurement: The Past Twenty-Five Years*. Technical Report CASE Paper No. 42. London: Center for Analysis of Social Exclusion, London School of Economics.

Goldstein, Gary W. 1990. "Lead Poisoning and Brain Cell Function." *Environmental Health Perspectives* 89:91–94.

Gordon, Tuula. 1994. *Single Women: On the Margins?* New York: New York University Press.

Government of Canada. 2005. "1944—Family Allowance Program: Supporting Canadian Children." Retrieved 15 January 2006 (canadianeconomy.gc.ca/english/economy/1944family.html).

Grall, Timothy S. 2003. "Custodial Mothers and Fathers and Their Child Support: 2001" (Current Population Reports P60-225). Washington, D.C.: U.S. Census Bureau, U.S. Department of Commerce.

Grall, Timothy. 2005. "Support Providers: 2002." Retrieved 11 December 2005. U.S. Census Bureau (http://www.census.gov/prod/2005pubs/p70-99.pdf).

Gray, Ronald F., Alka Indurkhya, and Marie C. McCormick. 2004. "Prevalence, Stability, and Predictors of Clinically Significant Behavior Problems in Low Birth Weight Children at 3, 5, and 8 Years of Age." *Pediatrics* 114(3, September):736–43.

Hadley, Jack. 2003. "Sicker and Poorer—The Consequences of Being Uninsured: A Review of the Research on the Relationship Between Health Insurance, Medical Care Use, Health, Work, and Income." *Medical Care Research and Review* 60(2, June):3S–75S.

Hamelin, Anne-Marie, Jean-Pierre Habicht, and Micheline Beaudry. 1999. "Food Insecurity: Consequences for the Household and Broader Social Implications." *Journal of Nutrition* 129:S525–28.

Hamilton Brady E., Stephanie J. Ventura, Joyce A. Martin, and Paul D. Sutton. *Preliminary Births for 2004. Health E-Stats.* Hyattsville, MD: National Center for Health Statistics. October 28, 2005. (www.cdc.gov/nchs/products/pubs/pubd/hestats/prelim_births/prelim_births04.htm).

Hancock, Ange-Marie. 2004. *The Politics of Disgust: The Public Identity of the Welfare State.* New York: New York University Press.

Hardy, Melissa A. and Kim Shuey. 2000. "Retirement." Pp. 2401–10 in *Encyclopedia of Sociology*, 2nd ed., edited by E. F. Borgatta and R. J. Montgomery. New York: Macmillan.

Harrington, Michael. 1963. *The Other America: Poverty in the United States.* New York: Penguin.

Harvey, David L. and Michael H. Reed. 1996. "The Culture of Poverty: An Ideological Analysis." *Sociological Perspectives* 39:465–95.

Hashima, Patricia Y. and Paul R. Amato. 1994. "Poverty, Social Support, and Parental Behavior." *Child Development* 65:394–403.

Haskins, Ron. 2001a. "Liberal and Conservative Influences on the Welfare Reform Legislation of 1996." Pp. 9–34 in *For Better and For Worse: Welfare Reform and the Well-Being of Children and Families*, edited by G. J. Duncan and P. L. Chase-Lansdale. New York: Russell Sage Foundation.

———. 2001b. "Effects of Welfare Reform at Four Years." Pp. 264–89 in *For Better and For Worse: Welfare Reform and the Well-Being of Children and Families*, edited by G. J. Duncan and P. L. Chase-Lansdale. New York: Russell Sage Foundation.

Haveman, Robert, Barbara Wolfe, and Kathryn Wilson. 1997. "Childhood Poverty and Adolescent Schooling and Fertility Outcomes: Reduced-Form and Structural Estimates." Pp. 419–60 in *Consequences of Growing Up Poor*, edited by G.J. Duncan and J. Brooks-Gunn. New York: Russell Sage Foundation.

Haveman, Robert and Barbara Wolfe. 1994. *Succeeding Generations: On the Effects of Investments on Children*. New York: Russell Sage Foundation.

———. 1995. "The Determinants of Children's Attainments: A Review of Methods and Findings." *Journal of Economic Literature* 33(4):1829–78.

Head Start Bureau. 2005. "Head Start Program Fact Sheet" Retrieved 7 February 2006 (http://www.acf.hhs.gov/programs/hsb/research/2005.htm).

Herrnstein, Richard and Charles Murray. 1994. *The Bell Curve: Intelligence and Class Structure in American Life*. New York: Free Press.

Heymann, Jody, Alison Earle, Stephanie Simmons, Stephanie M. Breslow, and April Kuehnhoff. 2004. *The Work, Family, and Equity Index: Where Does the United States Stand Globally?* Boston: The Project on Global Working Families.

Hill, Shirley A. 1999. *African American Children: Socialization and Development in Families*. Thousand Oaks, CA: Sage Publications.

Hofferth, Sandra L., Lori Reid, and Frank L. Mott. 2001. "The Effects of Early Childbearing on Schooling Over Time." *Family Planning Perspectives* 33(6):259–67.

Holahan, John and Johnny Kim. 2000. "Why Does the Number of Uninsured Americans Continue to Grow?" *Health Affairs* 19:188–96.

"Home Life Affects Children's Health." 1998. *Gainesville Sun*, 10 February, A10.

Hotz, V. Joseph, Charles H. Mullin, and John Karl Scholz. 2001. "The Earned Income Tax Credit and Labor Market Participation of Families on Welfare." Newsletter. *Poverty Research News* (Northwestern University/University of Chicago Joint Center for Poverty Research), May–June, pp. 13–15.

Hughs, Colin and Kerry McCuaig. 2000. "When Mom Must Work: Family Day Care as a Welfare-to-Work Option." Ontario Coalition for Better Child Care Retrieved 9 September 2004 (http://www.childcare.org/CPAG_CCEF/moms_welfare/).

Hunt, Matthew O. 1996. "The Individual, Society, or Both? A Comparison of Black, Latino, and White Beliefs About the Causes of Poverty." *Social Forces* 75:293–322.

Iceland, John. 2003. *Poverty in America: A Handbook*. Berkeley, CA: University of California Press.

Internal Revenue Service. 2005. "Earned Income Tax Credit (EITC) Questions and Answers." Retrieved 26 June 2005 (www.irs.gov).

———. 2006. "Claiming the Child and Dependent Care Credit." Retrieved 6 April 2006. U.S. Department of the Treasury (www.irs.gov/newsroom/article/0,id= 106189,00.html).

Isaacs, Stephen L. and Steven Schroeder. 2004. "Class: The Ignored Determinant of the Nation's Health." *New England Journal of Medicine* 351:1137–42.

Jansson, Bruce S. 1988. *The Reluctant Welfare State: A History of American Social Welfare Policies*. Belmont, CA: Wadsworth Publishing Co.

Jean, Renee. 2005. "Woman Struggles Out of Poverty, Helps Others." Retrieved 12 December 2005. Park Hill, MO/Daily Journal Online (www.dailyjournalonline.com/articles/2005/12/07/community/news3.txt).

John, Robert. 1988. "The Native American Family." Pp. 325–66 in *Ethnic Families in America: Patterns and Variations*, 3rd ed., edited by C. Mindel, R. Habenstein and R. Wright, Jr. New York: Elsevier.

Johnson, Julia Overturf. 2005. "Who's Minding the Kids?" *Childcare Arrangements: Winter 2002* Current Population Reports No. P70–101 Washington, D.C.: U.S. Census Bureau (www.census.gov/prod/2005pubs/p70–101.pdf).

Joint Center for Housing Studies. 2003. "State of the Nation's Housing, 2003." Harvard University. Retrieved 17 March 2005 (www.jchs.harvard.edu).

Kaiser Commission on Medicaid and the Uninsured. 2003. "The Uninsured and Their Access to Health Care." Retrieved 10 March 2006 (www.kff.org/ uninsured/1420-05/cfm).

———. 2005 November. *State Fiscal Conditions and Medicaid.* Washington, D.C.

Kamerman, Sheila B. and Alfred J. Kahn. 1978. "Families and the Idea of Family Policy." Pp. 1–16 in *Family Policy: Government and Families in Fourteen Countries*, edited by Sheila B. Kamerman and Alfred J. Kahn. New York: Columbia University Press.

Kamerman, Sheila. 2003. "Welfare States, Family Policies, and Early Childhood Education, Care and Family Support." In *Consultation Meeting on Family Support Policy in Central and Eastern Europe.* Budapest, Hungary: UNESCO and the Council of Europe, 3–5 September.

Kamerman, Sheila and Shirley Gatenio. 2002. "Tax Day: How Do America's Child Benefits Compare?" In *Issue Brief.* Retrieved 15 July 2002. Columbia University/The Clearinghouse on International Developments in Child, Youth, and Family Policies (http://www.childpolicyintl.org/issuebrief/issuebrief4.htm).

Kaplan, April. 1997. "Transportation and Welfare Reform." Welfare Information Network. Retrieved 10 March 2006 (www.financeproject.org/publications/transita.htm).

Kasarda, John D. 1990. "Structural Factors Affecting the Location and Timing of Underclass Growth." *Urban Geography* 11:234–64.

Katz, Michael. 1986. *In the Shadow of the Poorhouse: A Social History of Welfare in America.* New York: Basic Books.

Kessler-Harris, Alice. 1982. *Out to Work: A History of Wage-Earning Women in the United States.* New York: Oxford University Press.

Korenman, Sanders, Jane E. Miller, and John E. Sjaastad. 1995. "Long-Term Poverty and Child Development in the United States: Results from NLSY." *Children and Youth Services Review* 17:127–55.

Kotlowitz, Alex. 1992. *There Are No Children Here: The Story of Two Boys Growing Up in the Other America.* New York: Doubleday.

Kozol, Jonathan. 1992. *Savage Inequalities.* New York: HarperCollins.

Ladner, Joyce A. 1998. *The Ties That Bind: Timeless Values for African American Families.* New York: John Wiley.

Levin-Epstein, Jodie. 2003. "Welfare, Women, and Health: The Role of Temporary Assistance to Needy Families." Kaiser Family Foundation. Retrieved 10 December 2005. (www.kff.org).

Lewis, Oscar. 1966. "The Culture of Poverty." *Scientific American*, 215:19–22.

Link, Bruce G. and Jo C. Phelan. 1995. "Social Conditions as Fundamental Causes of Disease." *Journal of Health and Social Behavior* extra issue:80–94.

London, Andrew, John Martinez, and Denise Polit. 2001 May. *The Health of Poor Urban Women: Findings from the Project on Devolution and Urban Change.* New York: Manpower Demonstration Research Corporation.

London, Rebecca A. 2003 February. "Which TANF Applicants Are Diverted and What Are Their Outcomes?" Cited in Fremstad, S., "Recent Welfare Reform Research Findings," Center for Budget and Policy Priorities, January 2004. Retrieved 12 December 2005.

Loprest, Pamela. 2003 August. *Fewer Welfare Leavers Employed in Weak Economy.* (www.cbpp.org/1-30-04wel.htm) Washington, D.C.: Urban Institute.

Lutz, Steven, Janet R. Blaylock, and David M. Smallwood. 1993. "Household Characteristics Affect Food Choices." *Food Review* 16(2):12–18.

Macurdy, Thomas, Grecia Marruto, and Margaret O'Brien-Strain. 2003. *What Happens to Families When They Leave Welfare?* San Francisco: Public Policy Institute of California.

Manpower 2005. "Profile." Retrieved 3 October 2005 (www.us.manpower.com/uscom/contentSingle.jsp?articleid=297).

Markowitz, M. 2000. "Lead Poisoning." *Pediatrics in Review* 21(10):327–35.

Martin, Joyce A., Brady E. Hamilton, Paul D. Sutton, Stephanie J. Ventura, Fay Menacker, and Martha L. Munson. 8 September 2005. *Births: Final Date for 2003.* Technical Report No. 54(2). National Vital Statistics Reports. Hyattsville, MD: National Center for Health Statistics.

Marx, Karl and Friedrich Engels. 1968. *Selected Works.* New York: International Publishers.

Massey, Douglas S. and Nancy A. Denton. 1993. *American Apartheid: Segregation and the Making of the Underclass.* Cambridge, MA: Harvard University Press.

McCaine, Margaret Norrie and J. Fraser Mustard. 1999. "Early Years Study: Reversing the Real Brain Drain." Retrieved 14 February 2005. Publications Ontario (http://www.childsec.gov.on.ca/newsrel/resporten.pdf).

McCubbin, Hamilton I. and Marilyn A. McCubbin. 1988. "Typologies of Resilient Families: Emerging Roles of Social Class and Ethnicity." *Family Relations* 37:247–54.

McCubbin, Hamilton I., Marilyn A. McCubbin, Anne I. Thompson, Sae-Young Han, and Chad T. Allen. 1997. "Families Under Stress: What Makes Them Resilient?" Commemorative Lecture. Washington, D.C. American Association of Family and Consumer Sciences (AAFCS) 22 June.

McLemore, S. Dale and Harriett D. Romo. 2004. *Racial and Ethnic Relations in America*, 7th ed. Boston: Allyn & Bacon.

McLeod, Jane D. and Michael J. Shanahan. 1993. "Poverty, Parenting, and Children's Mental Health." *American Sociological Review* 58:351–66.

———. 1996. "Trajectories of Poverty and Children's Mental Health." *Journal of Health and Social Behavior* 37:207–20.

McLoyd, Vonnie C. 1990. "The Impact of Economic Hardship on Black Families and Children: Psychological Distress, Parenting, and Socioemotional Development." *Child Development* 61:311–46.

Mead, Lawrence. 1992. *The New Politics of Poverty: The Non-Working Poor in America.* New York: Basic Books.

Meier, Matt and Feliciano Ribera. 1994. *Mexican Americans, American Mexicans: From Conquistadors to Chicanos.* New York: Hill and Wang.

Miller, Dorothy C. 1992. *Women and Social Welfare: A Feminist Analysis.* New York: Praeger.

Miller, J. Elizabeth. 2000. "Religion and Families Over the Life Course." In *Families Across Time: A Life Course Perspective*, edited by S. Price, S. McKenry, and M. Murphy. Los Angeles: Roxbury.

Mills, C. Wright. 1959. *The Sociological Imagination.* New York: Oxford University Press.

Mindel, Charles H. 1980. "Extended Familism Among Urban Mexican-Americans, Anglos, and Blacks." *Hispanic Journal of Behavioral Sciences* 2:21–34.

Mink, Gwendolyn. 1995. *The Wages of Motherhood: Inequality in the Welfare State 1917–1942.* Ithaca, NY: Cornell University Press.

Mintz, Steven and Susan Kellogg. 1989. *Domestic Revolution: A Social History of Family Life.* New York: Free Press.

Mishel, Lawrence, Jared Bernstein, and Sylvia Allegretto. 2005. *The State of Working America: 2004/2005.* Ithaca, NY: Cornell University Press.

Mitnik, Pablo A., Matthew Zeidenberg, and Laura Dresser. 2002. *Can Career Ladders Really Be a Way Out of Dead-End Jobs? A Look at Job Structure and Upward Mobility in the Service Industries.* Madison, WI: Center on Wisconsin Strategy.

Morgan, Leslie and Suzanne Kunkel. 1998. *Aging: The Social Context.* Thousand Oaks, CA: Pine Forge Press.

Mouradian, Wendy E., Elizabeth Wehr, and James J. Crall. 2000. "Disparities in Children's Oral Health and Access to Dental Care." *Journal of the American Medical Association* 284:2625–31.

Moyniban, Daniel P. 1965. *The Negro Family: The Case For National Action.* Washington, D.C.: U.S. Government Printing Office.

Murphy, J. Michael, Cheryl A. Wehler, Maria E. Pagano, Michelle Little, Ronald E. Kleinman, and Michael S. Jellinek. 1998. "Relationship Between Hunger and Psychosocial Functioning in Low-Income American Children." *Journal of American Academy of Child and Adolescent Psychiatry* 37:163–70.

Murray, Charles. 1984. *Losing Ground: American Social Policy, 1950–1980.* New York: Basic Books.

———. 1998. *In Pursuit of Happiness and Good Government.* New York: Simon and Schuster.

National Coalition for the Homeless. 2005. "Homeless Families with Children." In *NCH Fact Sheet #12.* Washington, D.C. (www.nationalhomeless.org/publications/facts/families.pdf).

National Low Income Housing Coalition. 2004. "Out of Reach 2004: Introduction." Retrieved 1 December 2005 (www.nlihc.org/oor2004/introduction.htm).

———. 2005. "Out of Reach 2005" (www.nlihc.org/oor2005/).

Needleman, Herbert L., Alan Schell, David Bellinger, Alan Leviton, and Elizabeth L. Allred. 1990. "The Long-Term Effects of Exposure to Low Doses of Lead in Childhood." *New England Journal of Medicine* 322:83–88.

NICHD Early Child Care Research Network. 2005. "Duration and Developmental Timing of Poverty and Children's Cognitive and Social Development From Birth Through Third Grade." *Child Development* 76:795–810.

———. 2000. "The Relation of Child Care to Cognitive and Language Development." *Child Development* 71:960–80.

Nord, Mark, Margaret Andrews, and Steven Carlson. 2004. "Household Food Security in the United States, 2003." In *Food Assistance and Nutrition Report, Number FANRR42. Economic Research Service, U.S. Department of Agriculture*. Washington, D.C.: U.S. Department of Agriculture. (www.ers.usda.gov/publications/fanrr42).

———. 2005. "Household Food Security in the United States, 2004." Economic Research Report No. (ERR11). USDA Economic Research Service (www.ers.usda.gov/publications/err11).

Nord, Mark, Nader Kabbani, Laura Tiehen, Margaret Andrews, Gary Bickel, and Steven Carlson. 2002 March. *Household Food Security in the United States, 2000*. Food Assistance and Nutrition Research Report No. ([FANRR] 21). Washington, D.C.: Economic Research Institute, U.S. Department of Agriculture.

NPR Online. 2001. "Poverty in America." In *NPR/Kaiser/Kennedy School Poll*. Retrieved 1 December 2005 (www.npr.org/programs/specials/poll/poverty).

Office for Oregon Health Policy and Research. 2006. "Profile of Oregon's Uninsured, 2004" (www.ohpr.state.or.us/DHS/OHPPR/RSCH/docs/2004HealthInsuranceReportFinalWeb.pdf).

O'Hare, William P. 1995. "3.9 Million U.S. Children in Distressed Neighborhoods." *Population Today* 22:4–5.

Orshansky, Mollie. 1965. "Counting the Poor: Another Look at Poverty." *Social Security Bulletin* 28:3–29.

Ostrander, Susan A. 1980. "Upper Class Women: The Feminine Side of Privilege." *Qualitative Sociology* 3:23–44.

Parker, Emil and Jane Malone. 5 April 2004. *Administration Should Seek Increased Funding, Not Propose Drastic Cut in Key Lead Poisoning Prevention Program*. Washington, D.C.: Children's Defense Fund and Alliance for Health Homes.

Parrillo, Vincent N. 2005. *Strangers to These Shores: Race and Ethnic Relations in the United States*, 8th ed. Boston: Allyn & Bacon.

Pavetti, LaDonna and Greg Acs. 2001. *Moving Up, Moving Out, or Going Nowhere? A Study of the Employment Patterns of Young Women and the Implications for Welfare Mothers*. Journal of Policy Analysis and Management (Fall) 20:721–36.

Pear, Robert. June 28, 2006. "New Rules Force States to Curb Welfare Rolls." The New York Times.com (www.nytimes.com).

Peisner-Feinberg, Ellen S. and Margaret R. Burchinal. 1997. "Relations Between Preschool Children's Child-Care Experiences and Concurrent Development: The Cost, Quality, and Outcomes Study." *Merrill-Palmer Quarterly* 43:451–77.

Peterkin, Betty. 1964. "Family Food Plans, Revised, 1964." *Family Economics Review* October 3:12.

Peterkin, Betty and Richard L. Kerr. 1982. "Food Stamp Allotment and Diets of U.S. Households." *Family Economics Review* 1(Winter): 23–26.

Peters, H. Elizabeth and Natalie C. Mullis. 1997. "The Role of the Family and Source of Income in Adolescent Achievement." In *Consequences of Growing Up Poor*, edited by G. J. Duncan and J. Brooks-Gunn. New York: Russell Sage Foundation.

Pew Hispanic Center and Kaiser Family Foundation. March 2004. "Survey Brief: Latinos in California, Texas, New York, Florida, and New Jersey" (pewhispanic.org/files/reports/15.6.pdf).

Phelan, Jo C., Bruce C. Link, Ana Diez-Roux, Ichiro Kawachi, and Bruce Levin. 2004. "Fundamental Causes of Social Inequalities in Mortality: A Test of the Theory." *Journal of Health and Social Behavior* 45:265–85.

Poikolainen, Anni. "Characteristics of Food Stamp Households: Fiscal Year 2004." *U.S. Department of Agriculture,198 Food and Nutrition Service, Office of Analysis, Nutrition and Evaluation, FSP-05-CHAR* (Kate Fink, Project Officer, ed., 2005).

Powers, Elizabeth T. 2003. "Children's Health and Maternal Work Activity: Static and Dynamic Estimates Under Alternative Disability Definitions." *Journal of Human Resources* 38:522–556.

Presser, Harriet B. 2003. *Working in a 24/7 Economy: Challenges for American Families*. New York: Russell Sage Foundation.

Prows, Susan L., Michael A. Kennedy, Barbara Porter, Michael D. Stickler, and Jessica Clark. 2002. *Department of Administrative Services, Office of Oregon Health Policy and Research, Oregon's Uninsured: Summary of Findings from the 2000 Oregon Population Survey* (Fall).

Quadagno, Jill. 1982. *Aging in Early Industrial Society*. New York: Academic Press.

———. 1988. *The Transformation of Old Age Security: Class and Politics in the American Welfare State*. Chicago: University of Chicago Press.

———. 1994. *The Color of Welfare: How Racism Undermines the War on Poverty*. New York: Oxford University Press.

Rank, Mark R. 1994. *Living on the Edge: The Realities of Welfare in America*. New York: Columbia University Press.

———. 2003. "As American as Apple Pie: Poverty and Welfare." *Contexts* 2(3, Summer):41–49.

Rankin, Nancy. 2002. "The Parent Vote." Pp. 251–64 in *Taking Parenting Public*, edited by S. A. Hewlett, N. Rankin and C. West. Lanham, MD: Rowman & Littlefield.

Rector, Robert. 2004. "Welfare Reform: Progress, Pitfalls, and Potential." Heritage Foundation. Retrieved 10 March 2006 (www.heritage.org/Research/Welfare/wm421.cfm).

Roosa, Mark W., Shiying Deng, Rajni L. Nair, and Ginger Lockhart Burrell. 2005. "Measures for Studying Poverty in Family and Child Research." *Journal of Marriage and Family* 67(4, November):971–88.

Ross, Catherine E. 2000. "Bad Neighborhoods Can Cause Depression" (Press Release for "Neighborhood Disadvantage and Adult Depression," *Journal of Health and Social Behavior*, 2000; 41:177–187.). Retrieved 1 December 2005. Center for the Advancement of Health (www.hbns.org/newsrelease/badneighborhoods6-20-00.cfm).

Rouse, Kimberly Gordon. 1998. "Resilience from Poverty and Stress." *Human Development and Family Life Bulletin* (The Ohio State University, College of Human Ecology), Spring.

Rowe, Gretchen and Victoria Russell. 2004. *The Welfare Rules Databook: State Policies as of July 2002*. Washington, D.C.: Urban Institute.

Ruggles, Patricia. 1990. *Drawing the Line: Alternative Poverty Measures and Their Implication for Public Policy*. Washington, D.C.: Urban Institute.

Ruhm, Christopher J. 1998. "Parental Leave and Child Health" (Working Paper 6554). Cambridge, MA: National Bureau of Economic Research. Retrieved 11 January 2006 (http://papers.nber.org/ papers/W6554.pdf).

Saluter, Arlene F. 1989. *Singleness in America*. U.S. Bureau of the Census, Current Population Reports, Special Studies No. Series P-23, no. 162. Washington, D.C.: U.S. Government Printing Office.

Schiller, Bradley R. 2001. *The Economics of Poverty and Discrimination*. Upper Saddle River, NJ: Prentice Hall.

Schiller, Jeannine S., Patricia F. Adams, and Zakia Coriaty Nelson. 2005. *Summary Health Statistics for the U.S. Population: National Health Interview Survey, 2003*. National Center for Health Statistics no. Vital Health Stat 10 (224). Washington, D.C.: U.S. Government Printing Office.

Schochet, Peter and Anu Rangarajan. 2004. "Characteristics of Low-Wage Workers and Their Labor Market Experiences: Evidence from the Mid- to Late 1990s: Final Report." Retrieved 13 October 2005. U.S. Department of Health and Human Services (aspe.hhs.gov/hsp/low-wage-workers04/index.htm).

Schulman, Karen. 2000. *The High Cost of Child Care Puts Quality Care Out of Reach for Many Families*, Washington, D.C.: Children's Defense Fund.

Schulman, Karen and Helen Blank. 2004. *Child Care Assistance Policies 2001–2004: Families Struggling to Move Forward, States Going Backward*. Washington, D.C.: National Women's Law Center.

Schweke, William. 2004. *Smart Money: Education and Economic Development*. Washington, D.C.: Economic Policy Institute.

Scott, E. K., A. S. London, and A. Hurst. 2005. "Instability in Patchworks of Child Care When Moving from Welfare to Work." *Journal of Marriage and Family* 67:370–86.

Seccombe, Karen and Cheryl Amey. 1995. "Playing By The Rules and Losing: Health Insurance and the Working Poor." *Journal of Health and Social Behavior* 36:168–81.

Seccombe, Karen. 2000. "Families in Poverty in the 1990s: Trends, Causes, Consequences, and Lessons Learned." *Journal of Marriage and the Family* 62:1094–113.

———. 2002. "'Beating the Odds' Versus 'Changing the Odds': Poverty, Resilience, and Family Policy." *Journal of Marriage and Family* 64:384–94.

———. 2007. *So You Think I Drive a Cadillac?: Welfare Recipients' Perspectives on the System and Its Reform*, 2nd ed. Boston: Allyn & Bacon.

Seccombe, Karen, Heather Hartley, Jason Newsom, Kim Hoffman, and Clyde Pope. 2005. *Final Report to the Agency for Healthcare Research and Quality: Access to Healthcare and Welfare Reform*. Center for Public Health Studies. Portland, OR: Portland State University.

Seccombe, Karen, Delores James, and Kimberly Battle-Waters. 1998. "'They Think You Ain't Much of Nothing': The Social Construction of the Welfare Mother." *Journal of Marriage and the Family* 60:849–65.

Seguin, Louise, Qian Xu, Louise Potvin, Maria-Victoria Zunzunegui, and Katherine L. Frohlich. 2003. "Effects of Low Income on Infant Health." *Canadian Medical Association Journal* 168(12, 10 June):1533.

Selis, Sara. 2003. "Life in Poor Neighborhoods May Signal Greater Mortality Risk." *Stanford Report*, 23 July. Retrieved 1 December 2005 (News-service.stanford.edu/news/2003/july23/socioeco.html).

Sered, Susan Starr and Rushika Fernandopulle. 2005. *Uninsured in America*. Berkeley, CA: The University of California Press.

Shapiro, Isaac. 17 October 2005. *New IRS Data Show Income Inequality Is Again on the Rise*. Washington, D.C.: Center on Budget and Policy Priorities.

Siefert, K., C. Heflin, M. Corcoran, and D. Williams. 2004. "Food Insufficiency and Physical and Mental Health in a Longitudinal Survey of Welfare Recipients." *Journal of Health and Social Behavior* 45:171–86.

Silliman, Ben. 1994. "1994 Resiliency Research Review: Conceptual and Research Foundations." Retrieved 16 June 2001 (http://www.cyfernet.org/research/resilreview .html).

———. 1998. "The Resiliency Paradigm: A Critical Tool for Practitioners." *Human Development and Family Life Bulletin* (Ohio State University, College of Human Ecology), Spring.

Smeeding, Timothy A. 1997. "Financial Poverty in Developed Countries: The Evidence from LIS." In *Final Report to the United Nations Development Programme*. Income Study Working Paper Series No. 155. Luxembourg.

Smeeding, Timothy A., Lee Rainwater, and Gary Burtless. 2000. *United States Poverty in a Cross-National Context*. Income Study Working Paper Series No. 244. Luxembourg.

Smith, J., J. Brooks-Gunn, and P. Klebanov. 1997. "Consequences of Growing Up Poor for Young Children." In *Consequences of Growing Up Poor*, edited by G. Duncan and J. Brooks-Dunn. New York: Russell Sage Foundation.

Smith, Kevin B. and Lorene H. Stone. 1989. "Rags, Riches, and Bootstraps: Beliefs About the Cause of Wealth and Poverty." *The Sociological Quarterly* 30:93–107.

Smith, Kristin. 2000. *Who's Minding the Kids? Child Care Arrangements: Fall 1995*. Current Population Reports No. P70-70. Washington, D.C. U.S. Census Bureau. 27.

Social Security Online, Office of Policy Data. 2004. "Social Security Programs Throughout the World: Europe, 2004." Retrieved 7 March 2006. Social Security Administration (www.ssa.gov/policy/docs/progdesc/ssptw/2004-2005/europe/).

Starfield, Barbara, Sam Shapiro, Judith Weiss, Kung-Yee Liang, Knut Ra, David Paige, and Xiaobin Wang. 1991. "Race, Family Income, and Low Birth Weight." *American Journal of Epidemiology* 134:11167–74.

Steinberg, Stephen. 1981. *The Ethnic Myth: Race, Ethnicity, and Class in America.* Boston: Beacon Press.

Sterner, Richard. 1943. *The Negro's Share: A Study of Income, Consumption, Housing and Public Assistance.* New York: Harper and Brothers.

Stinnett, Nick and John DeFrain. 1985. *Secrets of Strong Families.* Boston: Little, Brown and Company.

Strong-Jekely, Lara. 2006. Letter to the Editor. *Brain, Child*, p. 2. Budapest, Hungary, Winter.

Swanson, Mark C. A., Mahendra K. Agarwal, and Charles E. Reed. 1985. "An Immuno-chemical Approach to Indoor Aero-Allergen Quantitation: Studies with Mite, Roach, Cat, and Mouse Allergens." *Journal of Allergy and Clinical Immunology* 76:724–28.

Szanton, Peter L. 1991. "The Remarkable 'Quango': Knowledge, Politics, and Welfare Reform." *Journal of Policy Analysis and Management* 10:590–602.

Takeuchi, David T., David R. Williams, and Russell K. Adair. 1991. "Economic Stress in the Family and Children's Emotional and Behavioral Problems." *Journal of Marriage and the Family* 53(4, November):1031–41.

Tanner, Michael, Stephen Moore, and David Hartman. 1995. "The High Value of Welfare Benefits Keeps the Poor on Welfare." Pp. 75–82 in *Welfare: Opposing Viewpoints*, edited by C. Cozic and P. Winters. San Diego, CA: Greenhaven Press.

Teachman, Jay D., Kathleen M. Paasch, R. D. Day, and Karen P. Carver. 1997. "Poverty During Adolescence and Subsequent Educational Attainment." In *Consequences of Growing Up Poor*, edited by G. J. Duncan and J. Brooks-Gunn. New York: Russell Sage Foundation.

Thomas, Susan. 1995. "Exchanging Welfare Checks for Wedding Rings: Welfare Reform in New Jersey and Wisconsin." *Affilia* 10:120–37.

Townsend, M., J. Peerson, B. Love, C. Achterberg, and S. Murphy. 2001. "Food Insecurity is Positively Related to Overweight in Women." *Journal of Nutrition* 131:1738–45.

Townsend, P. 1980. "Research on Poverty." Pp. 299–306 in *Wealth, Income, and Inequality*, edited by A. Atkinson. New York: Oxford University Press.

Trattner, Walter I, 1999. *From Poor Law to Welfare State: A History of Social Welfare in America.* 6th ed. New York: Free Press.

U.S. Census Bureau. 2005. "Median Income for 4-Person Families, by State." Retrieved 25 October 2005 (www.census.gov/hhes/income/4person.html).

———. 2006 February 1. "Poverty Thresholds 2005." (www.census.gov/hhes/www/poverty/threshld/thresh05.html).

U.S. Conference of Mayors. 2004. "A Status Report on Hunger and Cities." Retrieved 11 December 2005. (www.usmayors.org/uscm/hungersurvey/2004/onlinereport/HungerandHomelessnessReport2004.pdf).

U.S. Department of Agriculture. 2004. "Official U.S.D.A. Food Plans: Cost of Food at Home at Four Levels, U.S. Average, January 2004." Alexandria, VA: U.S. Department of Agriculture, Center for Nutrition Policy and Research. Retrieved 17 November 2005 (www.cnpp.usda.gov).

———. 2005 December. "Food Stamp Program: A Short History of the Food Stamp Program." Retrieved 27 December 2005. Washington, D.C: U.S. Department of Agriculture Food & Nutrition Service (www.fns.usda.gov/fsp/rules/Legislation/history.htm).

———. 2006. "Program Data: Food Stamp Program." (www.fns.usda.gov/pd/fspmain.htm).

———. June 2006. "Official USDA Food Plans: Costs of Food at Home at Four Levels, U.S. Average, May, 2006." Center for Nutrition and Policy Promotion (www.cnpp.usda.gov).

U.S. Department of Commerce, Bureau of the Census. 2005. "Table POV01. Age and Sex of All Peoples, Family Members and Unrelated Individuals Iterated by Income-to-Poverty Ratio and Race." Retrieved 14 September 2005 (Pubdb3.census.gov/macro/032004/pov/new01_100.htm).

U.S. Department of Health and Human Services. 2004. "Temporary Assistance to Needy Families (TANF) Sixth Annual Report to Congress." Office of Family Assistance. Retrieved 4 April 2006. (www.acf.hhs.gov/programs/ofa/annualreport6.htm).

———. 2005a. *The 2005 HHS Poverty Guidelines*. Retrieved 2 January 2006 (aspe.hhs.gov/poverty/04poverty.shtml).

———. 2005b. "Welfare Rolls Continue to Fall." Retrieved 4 April 2006 (www.acf.hhs.gov/news/press/2005/TANFdeclinJune04.htm).

———. 2006. "TANF: Total Number of Families (Fiscal Year 2005)." Retrieved 4 April 2006 (www.acf.hhs.gov/programs/ofa/caseload/2005/family05tanf.htm).

U.S. Department of Housing and Urban Development. 2003. "Fair Market Rents for the Housing Choice Voucher Program and Moderate Rehabilitation Single Room Occupancy Program—Fiscal Year 2004." *Federal Register* (Washington, D.C.), 28 May, pp. 31870–73.

———. 2005. "Final FY 2006 Fair Market Rent Documentation System." Retrieved 1 December 2005. (www.huduser.org/datasets/ fmr/fmrs/index.asp?data=fmr06).

———. 2006. "Proposed FY 2007 Fair Market Rent Documentation System." (www.huduser.org/datasets/fmr/fmrs/index.asp?data=fmr07).

U.S. Department of Labor. 1994. "Employment and Earnings."

———. 2004. "Childcare Workers." Retrieved 12 July 2005 (www.bls.gov/oco/ocos170.htm).

———. 2005a. Retrieved 24 January 2006. "Women in the Labor Force: A Databook" (stats.bls.gov/cps/wlf.databook2005.htm).

U.S. Department of Labor, Bureau of Labor Statistics. 2006a. "May 2005 National Occupational Employment and Wage Estimates." (www.bls.gov/oes/current/oes_nat.htm)

———. 2006b. "Employment Characteristics of Families." Tables 5, 6 (www.bls .gov/news.release/famec.toc.htm).

———. 2006c. "Median Weekly Earnings of Full-Time Wage and Salary Workers by Selected Characteristics." Table 37 (www.bls.gov/cps/cpsaat37.pdf).

U.S. General Accounting Office. 15 January 1999. *Lead Poisoning: Federal Health Care Programs Are Not Effectively Reaching At-Risk Children*. Technical Report No. HEHS-99-18. Washington, D.C.: U.S. General Accounting Office.

———. 1995. "Welfare to Work: Most AFDC Training Programs Not Emphasizing Job Placement." *Report to the Ranking Minority Member, Committee on Finance, U.S. Senate* (May).

———. 2000. *Oral Health: Dental Disease is a Chronic Condition Among Low-Income Populations*. Technical Report. Letter report GAO/HEHS, 00-72, April 12. Washington, D.C.: U.S. General Accounting Office.

U.S. House of Representatives. 1996. *Green Book*. Washington, D.C.: U.S. Government Printing Office.

———. 1997. *Medicare and Health Care Chartbook*. Washington, D.C.: U.S. Government Printing Office.

U.S. Social Security Board. 1940. *Social Security Yearbook 1939: Annual Supplement to the Social Security Bulletin*. Washington, D.C.: U.S. Government Printing Office.

UNICEF Innocenti Research Centre. 2000 "A League Table of Child Poverty in Rich Nations." *Innocenti Report Card No. 1* (June).

United Nations Statistics Division. 2005. "Table 5c—Maternity Leave Benefits." In *Statistics and Indicators on Women and Men*. Retrieved 14 January 2006 (unstats.un. org/unsd/demographic/products/indwm/ww2005/tab5c.htm).

U.S. Census Bureau. 2001. "Poverty in the United States: 2000." In *Current Population Reports*. Series P60-214. Washington, D.C.: Government Printing Office.

U.S. Census Bureau Public Information Office. 2001a. "More People Have Health Insurance, Census Bureau Reports." Retrieved 15 February 2002 (http://www.census.gov/ Press-Release/www.2001-cb01-162.html).

———. 2001b. "Poverty Rate Lowest in 20 Years, Household Income at Record High, Census Bureau Reports." Retrieved 24 May 2001 (http://www.census.gov/Press-Release/www/2000/cb00-158.html.).

U.S. Census Bureau. 6 October 2004. *Press Release: American Indian and Alaska Native Heritage Month: November 2004*. Technical Report No. CB04-FF.20.

Valentine, Charles A. 1968. *Culture and Poverty: Critique and Counter-Proposals*. Chicago: University of Chicago Press.

Vandell, Deborah Lowe and Barbara Wolfe. 2000. "Child Care Quality: Does It Matter and Does It Need to Be Improved?" Special Report No. 78. Madison, WI: Institute for Research on Poverty (www.ssc.wisc.edu/irp/).

Vinokur, Amiram D., Richard H. Price, and Robert D. Caplan. 1996. "Hard Times and Hurtful Partners: How Financial Strain Affects Depression and Relationship Satisfaction of Unemployed Persons and Their Spouses." *Journal of Personality and Social Psychology* 71:166–79.

Vozoris, Nicholas T. and Valerie S. Tarasuk. 2003. "Household Food Insufficiency Is Associated with Poorer Health." *American Society for Nutritional Sciences, Journal of Nutrition* 133:120–26.

Walsh, Froma. 1998. *Strengthening Family Resilience*. New York: Guilford.

Walsh, Wendy, 2002. "Spankers and Nonspankers: Where They Get Information on Spanking." *Family Relations* 51(1):81–88.

Warner, Judith. 2005. *Perfect Madness: Motherhood in the Age of Anxiety*. New York: Penguin Group USA.

Weber, Max. 1925 (reprinted 1947). *The Theory of Social and Economic Organization*. New York: Free Press.

Weinger, Susan. 1998. "Poor Children 'Know Their Place': Perceptions of Poverty, Class, and Public Messages." *Journal of Sociology and Social Welfare* 25:100–18.

Weitz, Rose. 2001. *The Sociology of Health, Illness, and Health Care: A Critical Approach*, 2nd ed. Belmont, CA: Wadsworth Publishing Co.

Wells, John. 1982. "Alcohol: The Number One Drug of Abuse in the United States." *Athletic Training*, Fall:172.

Werner, Emmy E. 1994. "Overcoming the Odds." *Developmental and Behavioral Pediatrics* 15:131–36.

———. 1995. "Resilience in Development." *American Psychological Society* 4:81–85.

Werner, Emmy E. and Ruth S. Smith, 1989. *Vulnerable but Invincible: A Longitudinal Study of Resilient Children and Youth*. New York: Adams, Bannister, Cox.

———. 1992. *Overcoming the Odds*. Ithaca, NY: Cornell University Press.

Wertheimer, Richard. 2003. *Poor Families in 2001: Parents Working Less and Children Continue to Lag Behind*. Publication #2003-10. Washington, D.C.: Child Trends.

White, Lynn and Stacy J. Rogers. 2000. "Economic Circumstances and Family Outcomes: A Review of the 1990's." *Journal of Marriage and Family* 62:1035–51.

Medicaid. (2005, December 28). In Wikipedia, The Free Encyclopedia. Retrieved 28 December 2005 (En.wikipedia.org/wiki/Medicaid).

Williams, Norma. 1990. *The Mexican American Family: Tradition and Change*. Dix Hills, NY: General Hall.

Willie, Charles Vert. 1983. *Race, Ethnicity, and Socioeconomic Status: A Theoretical Analysis of Their Interrelationship*. Lanham, MD: Rowman and Littlefield Publishers.

Willie, Charles Vert and Richard J. Reddick. 2003. *A New Look at Black Families*. Lanham, MD: AltaMira Press.

Wilson, William J. 1987. *The Truly Disadvantaged: The Inner City, the Underclass, and Public Policy*. Chicago: University of Chicago Press.

Wilson, William J. 1996. *When Work Disappears: The World of the New Urban Poor*. New York, Alfred A. Knopf.

Winicki, Joshua and Kyle Jemison. 2003. "Food Insecurity and Hunger in the Kindergarten Classroom: Its Effect on Learning and Growth." *Contemporary Economic Policy* 21(2): 145–57.

Wise, Paul H., Nina S. Wampler, Wendy Chavkin, and Diana Romero. 2002. "Chronic Illness Among Poor Children Enrolled in the Temporary Assistance for Needy Families Program." *American Journal of Public Health* 92(9): 1458–63.

Wolin, Steven and Sybil Wolin. 1993. *The Resilient Self.* New York: Villiard Books.

Wood, P. R., L. A. Smith, D. Romero, P. Bradshaw, P. H. Wise, and W. Chavkin. 2002. "Relationships Between Welfare Status, Health Insurance Status, and Health and Medical Care Among Children with Asthma." *American Journal of Public Health* 92(9): 1446–52.

Wood, Robert G. and Anu Rangarajan. 2003 October. *What's Happening to TANF Leavers Who Are Not Employed?* Princeton, NJ: Mathematica Policy Research, Inc.

World Values Survey. 1994. *World Values Survey, 1990–1993.* Ann Arbor, MI: Inter-University Consortium for Political and Social Research.

Yeung, Wei-jun Jean, Miriam R. Linver, and Jeanne Brooks-Gunn. 2002. "How Money Matters for Young Children's Development: Parental Investment and Family Processes." *Child Development* 73: 1861–79.

Zedlewski, Sheila R. 2003 August. *Work and Barriers to Work Among Welfare Recipients in 2002.* Urban Institute Press.

Zimmerman, Shirley L. 2001. *Family Policy: Constructed Solutions to Family Problems.* Thousand Oaks, CA: Sage.

INDEX